PENGUIN BOOKS

THE MEDIA LAB

Stewart Brand is best known for founding, editing, and publishing the *Whole Earth Catalog* (1968–1985; National Book Award, 1972) and the *CoEvolution Quarterly* (now called *Whole Earth Review*; 1973–1984), but he has also had a longstanding involvement in computers and the media arts.

Following his degree in biology from Stanford in 1960, and two years as a U.S. Infantry officer, Brand became a photojournalist and multimedia artist, performing at colleges and museums. In 1968 he was a consultant to Douglas Engelbart's pioneering Augmented Human Intellect program at SRI, which devised now-familiar computer interface tools such as the mouse and windows. In 1972 for *Rolling Stone* he wrote the first article about computer lifestyle, entitled "Fanatic Life and Symbolic Death Among the Computer Bums," chronicling the fringes of computer science at Xerox PARC, the Stanford Artificial Intelligence Laboratory, and MIT. While editor in chief of the *Whole Earth Software Catalog* (1983–1985) Brand organized the first "Hackers' Conference," which has since become an annual event. Currently he is researching learning in complex systems and lives with his wife, Patricia Phelan, on a tug-boat in San Francisco Bay.

THE Media Lab

inventing the future at **MIT**

■ **STEWART BRAND**

PENGUIN BOOKS

PENGUIN BOOKS
Published by the Penguin Group
Penguin Books USA Inc.,
375 Hudson Street, New York, New York 10014, U.S.A.
Penguin Books Ltd, 27 Wrights Lane,
London W8 5TZ, England
Penguin Books Australia Ltd, Ringwood,
Victoria, Australia
Penguin Books Canada Ltd, 10 Alcorn Avenue,
Toronto, Ontario, Canada M4V 3B2
Penguin Books (N.Z.) Ltd, 182–190 Wairau Road,
Auckland 10, New Zealand

Penguin Books Ltd, Registered Offices:
Harmondsworth, Middlesex, England

First published in the United States of America
by Viking Penguin Inc. 1987
This edition with a new preface
published in Penguin Books 1988

10 9 8 7 6 5

Portions of chapters 10 and 12 first appeared, in slightly
different form, in *Whole Earth Review*.

Grateful acknowledgment is made for permission to reprint the
following copyrighted material:
Excerpt from "The Machine Stops," from *The Eternal Moment*, by E. M. Forster.
Copyright 1928 by Harcourt Brace Jovanovich, Inc.; renewed
1956 by E. M. Forster. Reprinted by permission of the publisher.
Excerpts and a line drawing from *Computers and Communications*, by
Koji Kobayashi. Translation © 1986 by the Massachusetts
Institute of Technology; copyright © 1985 by Koji Kobayashi.
By permission of the publisher, The MIT Press.
Excerpts from *Technologies of Freedom*, by Ithiel de Sola Pool.
Copyright © 1983 by the President and Fellows of Harvard
College. Reprinted by permission of Harvard University Press.

Color section designed by Betsy Hacker, MIT Design Services
Color section photographs by Dan Teplin, David Chen,
Adina Sabghir, Bill Gallery, and Tim Browne
Black-and-white photographs by Marie Cosindas

LIBRARY OF CONGRESS CATALOGING IN PUBLICATION DATA
Brand, Stewart.
    The Media Lab.
    Bibliography: p.
    Includes index.
    1. Massachusetts Institute of Technology. Media
Laboratory.   I. Title.
T171.M49B73   1988   302.2'3'07207444   88-5848
ISBN 0 14 00.9701 5

Printed in the United States of America
Set in Goudy Old Style and Eras
Designed by Liney Li

Dedicated to the drafters and defenders of
the First Amendment to the U.S. Constitution:

Congress shall make no law . . . abridging
the freedom of speech or of the press.

Elegant code by witty programmers.

CONTENTS

PREFACE TO THE
PENGUIN EDITION

How will we directly connect our nervous systems to the global computer?

—Rory Donaldson

The time to understand a subject whole is when it's changing. Understanding is easier then because everything—even the deep premise structure—is up for grabs. And with whole understanding there's a better chance that the changes will be directed toward improvement. Nicholas Negroponte, founder and director of the Media Laboratory at MIT, likes to say that all communications media and technologies are poised for redefinition. The Media Lab was set up to collect that process and lead it.

MIT—the Massachusetts Institute of Technology—moved across the Charles River from Boston to Cambridge in 1916 to show its neighbor Harvard a thing or two, and rapidly did. Seventy-plus years later it is the high church of technology in a nation and a century more driven by technology than any before.

The Media Laboratory is a brand-new facility, $45-million ambitious, housed in a sleek I. M. Pei edifice on MIT's East Campus, built around Negroponte's conviction that something big and convergent is happening to the whole gamut of communications media—television, telephones, recordings, film, newspapers, magazines, books, and, infesting and transforming them all, computers.

I went there to see if it might be so. Back in 1968 when I started an "access-to-tools" compendium called the *Whole Earth Catalog*, and for a few years following, I'd had a clear feeling of the "future" and what to do about it. By the time I'd done half a dozen versions of the book, ending with a *Whole Earth Software Catalog* in 1985, I had no idea whatever about futures and was operating strictly on reflex. ("It's un-comfortable to do things again and again, as you have set a world record for realizing," Marvin Minsky told me at MIT.) So at age forty-six I thought I'd try a sabbatical—work somewhere else on something else for a while. Where? Only one place came to mind.

I'd seen a dazzling presentation of Negroponte's a couple years before at a "Technology, Entertainment, Design" conference. Since then I'd heard that his Media Laboratory was mustering a number of people I had admired from afar: Marvin Minsky, the co-father of artificial intelligence; Seymour Papert, author of *Mindstorms* and of LOGO, benevolent influ-ence on computers in education; Alan Kay, whom I'd reported on back in 1972 when he was fomenting a revolution in personal computers that is still in progress; Jerome Wiesner, President Kennedy's Science Advisor and former MIT President; and highly intriguing-sounding others. In June 1985 I wrote Negroponte and asked for a temporary job. He wrote back that I could start in January '86 and, meanwhile, come to the dedication of the new Wiesner Building, where the Lab was coming to life.

I had thought of doing a magazine piece about the Media Lab as a by-product of working there. What I saw at the Wiesner Building ded-ication changed that idea to book. Too much too various was going on at the Lab to surround with an article, and that was just the activities. The potential consequences disappeared over the horizon in every di-rection.

What started as a job became a quest for hidden structure, both in the Lab and in the world. While I worked at being of help to the Vivarium and Electronic Publishing projects in the Lab, I was watching the whole place. I saw an abundance of impressive work that was touted as all fitting together, and it acted like it fit together, but I couldn't figure out *how* it fit together. That question organized the year of assembling this book and eventually organized the book itself.

By the time I left the Media Lab after three months of participation, I had a good idea how the place functioned in terms of personalities and workaday routines, but I was still uncertain where the Lab's work stood in the overall scheme of communication technologies, and the intellectual kernel of the place, if any, was a greater mystery than ever. I studied communication trade journals and the business press to catch up with the current state of consumer electronics and broadcast technologies—the Media Lab's technological context. Since it demonstrated that Negroponte was right in his predictions of a few years ago and it showed where a world without the Media Lab would be heading, that "newmedia" news comes near the front of the book in Chapters 2 and 4.

The rest of the first half of the text, and the photo section in the middle, is the kind of in-depth tour of the Lab's researches that Lab people wish they could give every visitor. In fact nobody gets such a tour because the visitor would need to see the demonstrations, hear the explanations, wait for understanding (months, often, for me anyway), and then see the demonstrations again. The material is not too technical to understand right away, it's too . . . I need a word between "fundamental" and "personal." Too *close.*

Maybe the reader will be quicker than I was to catch on to what's really going on in the Lab's glittery variety. For me the core of it took six months to emerge—from transcribing and sifting seventy hours of interviews, from reading papers and books by Lab people and by other researchers they pay attention to, and from some delving into the history of the Media Lab and MIT. All that comes together in Chapter 8, "The Room Who Will Giggle," and again, pointing at the future, in the last chapter, "Quality of Life." The research domain of the Media Lab may have no circumference, but it has a center.

The rest of the book explores "so what?" The Media Lab is taking a leading role in a complex array of communications technologies which are increasingly interlocked and all-encompassing. Communications media are so fundamental to a society that when their structure changes, everything is affected. The sheer pervasiveness of all that gives meaning to the Media Lab cliché about "inventing the future."

What we mean by the word "world" usually is the world encompassed by human communications. The world was one thing when word seeped around from tribe to tribe. It became another when traders and religious enthusiasts set forth journeying. So it progressed through centuries—mail service, print, telegraph, telephone, electronic credit. Each time the means of communication advanced, the "world" metamorphosed.

Consequently this book is about two media labs. It is about the specific five-story pile of equipment, academics, and ideas in eastern Massachusetts, and it is about the worldwide media laboratory in which we are all likely to be experimenters for the rest of our lives. Since an unprecedented convergence is occurring in both of them, MIT's Media Laboratory may serve as a metaphor and a prefiguration of the wider evolution. The world of the Media Lab and the media lab of the world are busily shaping each other.

At first glance the topic of media in the 1980s is froth. It's pop culture and ephemera, corporate fads and fast-lane finance. Anything you say about it is old news by the next paragraph. But the topic of media is also core, as boring as sewer systems and as basic. Cities are organized around their sewers. When the sewers need replacing, there's chaos to pay for years, but if the process of rebuilding is postponed, urbanity will move elsewhere.

The word "media" means broadcast news media to most people— radio, TV, newspapers, and sometimes magazines. In its broadest interpretation, such as in Marshall McLuhan's *Understanding Media,* it means nearly everything from zippers to credit cards. "Media" at the Media Laboratory means <u>electronic communication technologies</u>, period. The subject is how humans connect, how they are connecting faster and wider with new technology, and how they might connect better.

Peter Drucker, management scholar and insightful futurist, wrote in *Innovation and Entrepreneurship* in 1985:

We are indeed in the early stages of a major technological transformation, one that is far more sweeping than the most ecstatic of the "futurologists" yet realize, greater even than *Megatrends* or *Future Shock.* Three hundred years of technology came to an end after World War II. During those three centuries the <u>model</u> for technology was a <u>mechanical one: the events that go on inside a star such as the sun.</u> . . . Since the end of World War II, however, the model of technology has become the biological process, the events inside an <u>organism.</u> And in an organism, processes are not organized around energy in the physicist's meaning of the term. They are organized around information.

And we understand information processes far less well than mechanical ones. As evident in Chapter 11, "The Politics of Broadcatch," and Chapter 12, "The World Information Economy," there is no very good theory of how the world wags these days. It may take a decade or more for workable ones to emerge. In the meantime the Media Lab is designing ethical principles into communications technology in a way which can help preserve the health of the world information system while we figure out how it is trying to work.

Acknowledgments are always and necessarily a combination of gratitude and apology—gratitude to all who made the book as good as it is, apology to the same people that it isn't as good as it would be if it really represented all that they know. To the faculty, staff, and students of the Media Laboratory I owe particular gratitude for suffering a journalist in their midst with grace and warmth. Among those who commented on drafts of chapters to reduce errors of fact and interpretation were Walter Bender, Stephen Benton, Richard Bolt, Alan Kay, Andy Lippman, Tod Machover, Marvin Minsky, Russell Neuman, Seymour Papert, Christopher Schmandt, William Schreiber, Jerome Wiesner, and David Zeltzer. Tim Browne, the Lab's Director of Communications, managed the tangled traffic of drafts, illustrations, captions, etc., with diligence, diplomacy, and humor. Nicholas Negroponte helped see the entire project through from my original book proposal to final draft, and the rough design of the cover and the color photo section are his. He had much of the work of a co-author with none of the control of one. He would occasionally debate when our opinions differed, but mostly he just watched with interest to see what I would do on the limbs I talked myself out onto.

People outside the Media Lab who contributed enormously with their comments include: John Brockman, literary agent; Daniel Frank, editor at Viking; Daniel Hillis; Tom Mandel; Patty Phelan, my wife, who endured all that goes with a year of no weekends; Peter Schwartz; and Deborah Wise, a former reporter for *Business Week* (Silicon Valley beat), who took on much of the research for the book. For crucial advice late in the project I am grateful to Paul Hawken and Philip Morrison.

In addition I am indebted to three communities of people who gave me sanctuary during the course of the writing: the Media Lab; Group Planning at Royal Dutch/Shell headquarters in London (where I was *supposed* to be a full-time consultant on organizational learning); and the *Whole Earth Review* offices in California, for cheerfully putting up with an emeritus editor underfoot. (If this book has additional printings, it will offer a chance to fix lingering factual errors. Please send any corrections to me at Whole Earth: 27B Gate 5 Road, Sausalito, CA 94965. This edition incorporates forty-some minor corrections sent in by readers of the hardcover version. Abiding thanks.)

The color section in the middle of this book was designed by Betsy Hacker of MIT Design Services and photographed in large part by Dan Teplin, Bill Gallery, Julie Walker, Adina Sabghir, Tim Browne, and David Chen. The black-and-white photos of Media Lab people scattered through the text are by the esteemed photographer Marie Cosindas. Apple Computer, through Alan Kay in connection with my work on his Vivarium project, donated the Macintosh Plus and LaserWriter printer on which the book took fluid shape.

The Media Lab provided, finally, what I went for—a clear feeling of the future and some ideas about what to do about it. My sabbatical, of course, became permanent. The technologies and questions I discovered at MIT don't lead back to where I've been, to where any of us have been.

—SB
Sausalito, California
March 1988

THE Media Lab

PART ONE

The
World
of the
Media Lab

1 DEMO OR DIE

Everybody experiences far more than he understands. Yet it is experience, rather than understanding, that influences behavior.

—Marshall McLuhan

In the basement the inventor of the white-light hologram that flickers from America's credit cards is demonstrating the world's first projected hologram. It's an eighteen-inch Camaro parked in midair, and the sponsors from General Motors are pleased. One of them steps from the front of the car around to the back and then *has* to reach into it. His hand grasps satisfactory nothing. The information is in his eye, not in the air.

Out in the Wiesner Building's sunny atrium, seven-foot-long computer-controlled helium blimps are cruising the five-story space learning how to be like fish—feeding, schooling, seeking comfortable temperature habitats.

On the third floor, body tracking is in progress, a figure in ultra-punk black leather and studs twirling in sensitive space. The studs are position indicators (infrared-light-emitting diodes) being sensed and translated by a computer into an animated figure on the room-size screen dancing in perfect echo to the human. The computer is paying attention and remembering: this is how humans move.

On the fourth floor a violinist strokes once more into a difficult piece, trying it with a slower tempo. The piano accompanist adapts perfectly, even when the violinist changes tempo again in the middle of the piece. The uncomplaining piano player is an exceptionally musical computer.

In the Terminal Garden on the third floor a visitor pretends to be a schoolchild and types into a computer, "hedake." A computer voice says aloud, "Headache," and shows the word spelled correctly. "The hell with kids," says the visitor, "*I* need this."

Between the second and fourth floors two computers are chatting on the phone, scheduling an appointment between their human keepers, neither of whom is around at the moment.

That's a small sample of the variety of endeavors going on in the Wiesner Building, but it gives a glimpse of major themes in Media Lab research. Everything mentioned involves communication, empowers the individual, employs computers (the Camaro was not photographed from a model but generated out of pure computer bits), and makes a flashy demonstration.

Students and professors at the Media Laboratory write papers and books and publish them, but the byword in this grove of academe is not "Publish or Perish." In Lab parlance it's "Demo or Die"—make the case for your idea with an unfaked performance of it working at least once, or let somebody else at the equipment. "We write about what we do," comments Director Negroponte, "but we don't write unless we've done it." The focus is engineering and science rather than scholarship, invention rather than studies, surveys, or critiques.

The Lab is a fascinating visit, a techno-feast of goodies from "Movies of the Future," "Toys of the Future," "School of the Future," Et Cetera of the Future, drawing no end of visitor traffic. On one somewhat heavy day, a year after opening its doors, the Lab was toured by forty computer scientists from China, the Chief Scientist from IBM, thirty-five Japanese architects, fifteen members of a Japanese study mission, the Secretary of State from West Germany, and the president of the German Newspaper Federation. Industrial sponsors of the Lab come to see if they're getting their money's worth. Potential sponsors come to see if they should buy in ("Less than $200,000 it's not really worth our time," Negroponte observes). Journalists come looking for The Story and go away confused, but still with plenty to write about. Scientists and researchers come to see who's ahead or behind on what. Distinguished visitors come because this is the kind of technological excitement that America and MIT want them to see, and it's one of the few places where so much is so concentrated.

They see the demos and are suitably dazzled or puzzled, but what draws them here is that they've heard or sensed the Media Laboratory has a Vision, capital V.

□ *Amphibian*
□

■ Consider the visionary.

"You'll find that your left cuff link will be communicating with your right cuff link via satellite," Negroponte teases an audience. "With flat-panel technologies every license plate, wine label, or price tag will be a 'display.' " Asked about computers he replies, "There will be many more MIPS in the nation's *appliances* than in its computers." (MIPS is million-instructions-per-second, a standard measure of computer power.) What about broadcast, the broadcasters ask him. He breaks it to them ungently. "Sports and elections probably will remain synchronous and shown live. The rest won't. The rule might be: if you can bet on it, you won't see it out of real time. As for the motion picture industry, it is the smokestack industry of today's information world.

"The world faces a more profound transition than fiber optics replacing bicycles or electroluminescent panels displacing newsprint," he summarizes. "Monologues will become conversations; the impersonal will become personal; the traditional 'mass media' will essentially disappear." The audience shivers deliciously. What if he's right?

Why does that sound familiar? Ah yes, 1966; Tom Wolfe's celebrated article about Marshall McLuhan, of *Understanding Media*, was titled "What If He Is Right?"

There were many studs of the business world, breakfast-food-package designers, television-network creative-department vice presidents, advertising "media reps," lighting-fixture fortune heirs, patent lawyers, industrial spies, we-need-vision board chairmen—all sorts of business studs, as I say, wondering if McLuhan was . . . right. . . . IBM, General Electric, Bell Telephone, and others had been flying McLuhan from Toronto to New York, Pittsburgh, all over the place, to give private talks to their heirarchs about . . . this unseen world of electronic environment that *only he sees fully*.

Nat Rochester, a senior computer scientist for IBM and the central negotiator for IBM's early and large involvement with the Media Lab, told me, "Nicholas combines very great technical knowledge and creativity with an artist's eye and skill, and really world-class salesmanship. If he were an IBM salesman, he'd be a member of the Golden Circle— that's the inner group that's made ten Hundred Percent Clubs; from then on they're completely privileged. If you know what good salesmanship is, you can't miss it when you get to know him."

Indeed this is no rumpled, tweedy, musing scholar. *Fortune* magazine observed that he "looks more like a matinee idol than a walking paradigm of the state-of-the-art technologist." Negroponte does look a bit like a young Robert Wagner. He's meticulously groomed and dresses sharp. The child of an old Greek shipping family, he grew up in Switzerland and the stylish circles of New York and London. Magazines like M and W (formerly *Women's Wear Daily*) keep an eye on him. W recently described him—"more the style of a sophisticated successful international executive than a research scientist or academic involved in extremely advanced computer work."

At age forty-three Negroponte is young for his responsibilities at MIT. He rose fast by virtue of the quality of his research on computer interfacing, the single-mindedness of his effort—the Media Lab is essentially his life work—and how he's built on a peculiarity of his university. MIT is more merrily in bed with industry and government than any other academic institution in the world. Professors are not only permitted but encouraged to devote up to 20 percent of their time—"a day a week," as they say—to outside consulting and other profitable business interests such as starting companies.

Negroponte found it easy to mix with the chairmen, directors, and chief executive officers of major corporations and government research offices. Months on the road every year, he's acquired a business sense of the world. At the university he's an exotic with the moves of a jet-set executive and a businessman's get-on-with-it rigor. But in corporate boardrooms and on trade organization stages he's the prestigious professor, representing the lofty intellectual perspective and long view of the university. Negroponte is an amphibian, comfortable in both worlds, giving an amphibian's value to both worlds, taking an amphibian's advantage

Professor Nicholas Negroponte, Director of the Media Lab

of both worlds. (The tactic could have been disastrous if he had got it backward and combined academic languor with business shortsightedness.) Nevertheless in his origins and fundamental loyalty he's an academic.

He gets the public attention of a media maven as McLuhan did, but Negroponte is different in major ways. He doesn't comment in order to comment—his only books are two somewhat specialist tracts from the MIT Press and another one available solely in Japan, in Japanese. He comments in order to get money to invent, to enable the entire apparatus of the Media Lab and its people to invent.

If imitation is the sincerest form of flattery, invention is the sincerest form of criticism. Faced with the cacophony of media drift, the policy of the Lab is to seize the design initiative—"invent the future"—and deliberately turn most broadcast media inside out. Negroponte would use computer technology to personalize and deeply humanize absolutely everything. The effect on mass media would be for the viewer, listener, reader, student to take over what is seen, heard, read, learned—making everyone into editor, and of a vastly enriched communication spectrum.

Populist program. Who's cheering?

Nobody political has paid the slightest bit of attention to Negroponte or the Media Lab. Who's lined up at the door is the business studs. General Motors, ABC, NBC, CBS, PBS, Home Box Office, RCA, 3M, Tektronix, NHK (Japan's public TV network), Ampex, Harris, Mead, the Defense Advanced Research Projects Agency (DARPA), IBM, Apple Computer, Warner Brothers, 20th Century–Fox, Paramount, LEGO, Dow Jones, Time Inc., Polaroid, Kodak, Schlumberger, Hewlett-Packard, Digital Equipment Corporation, BBN (Bolt, Beranek & Newman), The Washington Post, The Boston Globe, Asahi Shimbun, NEC, Sony, Hitachi, NTT (Japan's AT&T), Sanyo, Fujitsu, Fukutake, Bandai (Japan's largest toy maker), Mitsubishi, Matsushita—a hundred sponsors, a few of them government, most of them corporate. Their interest is simple: they want to stay in business, and if what is called the business environment shifts, they have got to shift with it, preferably just ahead of it.

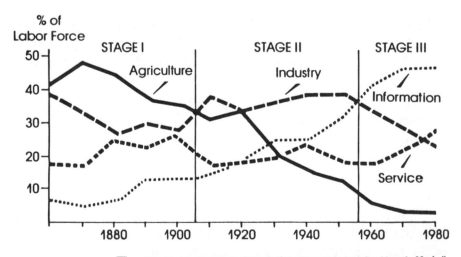

"The Post-Industrial Society: Shift in Economic Activity Already Made," reads the caption of this graph, shown widely by SRI International, indicating nearly 50 percent of the labor force involved in "Information" activities. This chart is taken from a 1976 doctoral thesis at Stanford University by Marc Porat.

Everyone in business has seen one version or another of this graph, which shows the "information" part of the economy outgrowing everything else, even the service sector. Everyone has heard the success stories—LEXIS grossing $150 million a year selling case law to lawyers electronically; Telerate making $150 million a year (thirty-nine-year-old founder Neil Hirsch now worth $65 million personally) selling financial information electronically; Apple Computer founded in a garage by phone phreaks; Sony coining money with audio compact disks; and on and on. And the failure stories—Knight-Ridder blowing $50 million on videotex before quitting; electronic gamer Atari losing an empire when "E.T." failed; Osborne Computer annihilated by a single marketing mistake; and on and on.

Once a new technology rolls over you, <u>if you're not part of the steamroller, you're part of the road.</u>

How does a corporation get to the front of this risky business without spending a hell of a lot of money? How can you peer ten years along a technological trendline that might devour or starve your present cash cows? How can you explore the crossover technologies where entire new businesses are being born without becoming one of the stillborn? You read in the *Wall Street Journal* or the *Boston Globe* how former industrial backwater Massachusetts is booming, with unemployment down to 3.6 percent and a state budget surplus, and it's all being attributed to MIT. Then Negroponte shows up keynoting somewhere with video demos of MIT researchers test-piloting the information technologies at the edge of the possible, flying in formation around a pattern vague and shifting but emerging, hypnotic . . . and you buy in.

☐
☐ *Teething Rings*

■ Negroponte's office is deskless. <u>There is only a round table surrounded by chairs, bearing the residue of recent meetings—scribbled notes, coffee cups, odd objects, *Variety*, and two telephones, one with a speaker-phone. A matched pair of Japanese pachinko games (vertical pinball, sort of) is set in a wall nearby, and two personal computers glow expectantly on a corner table—all computers at MIT are left on permanently; I don't know why. The door at one end opens to Jerome Wiesner's corner office; the door at the other end remains open to two secretaries that Negroponte keeps busy.

On one end wall is a long whiteboard covered with diagrams and words like "paralinguals," "kinesthetic knowledge," "intelligence = bandwidth." Above the whiteboard are four large clocks showing different times, labled Tokyo, San Francisco, Boston, and Athens (he has a summer home in the Aegean). In response to my request for a private version of his road show he sets up a self-contained slide projector and brings up the first image onto its screen.

"This is our marketing symbol." Negroponte sits back from the slide he's been explaining since 1979, which shows three overlapping circles labeled BROADCASTING, PUBLISHING, and COMPUTERS. "Muriel Cooper, who heads the Visible Language Workshop, calls it my teething rings. In fact this diagram is what launched the Media Laboratory. We foresaw the coming together of these three industries, which previously were completely distinct. I would give lectures about how nobody in the computer community had heard of 'Simpty,' the Society of Motion Picture and Television Engineers (SMPTE), or the AIGA, the American Institute of Graphic Arts. The three industries all have separate professional associations, separate journals, and separate heroes. A hero of

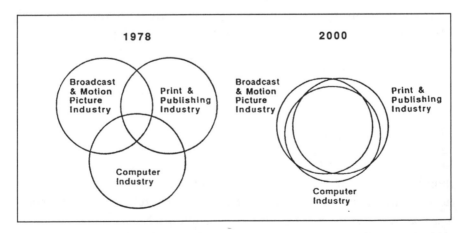

With these diagrams Negroponte made the case for the creation of a Media Laboratory at MIT.

broadcasting you've probably never heard of is Vladimir Zworykin. He invented much of TV. But the people in broadcasting or publishing have never heard of Alan Turing, who more or less invented computer programming. They have separate languages. You can talk to somebody for two minutes and if they use the word 'pixel' or the word 'pel,' you know where they come from. Both words mean the same thing—'picture element'—but 'pixel' is computer talk and 'pel' is television talk.

"The point is, while each of these fields will continue to grow—and then I'd show the Year 2000 slide—we saw the richest and most promising areas of research and development at their intersections. One of the goals of the Media Lab was to deal deliberately with the middle intersection, where you couldn't find much that was successful yet. Videodisks were in that area, but they came from the world of broadcast and motion pictures, and the computer people didn't get hold of them and make them interactive until too late. I think if the Media Lab had existed in the late '70s that wouldn't have happened."

Negroponte's vision: all communication technologies are suffering a joint metamorphosis, which can only be understood properly if treated as a single subject, and only advanced properly if treated as a single craft. The way to figure out what needs to be done is through exploring the human sensory and cognitive system and the ways that humans most naturally interact. Join this and you grasp the future.

It worked. Negroponte and former MIT President Jerome Wiesner toured and lectured and demoed and bargained for seven years, and raised the requisite millions. High aluminum walls, countless computers, attractive salaries were generated out of tense, soaring proposal words: ". . . New theories about signals, symbols, and systems will evolve from the merger of engineering, social science, and the arts. . . ." ". . . the intellectual mix of two rapidly evolving and very different fields; information technologies and the human sciences. . . ." ". . . a place where people will be expected to be equally familiar with lumens, leading, and lambda calculus. Graduates will be required to pursue studies in epistemology, experimental psychology, filmmaking, holography, and signal processing, as well as in computer science." Unlike the other forty-five laboratories at MIT, the Media Lab was aspiring to become an academic department as well.

The noblest phrase, and customarily the meanest practice, on any campus is "interdisciplinary." Yet sponsored research volume for the Media Lab in fiscal 1985–86 was $3.7 million; for 1986–87 it was $6 million. That's in addition to the academic budget provided by MIT of about $1 million each year.

Buying what? The boundaries keep shifting, but when counted in early 1987 the Lab was divided into eleven groups. Taking them in the order they appear in this book:

1. ELECTRONIC PUBLISHING gets $1 million, most of it from IBM. In the Terminal Garden are the electronic books and self-personalizing electronic newspapers, magazines, and TV broadcasts. Walter Bender runs the Garden.

2. SPEECH works with $500,000, mainly from the Defense Advanced Research Projects Agency (DARPA) and Nippon Telephone and Telegraph. Chris Schmandt invents such things as phones that know your friends and can converse with them in your behalf.

3. The ADVANCED TELEVISION RESEARCH PROGRAM is led by William Schreiber. Some $1 million comes to it from a consortium of television worriers—ABC, NBC, CBS (initially), PBS, Home Box Office, RCA, 3M, Tektronix, Ampex, Harris. Investigation centers on how gorgeous you can make television if you let the TV set have some computer intelligence.

4. MOVIES OF THE FUTURE gets about $1 million from Warner Brothers, Columbia, and Paramount, who suspect that computer digitalization will change their industry. Andy Lippman presides over the recording of "paperback movies" on compact disks, and other ambitions.

5. The VISIBLE LANGUAGE WORKSHOP, headed by design prize-winner Muriel Cooper, is trying to cure the chronic ugliness of computer graphics and visual design, working with $250,000 from Polaroid, IBM, and a German print technology firm called Hell.

6. SPATIAL IMAGING, otherwise known as holography, gets about $500,000, mostly from General Motors and DARPA. The leading light is Stephen Benton, who came from a couple decades of working at the right hand of Polaroid founder Edwin Land.

7. COMPUTERS AND ENTERTAINMENT is a fuzzy set containing a

fantasy called the Vivarium sponsored by Apple Computer, featuring Alan Kay, along with Marvin Minsky trying to godfather the next generation of artificial intelligence, and other fecund activities. Just as the Media Lab is considered by some to be MIT's lunatic fringe, this group is the Lab's lunatic fringe, and gets about $300,000 accordingly.

8. ANIMATION AND COMPUTER GRAPHICS, led by David Zeltzer, operates with $300,000, mostly from NHK and Bandai. The group is seeking the animator's holy grail: real-time computer animation. "Real-time" means live—the animation is created "on the fly" in the computer. It manages that by imitating some techniques of life itself.

9. COMPUTER MUSIC, running on $150,000 from the System Development Foundation, is in the process of becoming a major music research center exploring "music cognition" as well as new performance modes. Barry Vercoe and Tod Machover are in charge.

10. THE SCHOOL OF THE FUTURE, also called Hennigan School, led by Seymour Papert, gets a hefty $1 million, most of it originally from IBM, some from LEGO (of LEGO blocks), some from Apple Computer, MacArthur Foundation, and the National Science Foundation. The idea here is to find out what happens when you *really* put computers in a grade school.

11. HUMAN-MACHINE INTERFACE operates on $200,000 from DARPA, the National Science Foundation, and Hughes. Richard Bolt's machines can read your lips and eyes, which can feel like they're reading your mind.

The idea is that these disparate activities shall intersect like the teething rings diagram, and their people will collaborate gladly, defying hallowed academic custom. In fact the Lab is full of collaborative alliances which are generating much of the best work. But that's a little boring. What are the problems in utopia?

☐☐ *The Boggle Factor*

■ It is the dark side of the demos. It begins with sensory overload. Walter Bender would be demonstrating electronic publishing in the half-darkened Terminal Garden, the standard starting point for a Lab tour.

The cluster of visitors would be trying to concentrate on his workstation, where something marvelous is about to appear, but the room is seething with activity—other people's terminals around the room are already displaying mysterious colorful wonders, a computer-voice announces to the oblivious multitude, "Oh no! Oh three six oh!" a cat flashes past with tail straight up, and through the window where the really big computers are throbbing are perched two disembodied familiar-looking plaster heads.

Walter, radiating his customary sweetness, starts talking, and the group focuses on his computer screen, thinking—*this is the future*—squinting defensively—*what the hell am I seeing?* It's a gray picture of a motor or something. "It's an electronic book," says Walter, "of transmission repair, and you're having a conversation with the mechanic. You pave your own path through the material. It's got a lot of booklike attributes. There's a table of contents." He runs his finger over the picture on the screen, and parts of the transmission turn into bright color as he touches them. "Each of these is a different chapter." He touches a pictured box on the screen, and now there's text with pictures. Words in red turn into definitions when he touches them. The pictures turn into movies at his touch, slower, faster, forward, back; he touches one again and it fills the screen, the mechanic in the picture is explaining out loud—sound!— what he's doing wrong with the oil pan, which suddenly falls open and soaks him with oil. Laughter from the group, amazement, uncertainty— *That's terrific. Is that terrific?*

"How recent is this work?" someone asks. "It's five years old," says Walter in a voice that conveys he would love to stop giving this demo one of these years. "Can we see something more current?" Walter brings up a picture on his screen of a pretty girl with blue lines graffitied across her face. "This is eight-bit Pamela. It's compressed from twenty-four-bit color. The trick in that picture is, can you anti-alias the lines when the color repertoire is that limited?" One visitor asks, "Are all 256 colors being used?" Walter replies in Martian, "You build in a KD tree when you quantize the color space . . ."

Boggle. Too much coming too fast to sort out. Too many named new things. Too much that needs explanation to even understand what it is, much less what it's for or what's remarkable about it. Too much that appears too consequential or inconsequential to take lightly figuring out which is which. And *it's all connected,* so any piece of confusion infects everything else. You don't know what to be impressed by. You start to look for reasons to trust your guides, because the potential for being bamboozled is total.

In fact the Media Laboratory is scrupulously trustworthy, but one would like that to be self-evident, and there's no way it can be. I stayed boggled most of the three months that I worked at the Lab. I'm not boggled when I go there now, and I don't think someone who's read this book would be. It just takes time to build the context to digest the considerable news of the place.

I can recommend some cautionary attitudes that might be as helpful in this book as in the Lab. Be vigilant for "handwaving," an apt MIT term with much occasion for use. The word refers to what a speaker does animatedly with his hands as he moves past provable material into speculation, anticipating and overwhelming objection with manual dexterity—a deprecating "you-know" featuring a well-turned back of the hand, or a two-handed symmetrical sculpting of something as imaginary as it is wonderful. Sometimes handwaving precedes creation, sometimes it substitutes for it.

Watch out for overinterpretation, especially by me. "There's a natural instinct to see either a revolution or a conspiracy in every new technology that comes down the pike," Russell Neuman told me. Neuman is from MIT's Political Science Department, working with the Audience Research arm of the Lab's Advanced Television project, a warm fan of the Media Lab and a warm skeptic of media mania. "I think of the breathless rhetoric of people like Alvin Toffler and John Naisbitt," he went on. "To sell lots of copies of books you've got to wave your arms and talk about how 'information bombs are exploding and changing our basic psyche.' " He eyed me. "You may be faced with some decisions about how breathless to get in the first chapter of your book about the Media Lab."

The Media Lab aims to reframe the way the individual addresses the world and the world addresses the individual; is that handwave preceding a creation or substituting for it? Sponsors have put millions into the place expecting long-range but nevertheless commercial inventions or information; are they getting their money's worth? <u>If there is a clear idea at the heart of the Lab's research goals</u>, will it emerge crystalline and focusing or blend back into the blur of technological drift? What is that clear idea exactly?

The Media Laboratory is a huge public bet by MIT, by the myriad sponsors, by the researchers who are risking major portions of their careers. The idea that communication technologies are converging in the world, the idea of convening communication disciplines at MIT under one conceptual roof, the specific people that are gathering to work on it . . . they all have to be right to get a win. Demo or die.

2 NEWMEDIA 1— RECEIVING

> You can count how many seeds are in the apple, but not how many apples are in the seed.
>
> —Ken Kesey

The best way to understand what's special about Media Lab projects is to examine the range of what's going on outside in the communications marketplace. If Negroponte was right and communications technologies really are converging, you would look for signs that technological homogenization was dissolving old boundaries out of existence, and you would expect an explosion of new media where those boundaries used to be. Both would cause confusion on a grand scale.

This is the case.

There are so many new media forms each year now that the magazine *Channels of Communications* puts out an annual "Field Guide to the Electronic Environment." The 1986 issue, subtitled "A Time of Merging and Converging," listed twenty-six new kinds of public electronic media, including such things as MMDS (multichannel multipoint distribution system—called "wireless cable" TV) and CD-I (interactive compact disk). It barely touched revolutionary changes going on with telephone service and computer capabilities. The 1987 edition of the "Field Guide" observed that the last five years have been "the most turbulent in the history of media in America. Half a century has been compressed into half a decade."

Confusion abounds. Ask shoppers which videocassette format they prefer—VHS, 8mm, or VHS-C, not to mention the dying Beta or the upstart 4mm. Ask advertisers where they expect the center of their business to be in five years, or how much they're doing differently now from two years ago. Ask lawyers what's happening to copyright laws that were made back when media like print and television held still for a few years. (The advertisers are unhappy but the lawyers are happy—they feed on confusion.)

Despite the ferociously legislated distinction between telephone communications and broadcasting, cellular telephones now use broadcast frequencies that can be received on your TV set (a couple of UHF channels), and you can dial a "976" phone number for prerecorded entertainment ranging from children's stories, soap opera updates, and sports results to pornography for the ear.

The technical convergence that is dissolving boundaries comes in two overlapping stages: electronic, then digital. Less than one out of five words were delivered by print in America in 1977, according to Ithiel de Sola Pool's influential 1983 book, *Technologies of Freedom.* "The force behind the convergence of modes is an electronic revolution as profound as that of printing." The first era of communications, said Pool, was speech; the second, writing; the third, printing and other forms of making multiple copies such as phonographs and photography; and now the fourth era: "All media are becoming electronic."

And most electronic media are becoming digital. Telephones, radio, TV, and recorded music began their lives as analog media—every note the listener heard was a smooth direct transform of the music in the studio—but each of them is now gradually, sometimes wrenchingly, in the process of becoming digitalized, which means becoming computerized. You can see the difference in the different surfaces of long-playing records and compact disks: the records' grooves are wavy lines; the far tinier tracks of CDs are nothing but a sequence of distinct pits. Analog is continuous; digital is discrete.

With digitalization all of the media become translatable into each other—computer bits migrate merrily—and they escape from their traditional means of transmission. A movie, phone call, letter, or magazine article may be sent digitally via phone line, coaxial cable, fiberoptic cable, microwave, satellite, the broadcast air, or a physical storage medium such as tape or disk. If that's not revolution enough, with digitalization the content becomes totally plastic—any message, sound, or image may be edited from anything into anything else.

What will remain analog? Only live face-to-face conversation and performance—which may become newly valued. Even copy machines and photography are going digital. "Digital is a noise-free medium, and it can error-correct," comments Negroponte, referring to the capabilities that make digital reproductions as perfect as the original. "I can see no reason for anyone to work in the analog domain anymore—sound, film, video. *All* transmission will be digital."

Just as Negroponte and Wiesner proclaimed, communications media are not just changing, they're changing into each other, and when they get together, they breed. Since the process self-accelerates and self-branches, there's no reason to expect a new stability any time soon. It's a civilian version of what Arms Race specialists call "technology creep"— the uncontrollable surging ahead of invention past all attempts to predict it or legislate it. When the implements of the game keep changing the rules, you have to change with them or leave the game. "Invention," quoth Marshall McLuhan, "is the mother of necessity."

And the sheer volume of electronic information keeps soaring. The business would be growing radically even if it weren't changing in all the other ways. Astronaut Russell Schweickart explained the need for more communication satellites in simple supply-and-demand terms: "There's a runaway market for bits."

In Japan, expectably, the topic is of intense popular interest, sometimes reported under headlines with a thrilling futuristic word in compressed English: "NEWMEDIA." Japanese prosperity thrives on it, and it brings Japanese sponsors to the Media Lab by the dozen.

The area of communications that especially fascinates Media Lab people, where they see greatest room for improvement, is at the receiving end of broadcast media. There at the human/machine "interface" is where the prime event occurs. The broadcast and distribution apparatus comes up against the human mind, and a message gets through or not. It is a highly commercial event. Consumer electronics has been the locus of economy-swinging booms and busts for decades now—radio, TV, high-fidelity, "personal audio" (12 million Walkmen and equivalents loose in the world), personal computers (which are indeed communication devices), now CDs and VCRs (compact disk audio- and videocassette recorders), and more rapidly coming. The media laboratory of the world has been far from idle in this department.

□ □ *Digital Ears*

■ Compact disks with digital high-fidelity sound are being called the most successful consumer electronic product introduction in history, and small wonder. I remember the pleasure of buying into it. Perfectly lovely music came out of a relatively cheap box; the silent parts in the music sounded as if the electricity had gone off; the disks were conveniently small and so was the box; the music came in great long uninterrupted lengths (seventy-four minutes—Sony standardized the disk at a size that could hold Beethoven's Ninth Symphony) but still it could be scanned easily and preferred cuts found quickly; and *it didn't get old*—the two hundredth play would be just as good as the first.

Four years in, supply still cannot keep up with demand, and the original price of around $14 per CD disk has remained stable. Even so, U.S. sales of CDs in 1985 were triple 1984's, and 1986 tripled 1985. Meanwhile the $2.5-billion-a-year audiocassette business hit a compact brick wall—cassettes grew by half a billion dollars in '84; they grew zero in '85. Long-suffering long-playing record albums deepened the nosedive they've been in since 1981, losing yet another 20 percent in sales in 1985—the year analog music died. It used to be that new media supplemented old media; now they destroy them.

(A word about numbers. The above happen to come from *Billboard* in March '86, the *Wall Street Journal* in April '86, and the *Channels '87 Field Guide to the Electronic Environment*, but I'm not usually going to cite statistics sources in any detail. The figures I use have been gleaned from trade press such as *Broadcasting*, *Business Week*, *InfoWorld*, and the business pages of the *New York Times*, *Boston Globe*, *San Francisco Chronicle*, *International Herald Tribune*, and *London Times*, March '86 to January '87. Ephemeral as the weather report, they are the numbers that people in the businesses were quoting to each other in those months. I avoid using "future" numbers—like how the one CD disk factory in the U.S. in 1986 was expected to become twenty-two by 1990, forty-four worldwide—on the principle that this book is meant to be nonfiction.)

CD won big, but wait. Suppose you could get a digital audio medium that did everything CD does at comparable cost, only with *two* hours and more on a single cassette *half* the size of a regular audiocassette, *and you could record with it,* snatching perfect sound on your own? The advent of DAT (Digital Audio Tape) is one of the strangest in electronics history. Worldwide, eighty-four companies had agreed on standards and were poised to introduce DAT players and tapes in the summer of '86 and then, universally, they didn't. Many of them were in the CD business and wanted that market to mature at least a moment further before hitting the consumer with yet another new, scrumptious, incompatible format. Furthermore a whole new order of copyright problems loomed.

The recorded-music business was incensed, because it appeared that home listeners were about to be able to make copies precisely as good as the originals. The head of the Recording Industry Association of America told a Senate committee, "DAT has struck fear into the hearts of music industries throughout the world" because of an expected "quantum leap" in home recording. In the great late-twentieth-century struggle to maintain a commercial grip on the movement of commercially produced information, he was lobbying for royalties being collected from the sale of blank cassettes and of cassette recorders, or for a copy-preventing computer chip to be placed in all recording hardware. He was unsuccessful at the time. In the face of music industry wrath DAT is arriving anyway. Something like it always does, fortunately. Piracy is indeed a bad thing, but home manipulation of commercial information, as Media Lab projects show, is something worth encouraging.

☐
☐ *Dense Media*

■ However, don't write off CDs yet. CD players are cheaper than DAT players and they have that quick random access that tapes don't. *And* computers want to love them. Anything capable of 500 megabytes of random access data storage looks very tasty to personal computer users who are feeling cramped running 400 kilobyte floppy disks with 1/1200 the storage of that $14 CD disk.

(Brief reminder of numeric Greek: *kilo* is thousand, *mega* is million, *giga* is billion—they say a little DAT cassette may hold two gigabytes of data. A byte, you recall, is the eight bits a computer needs to define one character. This chapter, I just happen to know, has 36,067 bytes or 36 kilobytes of data in its text, a flea in the bathtub of a CD ROM.)

CD ROM stands for Compact Disk, Read-Only Memory. It's the same compact disk, only formatted for computer data instead of audio. The read-only part refers to its main limitation: you can't "write" on it any more than you can record on a phonograph record. If it really were a memory you could say it has enormous perfect recall, but you can't personally teach it a thing.

You can't teach anything to a book either, and on a CD you've got a cheap little parking place for 250,000 pages of text, the equivalent of 500 books—a truckload—instantly computer-searchable and publishable at one-fiftieth the cost of printing on paper. Some book publishers are riveted. "Dense media have the inherent characteristics necessary to cure some of publishing's greatest problems—excess inventory, short product life, high distribution costs, wasteful product returns, and insufficient shelf space to give new products a chance to thrive," observed publisher Barry Richman in a dandy 1986 survey text, *CD ROM.* "In the long run," he concluded, "dense media will replace paper as surely as papyrus replaced clay." To do that, he added quickly, we have to develop "affordable electronic forms that are as good as print at what print does best, and are better than print at what electronics does best." We're a long way from that right now, but it's exactly the kind of problem the Media Lab was designed to take on.

The first "popular" CD ROM publication onto the market in 1986 was Grolier's *Academic American Encyclopedia,* whose twenty volumes and huge index took up only one-fifth of a disk, costing $200. Dow Jones came up with a subscription service called CD/Newsline that mails out monthly updated disks to financial customers with detailed information on companies in four categories, at $9,600 a year for one category, $19,600 for all four. A few months later from PC-SIG came a $195 disk with 9,290 "public domain" (free) software programs for personal computers, using about one-third of the disk. This is clearly a medium still figuring out what it's best at.

I'm inclined to believe Barry Richman that the ideal content for CD ROMs is "the sacred texts of professional life—those specialized multivolume reference works and subscription services that are so expensive, so bulky, and often so complexly indexed that wrestling a set into the headquarters library is worthy of mention in the annual report."

The Media Lab is more interested in a different direction. "CD ROM is by definition an interactive medium," insists Negroponte. "It's really a cheap multimedia medium." Enter CD-I, Compact Disk Interactive, which can have on one disk a thousand video stills, a couple of thousand diagrams, six hours of high-quality sound, and ten thousand pages of text, along with a program to make it work as an organic whole, all intensely interactive with the user. The crippling limitation of the CD-I format, in Media Lab eyes, is that it can't do full-motion video. In 1987 Philips announced a CD video format called CD-V, and RCA demonstrated a CD video they call DVI (Digital Video Interactive), capable of holding a whole hour of full-motion video on a compact disk, thanks to signal compression techniques. Whoever wins the format wars, Lucasfilm, National Geographic, and Apple Computer have joined forces to develop programming for CDs and other laser-read media. That's a filmmaker, a magazine publisher, and a computer manufacturer right there—the red-hot center of Negroponte's teething ring diagram.

Negroponte respects CD ROM technology just as it is more than the industry does: "I marvel constantly at the industry's tendency to want to make read-only disks into write-once disks into read-write-erase disks— to make them like magnetic disks, failing to realize they are a publishing medium and that read-only is a virtue, not a liability. If you publish data, you want it inviolate and that it already knows about itself."

☐ ☐ *The E-Mail Proletariat*

■ This medium emerged from overlap with a circle not in Negroponte's teething rings diagram—telephones. A personal computer without a telephone line attached to it is a poor lonely thing. So far about a quarter of the 10 million computers in American homes have plugged into the phone system and tied into electronic mail ("e-mail"), computer teleconferences, and online databases. Even more of the same thing is going on in offices, where e-mail is becoming a way of life in some businesses.

In the months before I went to work at the Media Lab I was in daily touch with Negroponte via e-mail. One day when I knew he was traveling, I messaged him, "When you're on the road, who runs the Lab?" Three hours later I logged into the MIT system and found his reply: "The fact that I'm replying to you from Japan two hours after your question from California somewhat begs the question. The Lab doesn't know I'm gone." I later confirmed the fact when I worked there. Administratively, he isn't gone when he travels, any more than most of the Lab people are gone when they log in from home at odd hours. E-mail evaporates the tyranny of place, and to a considerable degree, of time.

The most surprising and consistent quality in e-mail communities is the human warmth they develop. They are a form of conversation. An author named Howard Rheingold was asked what he liked most about a regional computer teleconference system in the San Francisco area called The WELL, and he explained the permanent temptation to log in: "There's always another mind there. It's like having the corner bar, complete with old buddies and delightful newcomers and new tools waiting to take home and fresh graffiti and letters, except instead of putting on my coat, shutting down the computer, and walking down to the corner, I just invoke my telecom program and there they are. It's a place."

"The paperless office," so long predicted and designed for, ranks with "energy too cheap to meter" as one of the classic misdirections of technological forecasting. Computers have buried offices in paper. Nevertheless, estimates are that 250 million to a billion messages a year in the U.S. are going by electronic mail.

Via innumerable systems. On the local level you've got Bulletin Board Systems (BBS), which live in individual personal computers and take only one caller at a time. Wondrous subcultures flourish in them as people seek out other people who share their kink regardless of creed, color, address, or time of night. There is no quicker way to explore the bounteous variety of American enthusiasms. The odder the subject, the more warmhearted the people online.

Many of the Bulletin Boards are connected to each other through a grass-roots invention called Fidonet which routes messages from one Board to another across the country in the dead of night. It's so efficient that some businesses are starting to use it, and it's free.

Then there are the national teleconference systems which live in very large computers. Half a million American users may be found on Compu-Serve, Dow Jones, and The Source, messaging each other, meeting in SIGs (special interest groups, also called conferences on some systems), checking airline schedules, movie reviews, the national news, you name it. These are commercial services, far from free: rates range from $3 to $72 an hour, with additional monthly charges. Link systems called Use-net and the UUCP Network route messages and daily newsletters among 7,600 such systems worldwide. A portentous phenomenon is under way here, with whole new ways of life taking shape. It's the kind of revolution the Media Lab is fostering—people taking over a medium in convivial fashion—but clearly this is a revolution that will go on whether or not the Lab does. These are communications amateurs in the process of becoming communications professionals in professions that didn't exist before.

Take France, home of the world's largest e-mail system, a fascinating mix of socialism and capitalism, both rampant. The state-owned phone company, French Telco, responded to a government decree to put France in the forefront of the Electronic Age by handing out free computer terminals called Minitels to anyone who wanted them. The original idea was to provide a nationwide electronic phonebook (anything like that in the U.S. is forbidden until 1989 by Congress, lobbied by the American Newspaper Publishers Association, which doesn't want the phone companies "publishing"). Almost immediately the French began using the system for electronic mail, and traffic took off.

After four years France has two million Minitel terminals in use (10 percent are rented), twice the one million total subscribers to the whole fragmented range of "videotex" services in America. "Entrepreneurs get rich concocting new services for Minitel," noted the *Wall Street Journal*. Some 3,000 services are available—home banking and shopping, weather, airline and hotel reservations, games, TV schedules, real estate listings, magazines, on and on. The services cost up to $9 an hour, with three-eighths of the proceeds going to French Telco, the rest to the entrepreneurs.

"More than half the traffic," chortled the *London Times*, "consists of calls from people who are interested in sex. They are talking to companies offering 'personal services': sex counseling, computer dating, and *risqué* jokes." One can almost hear *Megatrends* author John Naisbitt murmuring, "High tech, high touch." Reportedly the French users courting by e-mail are developing remarkable writing skills.

Meanwhile French Telco is clearing over $100 million profit a year handing out the "free" $160 Minitel units to insatiable demand. Every year the operation more than doubles and profits increase by 25 percent.

The handful of videotex projects that failed gloriously in the U.S. did so by focusing on television rather than computer technology, resulting in crude color images, slow service, considerable expense, and an incommunicative role for the user. Customers tried to use the services for electronic mail anyway, which was about like burning money to make smoke signals. The fairly successful computer e-mail services like CompuServe are often referred to as "videotex," but they are quite different from the videotex that failed big on home TVs.

Russell Neuman at the Media Lab is dubious about the French system as an inspiration. "You need a trigger service or a trigger provider. The French example is plain not going to happen in the United States—the government is not going to pay for the terminals. If it happens by a provider, it's going to happen when the banks develop a standard and decide it's in their interest to pay the costs of getting the terminals out there. You need some kind of transactional service."

It was trigger services that brought online databases—the first true electronic publishing—into commercial reality. Financial professionals devour data, lawyers search infinite volumes for precedents and regulations, and both will do anything to get the information, even learn how to handle a computer terminal and acquire the arcane skills of data search, and pay generously. Since its beginnings in the late '60s this has become a $2-billion industry with 3,000 databases available—still only the beginning, everyone in the business assumes.

□
□ *The VCR Proletariat*

■ While e-mail and databases were making a quiet revolution out of public view, the noisiest media convulsion of the last decade was VCRs, the videocassette recorders that shocked Hollywood, the TV networks,

Associate Professor
W. Russell Neuman,
head of the Audience
Research Facility

and cable, and swept round the world in months. It's a fine example of customers taking over a communications medium, complete with an instructive counter-example in the fate of videodisks.

In the the mid-'70s movie studios decided it was time to resell films direct to the home, bypassing the networks and keeping more of the revenue. The technology they bought into was laser videodisks, which could be stamped out cheaply like long-playing records. Marketing stalled with a prolonged fight in the marketplace over incompatible standards— two kinds of disks that couldn't be played on each other's machines. (A fatal error the consumer electronics industry took to heart—witness the near-universal standards for compact disks and digital audio tapes.)

While confusion reigned among the videodisks, videocassettes arrived on the scene, also warring over several standards (VHS, which won, and Beta, which lost eventually). The VCRs had two crucial differences from videodisks, one in marketing, one in technology, both considered somewhat illicit.

The marketing difference was that videodisks high-mindedly es-

chewed dealing in pornography whereas VCRs built an industry on it—
a chapter in the history of commerce which has been noticed but never
examined. (It never is. Prehistoric cave art is replete with lovingly rendered vaginas, but they're not to be found in the books. Presumably
archaeologists of the future also will refer to twentieth-century porn as
"fertility symbols.") In the first years pornography made up over half the
prerecorded VCR business, though it's since settled back to 15 percent
as the rest of the business took off.

It's a nice case of a "trigger service." "Initially when tapes were very
expensive," notes Russell Neuman, "the only people who wanted to buy
an $80 prerecorded tape were people looking for something that could
not be gotten any other way—it wasn't available from broadcast, and
you had to go downtown to some sleazy pornographic movie house." An
interesting by-product is the gradual feminization of porn. Some 40 percent of the renters and buyers of video pornography are women.

More important, though, was the technological difference between
videodisk and VCR. \The disks delivered higher-quality reproduction,
but you could not record on them. The magnetic tape of VCRs was an
invitation to do-it-yourself. People recorded programs off the air and
watched them at their convenience, "zipping" the commercials (fast-
forwarding past them), comfortably pausing in mid-drama to answer the
phone or have dinner, collecting many more programs than they would
watch, sampling among them, looking for the best.

Videodisks had a related opportunity which was thrown away. They
can't be written on, but if a computer is attached the viewer can instantly
access any point on the disk, which is impossible with tape. It can be a
superbly interactive medium; the electronic book I mentioned in the first
chapter is a videodisk experiment. Videodisk lives on, mainly in schools
and industrial training, in interactive form, but VCRs captured the home.

"The only way I will watch TV is if it's been videotaped," declares
Media Lab scientist Alan Kay. "I haven't watched live TV in years,
except for football games, which I don't care about. I want to be able
to do all the things I do when I read—I want to be able to stop, to go
back, I don't want to be *taught* by it. I find VCRs liberating." The key
device is the "recording robot" that time-cues the VCR to watch TV
for you and play it back later. Mark Heyer in the CD ROM book recalled,

"Consumer acceptance was very difficult until time-shift recording with VCRs provided an unlimited source of apparently free software." (Revealing terminology. The content of all the storage media—music on audiocassettes and CDs, movies on VCRs, etc.—is now routinely referred to in the entertainment industry by the computer term "software." I wonder if doctors will soon be treating patients' "hardware" medical problems and sending the "software" problems to psychiatrists.)

Forty percent of all American homes now have a VCR, accelerating still. VCR penetration is even higher in parts of Europe, where broadcast channels are more limited. The income level of the customer is irrelevant. People with time and no money get it to fill their time. People with money and no time get it to make better use of the time they have. In many parts of the Third World, VCR *is* television.

Like electronic mail, it's a medium that <u>encourages the Mom 'n' Pop level of entrepreneuring</u> as well as the big guns. Thousands of VCR rental shops blossomed worldwide (along with a huge grass-roots black-market industry of tape piracy). The new medium unleashed hundreds of new legit publishers, 300 of them by now in the U.S., some with a staff of two, examining the far reaches of what the market is interested in. Reportedly <u>one-fourth of the business is "special interest" titles</u>. Opera is proving popular; so is jazz; even chamber music. Jane Fonda's original "Workout" tape in 1981 sold 1.3 million copies and inspired a sweaty horde of imitations, every one of them capable of selling 10,000 copies. Starting with video cookbooks, the how-to field is taking off. Libraries have to carry VCR tapes; so do bookstores (10 percent of the VCR business right there). Many of the myriad of tiny publishers sell by <u>direct mail</u>, taking extra advantage of the "efficiency" (minimum costs between producer and consumer) inherent in the medium.

<u>1986 was the year that VCRs surpassed theater box office in revenues</u> for movies, and the medium that was originally fought by the film studios (because of the copying) has been embraced passionately. Films are changing as a result. The home audience is seen as more adult and more segmentable than the theater audience, so a renaissance of good, strange movies is in the making, and classics are enjoying a rich revival.

People were also making home videos. Super-8 film disappeared from the Earth. The next round of videocassette standards—8mm and

VHS-C—was dramatically smaller to permit handier cameras. The VCR, like e-mail, is a homemade, people's medium, but the most personal-seeming of all media, the telephone, is another matter.

□ The Sun Never Sets on the Phone Company
□
■   One can imagine America functioning pretty well, maybe better, without television, but try imagining America, or the world, functioning at all without the telephone. Of all the communications media this $620-billion worldwide industry is the main event. With the breakup of AT&T's monopoly in America there was suddenly ferocious competition, new services every month, confused customers, and a giddy acceleration of the pace of phone technology in a business that used to be as conservative as banks used to be.

It was computers that led to the dismembering of AT&T, and it's computers that AT&T and the new regional phone companies are looking to for salvation. In the old days the phone company owned your telephone and was forbidden from purveying computers. When people got their own computers and hooked them to the phone system, the whole deal started to break down. One of the reasons AT&T went along with the divestiture without more of a fight was that it could at last get into the computer business.

So far AT&T has had no success selling computers, but they likely have a winner with the coming proliferation of computer-friendly digital phone service. The magic letters are ISDN—integrated services digital network. Once installed, the technology is, as usual, smaller, cheaper, safer, smarter, and higher quality than the old analog equipment. Voice and data can ride comfortably together on it. Pool anticipated accurately in *Technologies of Freedom,* "Subscribers can talk on the phone, have their utilities metered, watch a video picture on their television, and receive their electronic mail, all at once without interference. The loop is likely to be an optical fiber rather than copper wire because the fiber has the needed bandwidth at lower cost. This development may toll the bell for cable television, but perhaps not."

One of the newly separated phone corporations, Pacific Bell, has already run an ISDN-like test project in Danville, California. Still using the old twisted pair wires, they employed a technique called multiplexing (which layers messages on top of each other) to provide simultaneously two voice and five data channels to 200 test families. Via free Macintosh computers the families e-mailed and banked and shopped and data-searched to their heart's content. The experiment was deemed successful and is being expanded for a next round.

An enormous international effort is under way to link all the world's phone systems with an ISDN network capable of carrying every kind of signal, including television. Over 100 countries are involved, even the Soviet Union. Art Kleiner, a journalist who has specialized in telecommunications, reported Pacific Bell's plans for ISDN in the *San Francisco Bay Guardian*:

> If they ever digitize scent, it'll flow across the same channel that carries your voice. Some ISDN lines will have enough capacity to carry real-time video signals into your home or office. "You'll see the person you're talking to in video on one side of the screen," said Donald Simpson, an engineer who represents Pacific Bell at ISDN conferences. "You'll see a page of text on the other side, and you'll hear their voice on your phone receiver." ISDN will also process sound and image digitally—remove the silences in a recorded message, filter the hiss out of a piece of music, mute the color of Krystal's dress on "Dynasty," change a woman's voice to a man's. Your 15-digit ISDN phone number will travel anywhere with you from Alaska to Zimbabwe. "You'll carry your terminal and plug it into a wall jack," Simpson said. "The network will read your terminal and know who you are, and instantly deduct money from your account, not in dollars or yen but in Special Drawing Rights, decoupled from daily currency fluctuations."

Some of the services coming from Pacific Bell won't have to wait for the arrival of ISDN and are being offered in the late '80s: *Automatic Callback* (the phone keeps trying a busy line); *Distinctive Ringing* (your call makes a signature kind of ring at the other end); *Selective Call Rejection* (the unwanted caller gets a message instead of you); *Selective Call Forwarding* (certain callers go elsewhere automatically); *Customer Originated Trace* (*nail* the obscene caller); *Calling Number Delivery* (the caller's number is flashed before you answer—this already exists on a test service in Japan); and *Voice Mail* (a whole new medium is lurking there).

The elaborate ISDN treats will take longer to arrive, perhaps by the early-to-mid-'90s, as the phone companies gradually replace the existing $120-billion telephone plant in the U.S. with <u>digital switching equipment and optical fiber.</u> During that time cable television may be fighting for its life. Cable companies will try to take advantage of their existing installation by providing interactive services like banking, data search, and special video access as soon as they can. And they will lobby fiercely to have the phone companies prevented from competing.

My bet is that cable will live, and many houses will have two fat cables bearing data into them, but that the eventual advantage will go to the phone companies. Breaking up Mother Bell is widely viewed as a mistake, and full-service ISDN will be seen as a way to put the system functionally back together again.

It's all very ironic. Back in 1913 the government forced AT&T (American Telephone and *Telegraph*) to divest itself of Western Union and get out of the telegraph business because it was too repellent a monopoly. Thus perished Bell System's "grand design." According to Pool, "In 1910, the year of the merger (with Western Union), President Theodore Vail of AT&T described the new arrangement as 'One system with a common policy, common purpose and common action; comprehensive, universal, interdependent, intercommunicating like the highway system of the country, extending from every door to every other door, affording electrical communication of every kind, from every one at every place to every one at every other place.' " Seventy-seven years later, despite every effort to fragment and frustrate it, the grand design lives.

Art Kleiner told me in a letter, "The economic effect of the distribution of resources worldwide is going to be immense. I started to understand this when Don Simpson at Pacific Bell told me how you would be able to use the <u>central office phone-switching</u> computer as *your* computer with a special high-speed data line between your PC and their central computer. Through your terminal in Kenya you might access a program in Australia that drives a manufacturing plant in Pennsylvania."

The grand design keeps getting grander. A global computer is taking shape, and we're all connected to it. *How* we're connected to it is the Media Lab's prime interest.

3 TERMINAL GARDEN

FUNDAMENTAL UNIT OF TRUTH DISCOVERED

MIT researchers today announced the discovery of a new fundamental particle that is the basis for the widely-known phenomenon of information. Dubbed the "truon," this particle is vital to interactions involving the basic force of truth.

—Michael Travers,
Media Lab graduate student

The carpeted corridor floor clanks hollowly as you approach the Media Lab room called the Terminal Garden, signaling the kind of environment you're entering: wired.

Overhead maroon trays bearing cables veer suddenly through walls. As you enter the Garden's glass doors you spy a catastrophically short human . . . no, a human sticking out of the floor. One of the clanking squares of raised-floor has been removed and the human is busy rewiring something to something else. Down in the two-foot-high cellar is a spaghetti of video cables, power cables, networking lines, odd storage—archaeology of the Garden's rapidly layering past.

The light in the large, populated room is jungle twilight. Instead of using the fluorescents in the ceiling the fifteen workstations are lit by local lamps and large glowing monitor screens. Potted trees by the couch in the middle of the room suit the room's tropical sound—from each workstation comes a fluttery clicking of keys, like frogs on their lily pads, each with a different voice.

☐ *Personal Newspaper*
☐
■ Walter Bender is the Terminal Garden's keeper. A Media Lab veteran at thirty, he got drawn into the heady pace of invention at Negroponte's Architecture Machine Group back in 1978, when he was an undergraduate visiting from Harvard. Referred to as "Arch Mac" (pronounced "ark mac"), the Architecture Machine Group was the mainline predecessor to the Media Lab, the source since 1968 of nearly all the earlier research mentioned in this book. Arch Mac's Terminal Garden worked so well it was re-created in the Wiesner Building. Bender's husky voice, boyish look, and easy manner make him a natural demo-giver. He bears an exceptional burden of demo traffic because the zoo-like Garden is fascinating to visitors, and his domain of Electronic Publishing is a readily understandable one.

The standard opening demo for visitors is of NewsPeek, a selective home-publishable semiautomatic electronic newspaper that knows the reader, made of material drawn daily from Dow Jones News Retrieval, Nexis, XPress, and wire services, along with television news. Walter

Walter Bender,
responsible for Electronic
Publishing and for the
Media Lab's Terminal
Garden

punches it up on his monitor screen. Topic headlines in different colors indicate "International," "Technical," "Financial," "Mail," "People," etc. When he slides his finger across the screen, the image on the screen slides with him, revealing more text. He runs his finger across a lead paragraph, and that story fills the screen. He calls for other newsclips on the topic, and three come up, one of them colored pale yellow like aging newsprint, indicating it's an old item.

Illustrations on the screen in color, such as the map of Cuba or the photograph of the President, are drawn locally from a videodisk capable of holding 54,000 such images, the sort of thing that might be mailed out monthly by a subscription service. When Walter touches an article under "Today," suddenly the illustration comes to life, flames and smoke pouring up, a television voice announcing, "In Mount Bellevue, Texas, today there was an explosion at an oil refinery that set off a spectacular fire. Flames from burning propane, butane, and gasoline towered 800 feet . . ." The clip was captured from the evening news by NewsPeek and formatted into the presentation. The most significant item on NewsPeek's front page, Negroponte insists, is "Mail," where news from the user's own electronic mailbox is summarized. "It's news only to him, but it's the most important of all."

The demo is impressive but not as convincing as Negroponte and Bender would like because it can't be individualized for each visitor. That's a significant frustration, since the idea of intense personalization to the user is at the heart of most of the Lab's projects. Negroponte says, "I don't read newspapers myself. My wife, Elaine, reads them and tells me what I need to know because she's an expert on me. Artificial intelligence could do that, but in all the literature and programs I've come across I've never seen an expert system that pretended to be an expert about the *user*."

The Lab's current direction for the personal newspaper is exploring the nature of newsworthiness. Negroponte told an audience at Royal Dutch/Shell corporate headquarters in London, "If last night Mr. Gadhafi had invaded the United States and also last night you had had to cancel this meeting, in my morning newspaper the top headline would be: 'SHELL MEETING CANCELED.' Somewhere down below it would say, 'Gadhafi etc.' In *your* newspaper Gadhafi might have made the headline, but on your

front page someplace it would say, 'Negroponte Presentation Canceled.'
To nobody else would the cancellation be news. I was in Milano yesterday. If I had this newspaper printed out in my hotel room I would
expect to find somewhere in it a weather report for Heathrow Airport
in London, because I would have expected my travel-planning program
to have told my newspaper program my flight schedule."

What all of this might soon imply for newspapers is suggested in a
book called *Goodbye Gutenberg*, about the recent computer revolution
in newspaper production. Author Anthony Smith observed:

> Only about 10 percent of the total information collected every day
> in the newspaper's newsroom and features desk (all of which is held
> on-line, i.e., in continuous direct communication with a computer)
> is actually used in the paper, and yet, according to most surveys,
> the reader only reads 10 percent of what has gone into his paper.
> It seems, therefore, that the whole agony of distribution is undergone
> in order to feed each reader just one percent of the material that
> has been so expensively collected.

With an electronic newspaper, the whole 100 percent of what the
newsroom has could be accessed, and most of what would be selectively
delivered to the reader might be used. It's far more efficient at both ends.
The reader (the reader's machine, that is) has the additional advantages
of assembling material from a variety of sources and of getting versions
of articles of special interest that are much more in-depth than current
newspapers can offer. There would be only one copy of *The Daily Me*,
but it would have a devoted readership.

At the Media Lab the emphasis of research is not so much on the
content of the personal newspaper as on its interface with the user.
Negroponte tells what he learned from the *Wall Street Journal*: "I think
its middle column is the best international news synopsis in print, so I
made this arrangement to get it electronically when I was in Greece. I
was seeing it even before American readers did. But I found I just didn't
use it. I preferred to wait for the regular paper edition and read it there,
even though it was two days late. That printed column is a highly evolved
scanning device using four different type faces, two of them in its head-

lines, and it's a format I'm familiar and comfortable with. Electronic newspapers have to duplicate that level of sophistication, or they won't make it."

He adds, "The newspaper as a mass medium is going to die much less rapidly than broadcast television because you already have personalization in its design for easy scanning. Television is vulnerable because there is no personalizing so far except with VCRs."

☐ *Personal Television*
☐

■ Text and television media are constantly mixed at the Lab, in fine violation of their apartheid in the world. The same people and equipment are working on personalized television as on the personalized newspaper. One tool for that is a service called "closed-captioning," an optional service that some broadcasters provide for the hearing-impaired; lines of text appear along the bottom of the video image like foreign-film subtitles.

As Negroponte proposes, "One of the most hearing-impaired people I know is a computer. The computer could look at television all day for you, reading the closed-captioning, and when you get home at night, it says, 'I have twenty-five minutes of really great stuff I recorded today that you should look at. Your old friend so-and-so was on a talk show—he's just written a book. The company that you're competing with is reported to be going into Chapter 11. . . .' And if I like the 'Bill Cosby Show,' but I only have fifteen minutes, how about a fifteen-minute version of it, with skits and anecdotes it knows I'm interested in?"

The Lab already has a working program called NewsPrint that every night prints out the closed-captioning text of the "ABC Evening News" along with images it's taken off the air for illustration. (The news format is so predictable that the program can figure out pretty reliably when to capture the best television picture with each report—about a third of the way through each item.) NewsPrint could be expanded into kind of a personal *TV Guide* that summarizes graphically what the computer has collected for you today.

Many Lab visitors voice the fear that all this implies too much interactivity by the viewer. Walter Bender: "We had a guy from ABC here one night who was saying, 'When I get home what I really like to do is kick my shoes off, sit in a comfortable chair in front of the television, and veg out. I don't wanna interact, I don't wanna play games, I just wanna get fed.' But if the computer's been watching TV for you and knows what you're interested in, that's what you'll passively watch, instead of what everybody watches. That's Couch Potato Mode 1.

"Mike Bove, a graduate student here, is doing another level of generalization upon that, where he's not restricted himself to just television as input, but is using wire services, electronic mail, whatever. So if you're watching the news and it says, 'The stock market went crazy today,' then that's the appropriate time for your personal stock quotes to scroll across the bottom of the screen. That's called Network Plus—Couch Potato Mode 2."

Mike Bove fantasized further in a piece of e-mail addressed to the NewsPeek researchers: "I want to sit in an armchair reading the *Boston Globe* or the *New York Times*, and if any of the networks have any pictures to go with the story I'm currently reading, I want them to appear on the TV."

Grad student Judith Donath fantasized back:

Imagine the housewife, circa 1990, settling down for the afternoon soaps. She turns on "The Beating Heart." We left Brad and Allison yesterday in a dimly lit restaurant, just when Brad, as we knew he would, opened the box he had been holding out to her, revealing a sparkling diamond engagement ring, and Allison was acting oddly uncomfortable, not at all as if she was looking forward to this move. Today, we see them sitting there and then the screen dissolves into a flashback of that scene between Francesca and Allison—Allison crying, Francesca with that nasty superior smile, looking down at her.

"I hate that bitch Francesca," says the housewife to her chocolate. She touches Francesca's image on the screen. The video freezes and shrinks to a quarter of the screen. The rest of the screen is filled with the text of various magazines. There's *People* magazine's latest on Jessica Blackmore, the actress who plays Francesca. She's in the Coconut Lounge, sharing a two-straw drink with a large blond man. "I thought she was married to James Dealor," our viewer says to the cat. "What a cheating bitch." Sure enough, a photo in the next window—the *Post*'s gossip column—shows James Dealor being pulled off the large blond man. In another window is an article from *Soap Opera Digest*, from the time when the Allison/Francesca scene was news, analyzing the motivations of both characters and alluding to the possible repercussions.

Curiosity satisfied, the housewife touches the video still and it resumes action, filling the screen. About fifteen minutes later, just at the crucial moment when Allison is starting to tell Brad about the whole Francesca thing, two children come running in. "Mommy, he hit me!" "No I didn't! You're a liar!" "Mommy I am not he hit me I swear he did!" "Both of you stop screaming!" Finally it's all taken care of and Mommy can go back to her soap opera. She touches the screen and the video again freezes, and a transcript, starting at the current point in the script, appears at the side. She backs it up, finds where she was interrupted, and touches the transcript. In a moment the video again fills the screen, rewound to just where she had left off.

Donath would call it SoapBox.

"Interactive television," claims Andy Lippman, "represents a change as fundamental to the world of broadcasting as television itself was when introduced to the existing world of broadcast radio." A primary characteristic of interactive television is that it's asynchronous—stuff is broadcast at one time, viewed at another, just as people are doing now with VCRs. This could be a great relief to the broadcasters, who at present kill themselves trying to fill 8,760 hours a year with programs of potential interest to everyone. At the viewing end, interactive, asynchronous television could solve the major problem of viewers, which is scheduling. " 'Prime Time,' " predicts Negroponte, "becomes 'My Time.' "

A by-product of personal television would be conversation—what you see on *your* news may well be news to the rest of your office.

☐ *Broadcatch*
☐

■ In 1968 MIT's J. C. R. Licklider coined the term "narrowcasting" for what broadcast television should become—a much wider range of good programming targeted for specific audiences. The Carnegie report that his coinage appeared in led directly to the founding of PBS, America's highbrow TV channel. "Narrowcasting" soon came into general usage to describe what cable television was supposed to bring, and later it defined nicely what VCRs and satellite broadcasting in fact began to deliver.

The Media Lab is attempting something else entirely. If "narrowcasting" is the opposite of "broadcasting," we need a term that's the opposite of both. "Broadcatch" perhaps.

It's not utterly new. The station-selector buttons on a car radio are a kind of broadcatch device, since they are user customizable, but they only can select for source, not content. What's new at the Media Lab is the content-specific selectivity and repackaging at the receiving end that computer technology is offering. If printing and industrialization were revolutions that transformed civilization, a counterrevolution is under way.

The printing press mass-produced books, creating the mass audience, and to some extent, nations. The industrial revolution mass-produced hardware, creating mass consumers, and to some extent, world wars fought with massive hardware. But the most recent world war was won primarily by information—enemy signals captured from wireless transmissions and decoded by the world's first electronic computers. Winston Churchill was reading Hitler's orders before the German field commanders they were addressed to. Power was shifting from the material world to the immaterial world.

The first two decades of computer science following World War II were funded almost entirely by the American military. (Why this is not a major theme in contemporary history books I'll never know.) The direct, intentional result was the computerizing of society, and then the funny thing happened. Computing power dispersed. It went from the middle to the edges, from the broadcaster toward the broadcatcher. Thanks to the deliberate grass-roots revolt of the creators of personal computers and the lavish cleverness of the makers of consumer electronics, the bit business began to be taken over by citizens and customers.

When you shift perspective from how information is sent to how it is sought, a different pattern takes shape.

Some of the Media Lab researchers like to quote an optical disk prophet named Mark Heyer on the subject of information seeking. From Heyer's chapter in the book *CD ROM*:

> In my view, there are only three ways in which we gather information—by grazing, browsing, or hunting.
>
> *Grazing* is the well-known activity of sitting in front of the TV in an alpha trance, eyes wide open, with information, good or bad, flowing in. The networks used to point with pride to the fact that viewers who tuned in at 7 p.m. were most likely to watch the entire evening without bothering to change the channel.
>
> *Browsing* means scanning a large body of information with no particular target in mind. Newspapers and magazines are the high-technology browsing media today. They have lots of instantly accessible 2-D bandwidth. Browsing on TV has become popular with the advent of cable. During a 30-second commercial I can check out 15 different channels for 2 seconds each.
>
> In the *hunting* mode we are seeking specific information. Computers are superb hunting tools. Time-shift recording on VCRs is also hunting, although many people quickly find that they don't want their evening info-graze to become a hunt.

Broadcatch technology will change or accelerate each of the modes. Grazing—Couch Potato Mode—is intensified and perhaps made even more attractive by having an inquisitive robot do one's selective browsing all day, all night. Hunting by computer at present is an exhausting business, frequently jobbed out to data-search specialists. But much of what they do can be automated by broadcatch technology and soon will be.

What can't be automated, quite, is quality detection. The computer may be told, or even find out for itself, what subjects you're interested in. It will have a hell of a time detecting which of the infinity of junk out there you will consider, quote, *good*. The way around this, of course, is citation and review. The computer can query people whose opinion you share or respect on which of the junk is good. I can usually rely on the movie reviews of Sheila Benson in the *Los Angeles Times* or Jay Carr in the *Boston Globe*. I would inform my movie-search program of this.

One of the unexplored prospects of broadcatch is how opinion about quality will spread laterally among the populations of broadcatchers. Imagine innumerable highly specialized, highly judgmental *TV Guides*. Are fortunes to be made in that industry, or is it necessarily amateur? I would predict both, with successful amateur reviewers gradually becoming professional, as is already happening in the world of e-mail. Another question is whether broadcatch will exacerbate the excesses of best-sellerdom—popularity feeding on popularity and reducing variety—or will it provide a cure?

Meanwhile, part of what is driving the technology of broadcatch into existence is simple economics. More of the information at the source becomes potentially salable. If the filmmaker's cutting-room floor, the reporter's notes, the musician's outtakes, the author's earlier or longer drafts, can be accessed by inquiring audiences, then they will be.

At attractive prices, probably. Negroponte: "In principle it's much cheaper to get information this way." Take text. Pool noted, "Of the four distinguishable functions in the processing of words—input, storage, output, and delivery—storage is already cheaper in computers than in filing cabinets."

Electronic delivery of text is conspicuously cheaper than doing it on paper, and the booming of the laser printer market suggests that newspapers, magazines, and books will soon be more efficiently and conveniently manufactured in home and office than at printing plants. "The paper industry has cause for optimism," observed Pool. The printing industry does not.

Anticipating all that, the Media Lab is driving the quality end of broadcatch technology as far as it can. Lab doctrine states that everything you can see on present-day television and computer screens is unacceptable, both technically and aesthetically, and it says the same about what the Lab has produced so far. Andy Lippman: "The images should be perfect—*no* artifacts." Walter Bender: "Some of the things we've done are presenting information, not *selling* it, not doing what an alert salesman does."

Negroponte wants interactivity between humans and machines explored down to the finest nuance.

☐
☐ *Conversational Desktop*

■ I had heard bits and pieces of the Media Lab party line about interactivity for so long that I finally asked Andy Lippman for the full story and taped his answer. Lippman is an old Media Lab hand, dating back to the early '70s with the Architecture Machine Group. He has the Lab's finest mustache and a debate-loving manner of speaking. Our discourse in my office one day became what Gregory Bateson called a "metalogue"—a dialogue that is its own example, an explanation and a demonstration simultaneously.

The conversation about conversation that Lippman and I fell into

Andrew B. Lippman,
head of the "Paperback
Movies" project

is here presented verbatim. Be warned. Reading how people actually talk to each other is somewhat embarrassing, like watching someone throw up to see exactly how he manages it. But the point is in that very awkwardness, the perpetual mutual trespass of real conversation. Conversation with Lippman is a workable example in print because he is exceptionally articulate; when he says there are five corollaries, five show up. If the discussion seems too detaily and theoretical, bear with it. Getting detailed principles like these right is precisely the real work of the Media Lab, and the principles in this discussion have wide relevance.

STEWART BRAND: What does "interactivity" mean?

ANDY LIPPMAN: We have a clear working technical definition of the term "interactivity" that we've argued about for years.

SB: Which is?

AL: "Mutual and simultaneous activity on the part of both participants, usually working toward some goal, but not necessarily." There are five corollaries.

SB: Which are?

AL: One is interruptibility, which says that each one has to be able to interrupt the other, because we're trying to distinguish between what's interactive, which means mutual and simultaneous, versus alternating. And it's very clear that systems which use videodisks have missed that point, because what they call interaction is really an alternation—"your turn, my turn."

The model of interaction is a conversation versus a lecture. So the question is, what's the granularity of the interactive system—i.e., what's the smallest atomic element below which you can't interrupt? In conversation what is it? It may be the word or it may be the phrase. If you interrupt me while we're talking, I'll be able to finish the word. (**SB:** "Mm hm.") I might even finish the sentence, but you'll still have interrupted me, right? ("Mm hm.") There's some human interval in there, that you understand you're not being ignored, or . . .

SB: Or you'll say, "I'll get to that" or "Just a minute" or . . .

AL: Oh, you acknowledge the interrupt always. ("Yeah.") The question is acknowledgment, not whether you act on it. ("I see. Okay.") But the question is, when do I stop? Right? Okay?

SB: Interesting. Okay.

AL: So in human conversation it's probably the word or phrase. ("Mm hm.") In movies for example . . . well it's clear it's not the scene, that's too big. ("Mm hm.") If you're watching the movie and you poke the movie and it went all the way to the end of the scene, that's clearly too big. ("Mm hm.") So what is the size of those primitive elements is usually the key determinant to whether a system succeeds at being interactive or fails. And . . .

SB: A successful one sets a smaller grain.

AL: Yeah, but there's a grain size below which you don't have to go. I mean, if somebody's talking, they don't have to stop ("Mm hm.") . . . in the middle of a word. But it's clear if they go on to the end of the paragraph or the thought, that it's really becoming a lecture, that they've deferred, you know . . . Now, the other is graceful degradation. This one is Backer's addition to it, because he was writing this into his thesis for a time. ("Who?") And that was . . . Dave Backer. ("Mm hm.") Um. That has to do with, well, we're none of us geniuses, and we don't have everything we know at our fingertips. So it's clear that in any interaction you can always make some sort of request that can't be answered. (Laughter from SB.) It isn't necessarily a non sequitur. But does that halt the interaction? And the answer is, not if the system degrades gracefully. In the sense that it can fold in what it can't do. It'll say, "I'll answer that in a minute." ("Mm hm.") You know, because it can't answer it immediately. Somehow you have to productively handle the twists and turns that you haven't . . . that you don't know about, right?

SB: Okay, this is "not losing the thread"? (**AL:** "Well . . .") Or is that something else? ("No . . .") Is interruptibility . . . ?

AL: No, not losing the thread has to do with having a global vision of where you really want to go, and there's no guarantee that an interaction is going to end up where it thought it would when it started, and it needed in order to be an interaction.

SB: Thread is something besides goal. Um . . . ("I see. Okay.") I'm not sure what it is yet, but maybe it'll emerge. ("Okay.") So, what is this third one, "degradation of . . . ?"

AL: Graceful degradation. It doesn't blow the system away. Or personally, in a conversation, can you handle that ("Mm hm.") in such a way that the interaction continues, or does that cause things to collapse?

SB: I get why it's graceful. Why is it degradation?

AL: I don't know. It seemed like a good thing to call it. How does it degrade when it can't handle what it should, when it can't do what it ought to do? ("Okay.") In what manner does it degrade, productively or not?

SB: If it can't be brilliant ("Yeah."), it's being sort of bright repartee.

AL: Right. That's one way of putting it. Another one was limited look-ahead. ("Limited look-ahead?") Yeah. ("What's that?") In the sense that this is another corollary. Um. You can't have precomputed everything you're going to say. In a conversation, how far ahead of where you're talking are you really thinking? You have a goal, but since it's interactive, and each one of us is going to interrupt the other, we can't anticipate ever reaching that goal or where we're going to go or how far we're going to digress, so you don't look that far ahead in composing the interaction.

From the point of view of programming it would mean that you wouldn't necessarily string together the entire database. Okay? But you'd start to draw upon the whole database on the fly, to compose what your responses would be. See? It has to be on the fly. ("Mm hm.") And . . .

SB: "Limited look-ahead" and "on the fly" are related concepts.

AL: Sure, and another one that's related but perhaps distinct, I haven't ever really thought about it in this way, is the no-default. Okay? ("No-default?") When you build the system, you want to avoid building a system that sort of has this default path that you're going to go down unless you change it. ("Mm hm.") You really do want it to happen on the fly ("Mm hm.") because defaults are, I don't know what, boring.

(Excuse a written interruption to this oral event, but it's useful to know that the following remarks about a "Movie Map" refer to one of the Architecture Machine Group's most celebrated demos, which Lippman directed, a 1978 videodisk containing the entire town of Aspen, Colorado. With it the viewer drives at will down any street, turning any direction at any corner, and the appropriate film is shown. You can shift the scene any time to any season, look forward, to the rear, or either side, and stop and explore many buildings. It was a tour de force piece that compelled the optical disk industry to realize how interactive the medium could be. Nine years later the "Aspen Movie Map" still hasn't been surpassed.)

AL: The other corollary was: you have to have the impression of an infinite database. Okay? That is to say . . . look at the Movie Map, which is the thinking that we derived this definition from. ("Mm hm.") At every instance you have eleven choices. You can: continue, back up, change your view, change the season, or talk to any of ten buildings—there's fifteen different things you can do at every instant. ("Mm hm.") Now, if I made you wait till the end of the block—you couldn't touch the buildings, all you could do is control the direction you drive ("Mm hm."), okay? then it's not interactive, it's selective, because you make the decision to go down that street, and having made that decision there's no productive thing you can do until the end of it, until it's your turn again.

SB: It's a one-block granularity.

AL: Yeah, and that's clearly too big. ("Mm hm.") But the other is, if you only have these two choices at every instant the outcome of which after a while becomes obvious, then it's not interactive either. It wins because there are fifteen things you can do at every frame ("Mm hm."), each one of which is different. There's an appearance of an infinite database. You can touch a building and go into it, and you can't know what's there if you haven't been there before. If all you can do is drive and turn, you know what each input's going to do. If it becomes readily apparent that it's going to converge, then it's not interactive anymore ("Mm."), right? because there's no value in the interruption, because you know where you're going to get to—it's as if it has to have infinite look-ahead. It's all pre-computed. If nothing you can do can change that, what's the point of interacting?

Transcribing a verbatim conversation like this is astonishingly difficult—the mind wants to smooth over the awkwardnesses, edit them into convenient clarity. Yet in the course of writing this chapter I must have read the Lippman conversation fifteen times and learned something new each time—partly because it is its own example, partly because the whole Media Lab is its example. You can, for instance, see the ideas on interactivity employed with great effect in the Lab's Speech Research.

The director of Speech Research is Chris Schmandt, a former college dropout who spent five years hitchhiking across Africa, the Mideast, and India before rejoining MIT and the Architecture Machine Group. Big and brisk, at thirty-five he is still a keen hiker, vanishing frequently to the Arizona desert, Washington's Cascade Mountains, or the last snowshoeing of the season in northern Vermont. He explained the Lab's demo-or-die rationale: "To some extent these demos are our work. Ideas are cheap. I don't put much currency in ideas. You have to instantiate your idea, and that's what this kind of a demo system is. All kinds of things happen—one idea interferes with another idea.

"There's a general atmosphere here that prototyping is cool—it's our experimental method. If you think something might be a neat idea, go spend a couple weeks working on it and see if you can come up with a preliminary demo. Because we're not constrained by trying to build something with immediate applicability, we can handwave around a bunch of issues that have to do with current technology and focus more on deeper or background issues. Like, 'What is a conversation?' Or, 'If you could talk to a computer, what kinds of things would you talk about? How do you want it to act to you?'

"The demos come out, as a result, much flashier. We're known for that flash—it's not an accident. We're not making a product, we're making an idea, which can be convincing through its manifestation in

Christopher M.
Schmandt, head of
Speech Research

a demo. We should be challenging the way people think. What's wrong to say is, 'That's much too expensive.' You've missed it."

In 1985 Schmandt and cohort Barry Arons put together one of the Lab's more impressive demos, called "Conversational Desktop." The idea was to machine-emulate a good secretary. The videotape of the demo begins with Barry Arons in his office, wearing a microphone headset. He turns to his desktop computer and says,

"I'm here."

"HI, BARRY. REMEMBER TO . . ." (And the computer plays back Barry's own voice:)

"Get a gift for Steve before my flight to California."

The computer (in capital letters) speaks with a natural-sounding woman's voice. In fact it's "stored speech"—a number of phrases are recorded separately and then assembled into meaningful sentences as needed.

What's exciting here is that the machine is not just recognizing the speech but recognizing the speaker—"HI, BARRY." Barry continues,

"When I talk to Chris, remind me to . . ."

"READY TO RECORD."

". . . tell him how my parser aids recognition."

"OKAY, GOT IT." (The view flashes to his schedule for the day on his computer screen, which adds in blue a note about Chris.)

A lady in a blue dress walks in: "Hi, Barry, do you have a minute?"

He looks around. "Sure, what's up?"

Amazing. How does the computer know it isn't being addressed when Barry speaks to the visitor? Schmandt: "Good question. And we came up with a great hack to solve it. Speech as it comes out of your head is fairly directional. With a couple of microphones behind Barry we assigned directionality to the system, so the computer knows when you're talking to it. It worked like a charm." When Barry and the visitor decide they need to meet with Walter Bender, Barry turns to the computer and asks,

"When can I meet with Walter this afternoon?"

"WITH WHOM DO YOU WANT TO MEET THIS AFTER-NOON?"

"Walter."

"WALTER IS AVAILABLE TODAY AT ONE."

"Confirm it." (Shot of Barry's schedule; 1 p.m. fills in with Walter.)

"MEETING WITH WALTER SCHEDULED TODAY AT ONE."

The computer knows about Walter and how to reach his computer. Notice how the computer guides the conversation to be sure it's under-standing—"WITH WHOM DO YOU WANT TO MEET THIS

AFTERNOON?"—just as I did when interrupting Andy Lippman, "Limited look-ahead?" The two machines negotiated the meeting time with computer-quick speed. Barry's visitor leaves and his computer reports,

> "WHILE YOU WERE BUSY I TOOK A MESSAGE FROM TODD . . ."
>
> > "Hey Barry, you still want to have lunch? I'd love to get a bowl of chowder at Legal."
>
> Barry to computer: "I'm going to Legal Seafood."
>
> "ENJOY YOUR LUNCH."

Barry's computer knew that he was having a meeting, recognized Todd's voice, and knew that Todd was not high enough on Barry's priority list of friends to warrant interrupting the meeting, and so it politely took a message and told Barry as soon as it knew the meeting was over. If higher-priority Negroponte had called, the computer would have put him through. The video continues with the phone ringing in Barry's empty office.

> "HELLO, BARRY'S TELEPHONE SPEAKING. WHO'S CALLING, PLEASE?"
>
> "Hi, this is Mike McKenna."
>
> "WHAT'S THIS IN REFERENCE TO?" (Barry's computer screen shows an incoming call and a sequence of headings in a row: Name, Subject, Phone, Time, Message. "Name" now has a blue square under it.)
>
> "Your conversational messaging system." ("Subject" now has a blue square.)
>
> "HE'S NOT AVAILABLE AT THE MOMENT, BUT HE LEFT THIS MESSAGE . . ."
>
> > (Barry's voice:) "I'm at lunch. I'll get back to you as soon as I return."

"AT WHAT NUMBER CAN HE REACH YOU?"

This process works astonishingly well. The computer *isn't* understanding the speech, it's interjecting questions in the caller's pauses and then recording the answers whatever they may be and labeling them accessibly on the screen. As Schmandt says, "Audio is a hard medium to file, it's a hard medium to wander through, and it's a hard medium to label." Barry returns to the office.

"I'm back."

"HI, BARRY. YOU HAVE NEW MESSAGES . . ." (Barry touches the screen by the top call—there's no name there, since the computer didn't recognize the caller's voice.)

"Hi, this is Mike McKenna."

(Barry touches the blue square under "Message.")

"I'm interested in systems that emulate human conversation. I'd like to talk to you about your current work."

Barry takes the rest of the message and then asks the computer,

"When's my flight?"

"YOUR PLANE TO SAN FRANCISCO LEAVES IN ONE HOUR FIFTY-FIVE MINUTES. TRAFFIC TO THE AIRPORT IS HEAVY. SHOULD I CALL YOU A CAB?"

That kind of flash gets an audience murmuring. Then Schmandt or Negroponte can explain how that last bit was pulled off, like the rest, without faking. The Boston area has a data service called "Metro Traffic" that the computer checked on, and flight information was from the Official Airlines Guide available on CompuServe and elsewhere.

Since the making of the Conversational Desktop demo, Barry Arons moved on to Hewlett-Packard in California and Chris Schmandt has set about exploring the uses of "paralinguals"—the way speech is stressed, pitched, accented, as well as all the information carried in stutters, pauses, gulps, tones of voice. "I'm trying to bring up a system now to do 'grunt' recognition. Hypothesis: in general, confirming responses (to, say, someone giving you directions how to drive to MIT from Logan Airport) are shorter than negative ones—'uh-huh' versus 'what was that?' If that's true, I can build a very nice speaker-independent (in fact word-independent) direction-giver."

He's aspiring to ever finer secretary emulation. "I would like the machine to pick up that I'm not having a particularly good day and be supportive or something . . . ask me what's wrong . . . ask me if I'd like a sandwich. If you're having a bad day and somebody does some little thing for you, it can really swing your whole day around. Or the machine could detect a one-sided phone conversation and interrupt with a back-ground voice reminding me of a pending meeting, to give me an excuse to hang up. Then there's an idea called Phone Nag: 'Don't you think you ought to call your mother? You haven't talked to her for a month, you know. Here, let me dial the number for you.' "

Notice that none of this is total speech recognition yet, which nobody at the Lab expects to see in the 1980s. The Conversational Desktop only recognizes about 150 words in some thirty commands, though it can distinguish and identify a couple dozen different speakers. (As this technology gets into the market one can anticipate a sort of computer pidgin English becoming hip for a while. Jokes and urban legends will flourish—"So this lady sez to her car . . .")

Negroponte sees no reason to wait for complete speech recognition. "When you talk about speech, everybody thinks 'natural language'—the computer's going to understand English, we'll build a typewriter that you can speak into. That's wonderful, and I'm sure someday we'll all have them—at least our children will have them—but it's misleading and has sidetracked some very interesting and immediate applications of speech.

"The interesting applications fall into three categories that are un-dersold, little-understood properties of speech. One is that speech is a long arm, the longest arm you've got. I can talk to somebody twenty feet away and around corners and up stairs. Another is that speech has the very simple property of being another channel. If you're working on an oscilloscope with a couple of probes, looking around at the meter may be awkward, and you'd like to be able to say, 'Volts. Amps,' and have the meter just talk to you. It's purely a decluttering feature. And thirdly, the paralinguals allow you to put a lot more information in the channel. That's why printed speeches in newspapers are so unsatisfactory. You might be reading a quote from a speech by Reagan in an electronic newspaper and wonder aloud, 'How did he say that?' The computer sees where your eyes are looking, and lo and behold the voice comes forth.

"I would like to get up in the morning, walk by my personal computer and say, 'Is there any electronic mail?' Then as I'm brushing my teeth it says, 'Yes, you have three messages, and one was from Jerry Wiesner.' In neither case am I required to sit down and focus. I can do it in parallel. Doing things in parallel is what humans do naturally."

That may explain some of the attraction of the Terminal Garden. Programming requires enormous concentration, but many Lab people leave their quiet private offices to work in the melee of the Garden, focusing intently on their workstation screen, but all the time monitoring in parallel the action around them.

What the public sees of the Media Lab is demos, but what those demos are made of is endless computer programming, often as ingenious as the ideas being demonstrated, but invisible. Below decks with the apparent galley slaves—the student programmers—is where the real Media Lab action is, especially at night.

☐ *Why Programmers Work at Night*

■ Hackers invented themselves at MIT in around 1961, an event chronicled in Steven Levy's *Hackers: Heroes of the Computer Revolution*. Seymour Papert, who co-headed MIT's Artificial Intelligence Lab in the later part of those days, recalls, "The hackers were creating the front of computer science. Without specifications they would just start programming, quick and dirty. They did the first computer graphics, the first word-processing, the first computer games, the first time-sharing. If you tried to tell them what to do, you got nowhere at all. You could engage their interest, though."

At MIT these days there are still some hackers, but mostly what remains is the glorious tradition. Marvin Minsky, who was a perceptive defender of hacker freedom back then, notes, "The hackers had to drop out in the early '60s because they knew more than the professors. Now they don't necessarily know more than the professors." There are other differences in present MIT programmers, readily apparent in the Terminal Garden, even though hacker lingo ("flame," "wedged," "mumble," "device null") still prevails. Hackers used to be fat guys. This crowd tends to slimness, and a number of them are female (one-third of the 1986 MIT freshman class were freshwomen). They're frequently told what to do, and they do it. But the hacker zest for headlong group exploration abides.

I asked Walter Bender what the appeal of the Garden was. "It's where the interesting equipment is, and I guess I like being with people. With the newest, best equipment there's always only one, so there's competition to get on it." There's competition even for the machines present in abundance—the Sun workstations, the $100,000 Lisp machines from Symbolics, the new Bobcats from Hewlett-Packard.

The various workstations on the Garden network, with their distinct projects and personalities and customary users, are named "Almost Home," "Zuzu," "Vienna Finger," "Chip Ahoy," "Oreo," "Fig Newton," "Double Stuff," "Lorna Doone," and the ever-popular "Famous Amos." Cookies. Bender explained, "There used to be a tradition of sending out graduate students for cookies in the late afternoon when Arch Mac was across from the Coop (campus store)." Frequent brain sugar and then group runs for Chinese food are renowned hacker food habits. Minsky has a theory: "What's the most significant feature of Chinese food besides the food itself? It's a group decision. Contrary to common belief, hackers are more social than normal people. And then there's the adventure of eating mysterious unnamable things."

Programmers still shack up with the computers in hacker fashion, moving in and spending the night or a week straight welded to the keyboard. This gives the Terminal Garden and other programming environments around the Lab a lived-in look that I find appealing but which sponsors are expected not to. Walter Bender waxes wroth via e-mail on occasion:

There is a MAJOR site visit by IBM on Friday. These are the guys paying your tuition, so we'd best be prepared. At Monday's meeting everyone should have a status report ready detailing what they will be able to demonstrate/handwave on Friday. In accordance with which there will be a major depigging of the Garden Thursday afternoon. Anything that doesn't belong there (shoes, old food, blankets, et cetera) will be burned on the loading dock at 5 p.m.

I could always tell when a sponsor visit was scheduled. Implicated researchers were in ties and slacks instead of the customary native garb of running shoes and jeans.

The working hours of programmers are like those of musicians— late afternoon to God-knows-when a.m. This is not too surprising considering that many programmers *are* musicians. Daytime, it is understood, is for administration. Nighttime, with fewer phone calls, longer cycles available on the big computers, is for concentration. The all-night brigade in the Terminal Garden may take breaks together and socialize, but the main event is focused work, and everyone up at that hour knows that and respects it.

Programming (or making music) at night is dreamtime, a period exclusively mental, utterly absorbed, sustained and timeless, placeless, disembodied. "Electronic man has no physical body," proclaimed Marshall McLuhan presciently. A famed hacker and co-designer of the Macintosh computer named Andy Hertzfeld described the attractions of the programming state of consciousness in *Programmers at Work*:

It's the only job I can think of where I get to be both an engineer and an artist. There's an incredible, rigorous, technical element to it, which I like because you have to do very precise thinking. On the other hand, it has a wildly creative side where the boundaries of imagination are the only real limitation. . . . It takes incredible concentration and mind space. Just keeping all the different connections in your brain at once is a skill that people lose as they get older. Concentration is a gift of youth.

Is there still debate going on about whether computers will augment human intellect? Computers enable programmers to live at the very edge of their intellectual abilities, constantly pushing that edge further. Like centaurs of myth they become temporary cyborgs, part human, part machine.

Programmers, even more than most MIT students, have the romance of the alien going for them. The lavatories on the Media Lab's third floor have Martian-creature silhouettes replacing the conventional male and female insignia on the doors. Life is question. "I wonder why we get bags under our eyes when we're tired. Why there?" Steve Strassmann would ask me, strolling somewhere after he'd spent a night adding five new features to his thesis program. Like tourists to Earth, the students speak with a bemused self-inquiry, as if noting, "Isn't it interesting that here we are talking in English, and it even sort of works, but what an odd way to communicate." Many talk in sustained blurts, a surging torrent of words that doesn't bother with interruptions. Two or three will rattle on simultaneously, apparently sending and receiving at the same time. And MIT students work harder than any others I've seen in America. The university colors of maroon and gray are referred to as "blood on concrete."

"Students tend to be the glue that keeps this place together," says Negroponte. "They drift between groups." Of the Lab's 140 people, sixty-five are graduate students getting degrees in Media Arts and Sciences. Another thirty-seven are "UROPers," kids from MIT's Undergraduate Research Opportunities Program, which enables undergraduates to participate in the serious research going on in any of the forty-five laboratories on campus, earning $5.50 an hour.

MIT's attitude toward its students shocked me. When I fled universities back in 1960, it was largely because of the routine institutional disdain, even contempt, for students. Now I was hearing people like ex-President Jerome Wiesner saying, "The new interdisciplinary things are done by students, not by faculty. We can sit around and dream, but some kid will elect himself a program as a graduate student, and it will have certain characteristics attractive to other students, and pretty soon you'll see a movement. That happened with biophysics, biochemistry, and computer modeling of the economy, just to mention three."

In the midst of a heated argument at a meeting, one Lab professor remarked as an aside, "MIT's secret of success is: we have the best students in the country. What we teachers do, or how, seems almost irrelevant." His opponent agreed vigorously with that point before counterattacking on the disputed topic. Wiesner predicts there'll be one sure measure of Media Lab success or failure: "We'll know whether we're right by whether good students flock here."

"I believe in the Elixir of Youth. I believe in the Absolute Truth," remarks the screen that grad student Steve Strassmann is using to demo his "Brushes That Change" thesis project. ("Hardwired: the wrath of God," the screen says the next time.) Strassmann has taught the computer to make Chinese/Japanese-style *sumi-e* ink drawings by modeling the behavior of ink and the individual bristles of the brush.

As he makes sweeping motions on the screen via a "mouse" on the desktop, Strassmann explains, "Now I can dip the brush in a different kind of ink, or I can change the dryness of the brush so it gets drier earlier. I can change the texture of the 'paper,' so it's more like a charcoal sketch. I can go back and blur the stroke like a watercolor. As the brush turns a corner it can shpritz a little ink out in droplets." A delicate Oriental image of a bird wisps into existence. "Next month I'm going to try to make a movie—a traditional Chinese scene with mountains and clouds, and a heron preening its feathers. Later on I'd like to make ink-brush strokes in three dimensions, like a syringe through Jell-O."

Brushstrokes in three dimensions like a syringe through Jell-O. Is that what NBC and Paramount Pictures want from this place?

4 NEWMEDIA 2— SENDING

The word "broadcast" comes from agriculture: it's what the sower of seeds does. Her arm makes a centrifugal strewing motion and an arc of uniform vegetable information intersects the soil, planting consequence shallow but wide. Nature plants the same way, strewing dandelion seeds, tadpoles, cocoanuts, and viruses. Broadcast is heedless. It keeps the world packed with news, welcome or not.

—Susan Braintree

Mass broadcasting, often portrayed by Negroponte as doomed, is at least in a state of upheaval set in motion by major changes in its infrastructure technology.

The curious attributes of electronic broadcasting are neatly summarized by Sydney Head in *World Broadcasting Systems*. Broadcast is: *ubiquitous*—it reaches everywhere, cheaply; *immediate*—always available, constantly unfolding; *voracious*—a bottomless maw for programmers to fill; *flexible*—local can become national with the flip of a switch; *voluntary*—the audience must decide to tune in, and it invests in part of the system, the receiver; *potentially controlling*—governments perceive the power of the instrument; hence, *regulated*.

From Media Lab perspective, broadcast is not nearly voluntary enough. It's a streetcar: you can be on or off it, and you can pick your stop (channel, station), period. Why can't you drive it like a car, anywhere you want? The immediacy is a problem, too. You have to abide by the streetcar's schedule. And regulation can be a hazard for inventors. The government doesn't usually want anybody messing with the streetcars.

Since the coming of Reagan the government has been highly deregulatory for the first time in decades. The FCC—the Federal Communications Commission—effectively told television and radio, "Do what you want." Mark Fowler, the FCC Chairman for six years, said to the broadcasters, "Your calling is to the market, which is the people, and to the truth. You don't need, and shouldn't have, an FCC telling you how to run your business." Upon Fowler's departure the *Wall Street Journal* noted, "Mr. Fowler found that many of his procompetitive moves . . . were opposed by business interests that profited from the regulatory status quo. 'Our biggest problems,' he said, 'have been with the Fortune 500 companies and not the Naderites.' "

The legions of communications lawyers in Washington were scared for a while by the relaxed FCC, but then they discovered there's even richer pickings in the chaos of newmedia, so the young ones learned the new terminology and the old ones retired. (Want to know where the action in a culture is? Watch where new language is turning up and where the lawyers collect, usually in that sequence.) Deregulation does encourage invention, at least until the next monopolies set in; then you have to regulate again to keep the marketplace working while new technology accumulates for the next round of invention-leading-to-deregulation-leading-to-invention.

TV broadcast these days is in turmoil while radio and the print media are relatively quiet. Newspapers have been turned by computers and satellites into national, even world, media. Magazines are as plodding as radio—cash machines for advertising to highly segmented markets. Book publishers flirted somewhat disastrously with personal computer software, then were surprised by the success of audio books—suddenly there's 20,000 book titles on audiocassettes, some of them selling over 200,000 copies, and you can't help wondering what that might be a portent of in Media Lab terms.

The content of electronic broadcasting fascinates. That's its job. Like the content of individual human consciousness, it's a headlong blur of amusements, warnings, and work. The work is expressed in skill-acquisition, access-to-tools, and countless numbers—temperature today, stock market today, inflation, unemployment, prices. The warnings are all the bad news that news is made of, which makes good sense when you consider that most of us learn from other people's mistakes rather than our own.

The amusements of broadcast consist mainly of songs, stories, and games, just as in tribal life. The songs and stories are mostly about courtship, the games mostly played by men, just as in tribal life. What's different is the scale, yielding the perfectly named phenomenon of Pop Culture—clouds of iridescent, fragile bubbles floating miraculously, reflecting each other lovingly, gone in a ping of brief dismay, constantly inflated anew. Perhaps the shallowness and self-obsession is the price of there being a single pop culture, a conveniently unified frame of reference for everybody tuned in to it.

Marvin Minsky takes a cheerful view: "Imagine what it would be like if TV actually were good. It would be the end of everything we know."

□□ TV Is Trying

■ The fate of broadcast TV is of direct interest to the Media Lab, given its network sponsors and its joyous meddling in the video medium. Speaking one day in the Bartos Theater in the Lab's basement was Frank Stanton, head of CBS from 1949 to 1979, still considered one of TV's leading intellectuals. At seventy-eight he has the look and sound of one who's earned the distinguished bags under his eyes.

"The question in my mind is whether you really need a network if you look down the road," he told the full house. He explained that what the networks were really made of was coaxial cable and later microwave towers linking the nation. The coming of cable television and satellites, along with tape used both by stations and in the home, has led to a progressive unraveling. With satellite and cable Ted Turner nabbed 36 million households for Cable Network News. VCRs take a big toll. "Hollywood might as well distribute itself now via satellite," Stanton said, a couple of months before 20th Century Fox launched "the fourth network." With transportable satellite uplinks, every local station is beginning to do some of its own world newsgathering, reporting direct from Geneva or Manila, leaving network news with not much special to offer. "Look at 'Entertainment Tonight,' " said Stanton, "if you want to see what the direction of network news might be. It's outrating the

three networks' news anchors. And that's coming out of Tinseltown."
His forecast: ever more glitz.

Though networks are battered by technological changes, some of
the new technologies are welcomed, at least by manufacturers, because
they require no major restructuring, just new equipment purchases by
everybody. One such is stereo TV, currently abloom. By virtue of signal
compression it offers better sound than you can get from FM radio—the
broadcaster uses computer technology to squeeze the signal, the receiver
expands it. Already popular in Japan and Germany, stereo TV is coming
faster in the States than color TV did in the '50s and '60s. Three-fourths
of American homes were getting some stereo broadcasting in late 1986,
and 5 percent had stereo sets. VCR manufacturers also are cheerfully
retooling for stereo.

There's also VBI—vertical blanking interval—ten whole lines of the 525
lines in the American TV image. When your picture rolls up on the screen
and you see a black band, that's the VBI. For the hearing-impaired some
broadcasters are using the VBI for "closed-captioning"—exploited at the
Media Lab for its Personal Television experiments. A few broadcasters in
farming states use VBI to broadcast agricultural prices.

□ Cable Is Trying
□

■   A full half of America's 86 million homes are wired for cable television, avenue of yet more exotic services. Twenty million of those homes
are customers of the Home Shopping Network or its competitors, where
the commercials, in effect, *are* the programming. See what you like,
phone in your order for a discount price (and the cable service gets a 5
percent commission). A recent feature on some systems is "photoclassified
ads" for regional use, reaching half a million cable subscribers. Another
service available by cable, perhaps a harbinger, is XPress. Styling itself
an "instant electronic newspaper," it provides up-to-the-minute wire

service news, stock quotations, financial data, weather, sports, etc., for $20 a month. All text. You don't get it on your TV, but on your personal computer hooked up to the cable.

Closer to the hearts of cable broadcasters is PPV programming—pay-per-view—the dream of cable from day one. It failed repeatedly in the early years until cable gave up and learned to charge by the month for the connection, leaving the valve open and unmetered. But with new "addressable" technology the nuisance factor is diminishing and viewers can expect a new round of experimentation. Except for major special events I doubt if there's much chance for it—too much free competition.

All this juicy variety and interactivity was forecast over twenty years ago when cable was first contemplated, inspiring hundreds of entrepreneurs to set about wiring America with coaxial cable. The business languished and languished and then suddenly took off. I asked Russ Neuman at the Media Lab what happened.

"That's easy. The industry knows that one," said Neuman. "The answer is two words: Jerry Levin. He was a middle-level executive at Time Inc. Time bought Home Box Office in '72. In 1975 Levin says, 'We're going to take a big gamble. Put HBO on the bird.' " In other words, broadcast by satellite to the cable services; they didn't have the requisite $100,000 satellite dishes, but they might be persuaded to get them if good movies were available. "Everybody sort of scratched their heads, and whammo, the industry took off." Suddenly distance was of no economic consequence. "It changed the definition of what was going on. The psychology of control between the networks and their local affiliates changed by going to the dish." Hollywood also was shaken as they watched ten years of very big bucks for movies going to someone else. "By the time Jerry Levin left the presidency of HBO, 50 percent of Time Inc.'s income was from television."

▢▢ *The Satellite Proletariat*

■ "Three billion dollars in backyard satellite dishes came out of the blue," a banker told me. No one expected that individuals would put up the $8,000 it took to assemble a ten-to-twenty-foot tracking dish and signal-amplifying equipment (later it was $3,000, now it's as low as $800). Since no major manufacturers were ready for such a market, hundreds of garage-based businesses rushed into the quasi-illegal vacuum. In twelve years home dishes went from zero to an estimated 2.1 million installed on the American landscape. "Estimated" because no one really knows how many of the wicked things are out there. Many are home-built, like chicken coops, by owners completely undaunted by the highness of the tech involved.

The reason is free riches. Beaming down onto North America from twenty-nine satellites are 114 channels of you-name-it television. You get regularly scheduled dog racing, harness racing, rugby, Australian-rules football, surfing, cheerleading, body-building, and lacrosse, plus all the regular sports. There are channels for blacks, Spanish, Jewish, Japanese, children, and hearing-impaired. You can escalate from pornography soft to pornograpy hard and then recover on any flavor of religious channel from Baptist to Mormon. There are channels for finance, art/culture, science/nature, health, live Washington politics, weather, news, home-shopping, and adult education. Along with quite a few movies—in any week you can take your pick of over 420.

Plus forty FM radio stations.

The reason that J. C. R. Licklider's vaunted "narrowcasting" didn't happen with cable is that most cable stations carry only some thirty-plus channels, few of them very specialized. So far there simply hasn't been enough advertising revenue to go around to cover the longed-for specialty broadcasting on cable.

The coming of VCRs was a partial cure for the viewer, but satellites have covered the waterfront even better by effectively turning each dish owner into a private cable service with countless channels. As far as the cable stations were concerned, that meant war. Cable lobby groups assailed Congress to outlaw private satellite dishes. Instead Congress legalized them, so long as the dish owners weren't selling what they captured.

So cable set about "scrambling" the signals going to and from the satellites so you would need a commercially controllable decoder at every dish in order to get decent reception. The dish owners' lobby group fought that without success. In early 1986 Home Box Office, followed by Showtime, scrambled its signals and frightened the backyard dish marketplace. It now appears a new equilibrium is emerging, with some satellite signals scrambled and most not, and some dish owners paying for the decoders and many not. Overall, the wealth of programming in the sky continues to increase.

Meanwhile satellite technology presses on. Most of the present satellite television is in the so-called C-band (4–6 gigaHertz—4 billion cycles per second; quite high frequency). It requires a 10-foot-wide dish to pull in properly. Already starting to arrive is Ku-band TV (11–14 gigaHertz), which you can collect with a 4-foot dish, costing down to $500. Coming sometime, no one knows when, is Ka-band (20–30 gigaHertz), which can serve a little antenna on top of the TV set. At Ka-band frequencies you can have no end of channels. Also starting to arrive are flat antennas for satellite reception that can live inconspicuously on roofs and walls.

In other satellite developments, remote imaging from space by civilian services is approaching military standards. The leader at present is France's SPOT satellite, whose pictures are appearing routinely in the news, showing such details as the unannounced damage and fire at the Chernobyl nuclear reactor. It's changing the secrets game.

☐ *Optical Fiber Strikes Back*
☐

■ Just when you think satellites have communications all wrapped up, fiberoptic cables arrive to confuse everything. This was dramatically demonstrated one noon at the Media Lab. Guests for lunch were two gents from the Bell Communications Research Group, Patrick E. White and Edward Arthurs, who were working with the capabilities of fiberoptic cable. Negroponte had invited a number of the Media Lab's researchers and posed the day's question to them thus: "What would you do with infinite zero-cost bandwidth?" We looked up from our plates in aghast silence.

The bandwidth bottleneck is the eternal bugaboo of communications technology: it governs the amount of data a medium can transmit per second. The reason we don't have wonderful cheap picturephones is that you can't squeeze all the information needed for good picture and sound through the "twisted-pair" copper wires of conventional telephone lines.

Similarly with bandwidth in the broadcast spectrum. Comparing FM with AM radio, the higher fidelity of FM takes ten times as much bandwidth per station as AM. Television channels require thirty-three times more bandwidth than FM—*anything* graphic requires enormous quantities of data, as we'll see again and again. Beating that game with ingenious compression techniques is one of the primary goals of the Media Lab, because defeating bandwidth strictures means delectable new levels of quality of image and sound could be transmitted through existing media.

Hence our stunned silence. Negroponte was saying the war was over: there was no war. The gentlemen from Bell had a rapt, skeptical audience. Fiberoptic cable, they informed us, could today deliver half a gigabit per second of data to every house, *and* Bell has the switching technology to manage four simultaneous interactive channels on it right now. Everybody's mental calculators fluttered.

I translated "half a gigabit" wrongly into 500,000 bits per second and was impressed. We read (you're reading now) at about 300 bits per second. Moving up to 1,200 bits per second telecommunicating with a personal computer (buying a 1,200-baud modem) is a big step, like getting long pants used to be. A channel over 400 times more intense than that simply awed me. When I mentioned this later to Negroponte, he was amused but gentle. "You're off by three orders of magnitude (1,000)." *Giga* is billion, not million. Half a billion is 500 *million*, not thousand, bits per second. Effectively, infinite bandwidth. "These things are changing by astronomical orders of magnitude," Negroponte consoled me. "We don't have any feel for such quantities. We can imagine a book a couple inches thick, but not a book a mile thick."

The Media Lab's best and brightest stuttered. One volunteered you could have a combination of television immediacy and newspaper depth and detail available any time through such a medium. Fine, that would occupy a teensy fraction of the bandwidth. What else? Uh, every house acquires its own broadcast capability. Uh, you could broadcast solids by having them fabricated at the receiving end. Uh, everything would be instantly available as super fax—a daily *National Geographic*-quality *New York Times* with today's news rather than yesterday's, manufactured at the breakfast table. Um . . . *half a gigabit per second? When?!*

Well, cable television has coaxial cable going to over half of American homes now. The men from Bell figured fiberoptic cable might reach that many homes by 1996, and 90 percent of homes by 2026. The luncheon adjourned in bemused confusion. Everyone went away with their data compression design problems intact, but with the promise of major data expansion problems to come: how *would* you fill infinite bandwidth with something useful?

Russ Neuman later told me how the scenario would have to go. "*If* the telephone operating companies—which are regulated monopolies— could throw the $60-billion cost of wiring each house for fiberoptic into the rate base—that is, charge for it as part of regular telephone service and get the Public Utilities Commissions and FCC to okay it—then universal fiberoptic would blow coaxial cable and satellites out of the water. You get bandwidth. There is a lot of optical fiber on the trunk lines now. Some skeptics argue that the phone companies will not want to replace all that twisted pair and stomp through all those rose bushes in people's yards. But they've been wrong before. Bell Southern has several experiments running right now."

The easiest place to lay cable is underwater, so coasts get the trunk services first. Trans-Atlantic fiberoptic cable is going into service in early 1988, trans-Pacific to Japan in late 1988, then most of the far Pacific, the Mediterranean, and the Caribbean by the end of the '80s. Countries that are rapidly putting in fiberoptic cabling include Japan, China, India, most of Europe (Poland strongest in the Eastern bloc), South America, and the U.S. So far it's for major traffic channels, not house-to-house.

When the Media Lab hosted a debate in the Bartos Theater between industry specialists, "Satellite vs. Fiberoptic," some of the issues became clear. International satellite use is highly regulated, with the rich countries expected to subsidize the poor ones, so comparative economics usually favor fiberoptic, which is relatively unregulated because it's not viewed as a broadcast medium. Furthermore fiber is far more secure from eavesdropping, it's easier to repair than something 22,300 miles away in orbit, and it doesn't have the time delay that a satellite necessarily does (the one-tenth of a second while your voice is beamed out to the orbit of synchronous satellites and back; it makes for jaggedy phone conversations sometimes, full of interruptions and empty pauses).

Nevertheless satellite has the advantage whenever you're trying to reach many places at once or you're dealing with a dispersed clientele. An archipelago like Indonesia is served well by satellite, poorly by fiberoptic. We may find soon that rural areas somewhat languish with one-way narrower bandwidth satellite communications while easy-to-wire urban areas have wide-band two-way fiberoptic communications of much greater richness.

However it regionalizes, the dominant late-twentieth-century fact is the wiring up of the world. The ring of eighty-plus communications satellites makes the Earth look informationally like Saturn. A poor island nation like Jamaica has 15,000 backyard satellite dishes. Over 90 percent of the homes in the world's developed nations have television. Telephones reach farther into hinterlands than electricity does. There are well over a billion radio receivers in the world.

The wired world is an astonishing accomplishment, and the Media Lab is surfing on the steep wave of communications industry success, but what interests the Lab most is the vast room for improvement. If quantity of communications is a given, then go for quality. Better still, investigate what we might mean by "quality" if we didn't settle for obvious solutions or the limitations of present technology.

5 THE SCIENCE OF APPARITION

Art is not a mirror.
Art is a hammer.

—Note on whiteboard in Media Lab's
Visible Language Workshop

One of the most conspicuously galling of the limitations of present communications technology is the standard television image. It's archaic, wretched, and everyone has to look at it. It will get spectacularly better, but the questions are when and how much better and whether viewers will have any say in the matter.

"If you walked up to the average person in the street and asked, 'What's wrong with TV?' they probably wouldn't say 'Artifacts!' " Andy Lippman was holding forth with customary relish. Artifacts are everything in the TV image that departs from true; there are a lot of them. Lippman: "We teach courses that deliberately ruin watching television and film for you."

Artifacts like what, I asked him. "Vertical aliasing—letters become unreadable as they scroll upward. Cross color—striped shirts generate rainbow patterns. Poor relative color resolution. Chrominance shift—colors are often blurred to the right. Cross luminance—leftover color in the brightness signal. Motion errors in converting movies to video. The color signal is very noisy (snowy) compared with monochrome. If you don't believe this, try playing with the color saturation control on your receiver." TV has shoddy-looking low resolution (not much detail). TV flickers perceptibly (sixty times a second). The TV image seethes like an ant nest when you get close to it. Lippman: "When you look at a big projector-TV image, all you see is rainbows and creepy-crawlies and junk."

None of that is necessary. All of it is built into the present TV standard, called NTSC ("Stands for 'Never the Same Color,'" says Walter Bender). The system dates back thirty-four years to 1953, when the National Television Systems Committee (NTSC, right) established the present U.S. color television standard. It was brilliant for its day, but "it contained the seeds of its own destruction," says Lippman, because advancing television technology began to expose its cute tricks in an ugly way. If you sit six inches away from a magician you see sleight-of-hand instead of magic—unless the magician's *really* good.

In 1981 the Japanese proved how much better TV could be by demonstrating a new high-definition television—HDTV—that they thought worthy of becoming the world standard for television. It is gorgeous, nearly the quality of 35mm motion picture film, complete with a wider, more cinemalike screen. The screen is nearly twice as wide as it is high, compared to the boxy four-by-three of current television, which is based on old movie dimensions. As Andy Lippman says, the wide-screen HDTV sets sell themselves even when they're turned off.

HDTV gets its high definition by having twice as many lines (1,125) down the screen as the U.S. standard (525). Not only is there vastly more detail, but the "interline twitter," the seething, isn't visible, so the image looks steady as well as rich. To see one is to want one. But the Media Lab is publicly opposing conversion to this HDTV standard.

Lippman: "The Japanese spent $200 million and ten years to develop HDTV. They were the only people doing it, the only ones with the

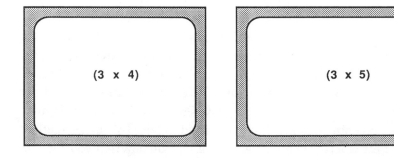

■ Regular TV screen (LEFT) and proposed Japanese HDTV screen (RIGHT)

foresight, and they're ten years ahead of everybody. But they woke the sleeping giant that is the rest of the world. Suddenly it's not a dead topic anymore, it's not an intellectually bankrupt area, and there's a tremendous amount of technological activity in television now."

Negroponte: "The Japanese HDTV format is outdated now, because they designed it at a time when VLSI (very large scale integrated) chips did not exist, so computation was not considered as a way to get a better picture. To get five times the resolution, they used five times the bandwidth, which would be dumb today."

☐☐ Intelligent Television

■ The activity at the Media Lab is called the Advanced Television Research Program, run by a highly regarded professor of electrical engineering named William Schreiber, author of the 1986 text, *Fundamentals of Imaging Systems*. Much of the current high technology of printing emerged from his work, of which more is said in Chapter 11. Schreiber, a compact and concise man of sixty-two, still has the street-feisty accents of his New York city origins. "Apparently the movers and shakers in the television industry came to the conclusion that the industry was falling behind relative to Japan and Europe because we had no national television laboratory. All civilized countries have national television laboratories. Since our sponsors normally compete with each other, they had to get Justice Department approval when they formed this project." The ten national television broadcasters and equipment manufacturers that sponsor the work first got together as the Center for Advanced Television Studies in 1981 and started the Advanced Television contract at MIT in 1983. Immediately the Media Lab found itself in the middle of the HDTV debate, an extremely high-stakes international controversy. The dispute is worth going into in a little detail, because it is a good example of the kind of standards debate from which the public is always excluded.

The Japan HDTV technology was being strongly proposed as a new *world* standard to replace the three different television systems now in use (not quite replace, the Japanese said, just let it be a production and

Professor William F.
Schreiber, head of the
Advanced Television
Research Program

transfer standard; everybody figured that meant replace eventually). Europe, especially France, was resisting HDTV. The U.S., led by CBS, was supporting the Japanese HDTV, despite Negroponte's lobbying against it at the State Department. The whole thing was to come to a decision at the May 1986 plenary meeting of the International Radio Consultative Committee (CCIR) in Dubrovnik, Yugoslavia. Don't be surprised if you've never heard of it: you weren't invited. There was no press on the matter outside of trade journals.

The leading U.S. proponent of HDTV, Joseph Flaherty at CBS, told *Broadcasting* magazine, "Standards serve users better than they serve manufacturers. . . . Competition is what you put in boxcars, but the rails have to be equal width all the way across the country, or you don't have a free market." He said that the Third World was interested in a new standard because they could leapfrog straight to it, and education would be served because the HDTV wide screen could show two pages of book text at a time. About the timing of the decision, he observed, "One of the problems with standards is taking it too soon, in which case you limit development, or taking it too late, when there are multiple standards."

Television in the late '80s may be a case of both too late and too early to make a new standard. Andy Lippman argues, "You establish a standard when a couple of things are stable. When you know what you're going to do with a technology, then you standardize so that everyone can do it. And when the rate of technological change is at a flat point, then you can standardize. Exactly the opposite is true in television today."

Schreiber: "Japan's version of HDTV has no new design principles in it. What they did is scale up the present system." Their proposal is bandwidth-greedy, requiring five times as much bandwidth as the present system—it would take five present television channels to carry one channel of Japanese HDTV. Despite the "infinite bandwidth" session with the Bell fiberoptic engineers, Negroponte explains the Media Lab's obsession with bandwidth problems in nearly apocalyptic terms: "To transmit video signals around the world is outrageously expensive because bandwidth costs. Bandwidth will probably cost forever. It is limited by the laws of physics. You can lay as many optical fibers as you want across the Atlantic Ocean, you'll never have enough bandwidth."

The Media Lab thinks it can deliver those gorgeous HDTV-quality images within existing TV bandwidths by clever data compression and image improvement. Says Schreiber, "It's ironical that the root cause of the NTSC (present system) problem is now fully understood and curable, and we'll probably abandon it just as we know how to fix it. One major problem is interlace."

The TV image has been interlaced since 1934. The electron beam in the TV tube paints a new picture thirty times a second, but if it painted the whole picture that way, it would flicker intolerably. So instead it first paints the odd lines of the 525-line screen, then one-sixtieth of a second later paints the even lines. Very smart: no flicker with half-resolution images sixty times a second. But the picture looks like it's boiling.

The Media Lab sees a way to solve that with computer intelligence at the receiving end. The solution is progressive scan (also called de-interlacing), performed in the TV set. Lippman: "Progressive scan is just:

paint all the lines in order, but twice as fast." To do that the TV set has to figure out what the extra lines "should" contain by examining what's nearby in space and in time and then putting it into the new lines. That can be done with what's called frame memory—using computer memory to hold the picture while working on it. The product is a steady image with twice the resolution. It looks great.

Lippman: "We can make TVs that give you absolutely stunningly wonderful pictures from standard broadcast—oh God." Schreiber: "When you see the two pictures side by side—sixty-frame progressive compared with thirty-frame interlaced—it's like night and day. You wouldn't believe how much it is shimmering until you see one that isn't. You try it, you like it." Lippman: "I believe that in the next three years there won't be an interlaced display sold in America. That's the wrong way to put it. In the next three years there won't be an interlaced television set sold in Japan."

The debate in Dubrovnik at the CCIR meeting on Japan's HDTV as the new world television production standard came to the momentous conclusion: "Not yet." The matter will be taken up again in 1990. Meanwhile HDTV production equipment is being used by a few television and film companies instead of 35mm film because of its field convenience and flexibility. If that goes on enough it will build a stronger case for 1990. The Media Lab also will be using that time to make its different case. Negroponte: "Thank God. It gives us four years. If CCIR had accepted that HDTV we would have been in the soup."

Postponing the decision also might give the public a chance to participate for a change. The great debate should merit at least a television special. A few Congressional hearings wouldn't hurt. If journalists ever discover standards debates, they'll find there's a whole world of them. It's true that nobody votes for technology: things like birth control pills, jet airplanes, and computers just arrive. But standards are agreements. They are a political process that, so far, has taken place far from the political arena of the public the standards will affect.

At the Media Lab the computerized interlace-fix is seen as a holding action while deeper, finer television solutions than Japan's HDTV are explored. Two major instruments at the Lab for doing that are nice examples of collaboration between disciplines. One, run by Russell Neuman from the MIT Political Science Department, is an Audience Research Facility to explore what normal people think of the Lab's and other people's advanced television. The viewers are recruited from the 25,000 shoppers a day at a mall in Danvers, Massachusetts, and walked to a living-room-like lab in the mall to watch exotic TV.

The other experimental instrument was invented by Steve Benton, head of holography projects at the Media Lab. It's an ingenious beam-mixing device that eliminates the shadowmask, the perforated wall just behind the TV screen that has blocked improvements in image resolution and brightness for decades. Benton describes it as the ultimate rubber TV set that can display a video image to match any standard, including ones not being considered so far. It can go all the way up to a resolution of 2,000 lines per inch—the equivalent of a 35mm slide. You view it in a kind of a booth.

Benton: "What you give up is, only one person at a time can see it. You have to be in the right sweet spot. For a simulator we figured that would be okay." I asked if he could turn that narrow view into a virtue, and he began smiling. "You could make the point of view so limited that it only includes one eye, and send something else to the other eye. Heh, heh, our motives were mixed." In other words, the rubber TV set might become a 3D TV set. In addition, though the image is only arm's length from the viewer it can be made to appear at infinity, like looking out a window.

Other experiments are going on. Schreiber: "We're making a demo where we change the duration of a scene by 20 percent, just to show it can be done." Movies are usually the wrong length to fit between ads. Duration adjustment in broadcast television now is done with the video equivalent of scissors. Schreiber's technique would leave the original intact, just imperceptibly quicker or slower. Then there's "extended definition." Your television set could collect a one-hour program over four hours at night and assemble it for super-high definition one-hour viewing at your convenience. Such extended-definition sets could play super-high definition videocassette tapes as well.

Negroponte bases all of his plans on the growing computer intelligence of the TV set itself. "You have 600 million TV sets out there. To put out another 600 million, each of which is an image processor that removes all the shadowing and ghosting and all that, is a big potential market. Twenty years from now your TV set will probably have 50 megabytes of random-access memory and run at 40 to 50 MIPS. It'll be basically a Cray computer." (The Cray is at present the world's most powerful supercomputer and costs a cool $15 million.) "It will not be receiving pictures. It will be receiving data, and it makes the pictures."

☐☐ Paperback Movies

■ The image-improving techniques discussed so far are fairly predictable. They take the engineering of signal processing a step or two further, but nothing radical is expected. Where the Media Lab sees a breakthrough possible is in technology coming from a different philosophy about information itself.

The idea of "information" has been changing lately, thanks in part to the computerization of communications. Back in the late '40s when Claude Shannon, then at Bell Labs, founded Information Theory, "information" was almost physical it was so objective—"*the information contained in a message unit is defined in terms of the average number of digits required to encode it*" (McGraw Hill Encyclopedia of Electronics and Computers). This was the science of signal and noise and the subtle art of extracting signal from noise.

Marvin Minsky tells an admiring tale of what happened to Information Theory: "They solved all the problems and new ones didn't come up. I was on this little board making the program selection for the 1965 International Information Theory Congress. We were looking at 140 papers to see which ones were acceptable. There were a couple that were marginal. We sat around trying to figure out how to adjust the threshold of acceptability, and Bob Fano said, 'Maybe it's all over. What would happen if we canceled the meeting?' Someone said, 'These arrangements have been made.' Someone else said, 'Well, have we paid the advance?' At the end of the afternoon we voted to cancel the field."

In 1979 anthropologist-philosopher Gregory Bateson offered another definition of "information": "*Any difference which makes a difference.*" He said, "The map is not the territory, we're told. Very well. What is it that gets from the territory onto the map?" The cartographer draws in roads, rivers, elevations—things the map user is expected to care about. Data, signal ("news of a difference") isn't information until it means something or does something ("makes a difference"). The definition of information I kept hearing at the Media Lab was Bateson's highly subjective one. That's philosophically heartwarming, but it also turns out there's a powerful tool kit lurking in the redefinition.

Conventional signal processing works strictly on objective signals. You can "compress" a transmission if you remove the redundancy from a message, send the important stuff cheaply through a narrow-bandwidth channel, and then reconstitute it at the other end. One time at dinner I was free-associating to Minsky about how a computer could list the words in a text by frequency, send the list numbers instead of the words ("2" for "the," "5" for "and," etc.), and expand at the other end. I was awed by my genius. "Ah yes," Minsky said, "Huffman coding." Standard signal processing.

The de-interlacing the Advanced Television group is working on at the Lab is still conventional signal processing. So is the Lab's work with "color space" compression, where three-dimensional graphs of the hundreds of colors in an image are systematically reduced by computer to a handful of the "right" colors. But Minsky and Negroponte are impatient with the limitations of the "electrical engineering" approach and are pushing for serious pioneering of a new kind of data compression which takes account of the *content and meaning* of the material being compressed.

In the politics of communication technologies, this is radical, Left Wing, dangerous thinking. Where better to try it out than with the Lab's most technologically conservative sponsors, the film studios. Movie studios are so conservative they still use huge wheels of 35mm tape for sound recording, unchanged from the 1950s. With the "Movies of the Future" project, directed by Andy Lippman, Negroponte sees as an opportunity to aim at an apparently impossible, highly desirable goal: the Media Lab is trying to put an entire feature-length color movie on a compact disk—where only eight minutes of conventional video could fit at present. That would be the paperback movie.

Negroponte tells audiences, "Films are being pirated, and that's annoying, but the thing that's much more devastating to the motion picture industry is *rentals*. The honest VCR rental shop buys one copy of a movie, pays the royalty once, and then rents it hundreds of times. The dishonest rental shop doesn't even buy it, they steal it. The real dishonest shop makes many many copies and rents them out."

Various protection schemes have been proposed—encryption, cassettes that don't rewind; all of them amount to some kind of lock. Negroponte: "We said, maybe the best way to solve the problem is to make the original cheaper than the copy. It's crazy to make xerox copies of paperback books—it's cheaper to buy one. The manufacturing cost of a compact disk is about thirty cents. If you could put a high-definition feature-length film on a compact disk, you'd have the equivalent of a paperback movie." Exit the film-rental business.

Negroponte to audience: "To do this you need a kind of data compression for which there's no precedent. It exceeds by a couple orders of magnitude what people can do with normal data compression. You have to get very deeply involved in the world of artificial intelligence and have the machine know something about the movie. The system would need to look at it several times, understand what's going on, what's in the background, what's in the foreground, when it's night, when it's day, who's doing what—and use a semantic data-compression technique. At this point it's an intuition. If we can do it, it might have enormous impact." The audience stares quietly. *Semantic data compression?*

I heard the word so often at the Lab that I finally asked Marvin Minsky, "What does 'semantic' mean?" He paused. "It's not a good word. It just means, 'My ideas are deeper than your ideas.' It's used in language study to distinguish between *syntax*, which is the way the words are arranged, and *semantics*, which is supposed to be what the words mean." The term has achieved buzzword velocity in the academic world. I even ran into it as a judge in a national contest of student design work. One contestant waxed eloquent about the "product semantics" of his submission. He meant the handles were cleverly designed to look like handles.

If a term is defined by its most extreme use, consider this speculation by Negroponte, telling me about the Greek island he spends time at.

He said, "You ask me, 'What's it like in Patmos?' And I tell you, *'It's like the last scene in the movie 'Kaos.'* " My mind filled with that extraordinary sequence—the children leaping/flying down a steep white sand dune into water so blue it might as well be sky. He went on, "That's maybe ten words, forty characters, just a few hundred bits. Clearly it's not a complete description. It only works if I know you've seen 'Kaos.' So a system that compresses that way has to know not only about the signal but about you. It's taking the hundreds of millions of bits needed for transmitting scenes of Patmos and reducing them to a few hundred."

"Analogy," I said, keeping my bits to the minimum.

He agreed. "Analogy is a wonderful way to think of semantic data compression: this signal is like that signal, and you got that signal already. It is a dramatic class of bandwidth compression that will start to emerge in computer science."

This sort of thing becomes more possible as movies become digital, and that seems to be under way anyway. Negroponte was showing me around the Bartos Theater in the Wiesner Building's basement, which he said was designed specifically for exploring digital film. "The movie industry doesn't want to make prints and ship them around. Film is costly to make, costly to deliver, and it deteriorates. They want to get into distributing digital signal by satellite and broadcasting into movie theaters." Bring it on. Incompetent projectionists and shoddy prints are the feeblest links in the showing of movies. Digital movies might also permit interactivity between the audience and the show. The floor of the Bartos Theater is raised a couple of feet and cabled underneath so that every seat is wired for potential action.

In another part of the Lab an All-Star baseball game is being converted into a database. That is, the entire game as recorded by a dozen NBC television cameras is being rendered into a digital totality. Andy Lippman imagines it would be interesting to show the game in three dimensions in a sort of aquarium so that you could walk around, peer in, and mess with what's happening.

Coming back to the present, on the fourth floor of the Lab in a windowless room is Keishi Kandori, a research affiliate visiting from Asahi Broadcasting in Japan. Looking over his shoulder at his large computer screen you see an orderly but complex array of jewellike little color movie stills which Kandori is manipulating. Negroponte explains, "The purpose of this is to invent new ways to edit film. If you think of these pictures as representing the scenes or cuts of the film, you can shuffle them like a deck of cards, push the button, and out comes the new film. We're taking the epitome of a sequential medium and making it random-access in the service of editing it. This is to a filmmaker what word processing is to an author."

I want one. "Uh, do you think this could be economically scaled to a home market?" I sublimate. "Oh God, yes," responds salesman Negroponte. "All personal computers will be video-processing machines, and you'll be able to transmit between them. You'll edit one of these things, and it'll be a birthday card for your grandmother."

Art for Invention's Sake

■ Artists have been manipulating images forever. Those skills, along with the restless creativity of artists, are seen as a resource for the Media Lab.

The Wiesner Building, originally called the Center for Arts and Media Technology, has its entire ground floor devoted to art—three galleries, the offices of the List Visual Arts Center, and the Council for the Arts at MIT, which Jerome Wiesner chairs. The building itself is art. Modernist architect I. M. Pei collaborated experimentally with artists Kenneth Noland (brilliant colors on the atrium wall), Richard Fleischner (elegant courtyard and outside furniture), and Scott Burton (lame concrete benches).

It's an attractive building, slick as a corporate logo, with somewhat the look of a modern appliance. The high, narrow atrium inside is pretty, but impersonal and cold. Best appreciated as habitable sculpture, the building doesn't work very well. Groups in the building that want to collaborate are kept isolated by the design, there's scant adaptability in the structure, and working floor space is in chronic short supply. One senses in the building the residue of campus politics and an architect perhaps more interested in the eye than the whole collaborating human.

But the groups collaborate anyway, and the point is made: art, science, and engineering are in alliance in reshaping communication technologies. Jerome Wiesner, a friend of Alexander Calder, Picasso, and others of their stature, has promoted art at MIT throughout his career. Negroponte was an architect originally and takes an artist's pains with the presentation quality of anything he's involved in. The attitude toward artists throughout the Lab is respectful but not worshipful— they're regarded as hackers minus computers, one of us.

There are a number of artists working in the Media Lab itself, especially in music and in the Visible Language Workshop run by Muriel Cooper, but most of the legions of artists that would like to get in and play with Lab goodies are turned away. "This is not an advanced art school, we don't have an art curriculum," explains Negroponte. It's a highly technical environment. If people with some art background prepare themselves academically to participate directly in technical innovation, then they're welcome. (And there's always some backdoor activity— Media Lab stuff is catnip to artists.)

Alan Kay draws the distinction: "The thing that attracted me to this place was the attempt to collide technology with the arts, rather than an attempt to collide technologists with artists. You're always better getting people who have already had that collision in themselves. However, this isn't a Renaissance culture here yet. It's a speckled culture."

The artists around the Lab have ideas about what to do with the technology, and the scientists have ideas about what to do with art. Negroponte: "The impact of computers on the arts will be bringing out the artist in all of us. Much of it will be like hanging the child's paintings on the icebox. It doesn't have any meaning outside the family circle, but it's very important to the local constituency. You'll see a return of the Sunday painter."

3D Comes Back

■ Holography at the Media Lab owes a great deal to artistic pioneering in the 1970s.

Take a look at the hologram on your credit card (if you have one). Look at it in the usual upright orientation. Then look at it rotated 90 degrees to left or right, so the right or left side is now up. Notice anything strange. Then come back.

From sideways the hologram still moves things behind each other as you move your head, but the depth *feeling* is gone, and you notice that things in the image move when you move your head up and down but not when you move from side to side. When you look at it normally, right side up, there *is* a depth feeling, and things in the picture move when you move your head side to side, but not when you move up and down.

What's missing is called "vertical parallax." The hologram does have "horizontal parallax," or change of line of sight, and that's what makes it work. Most people never notice the absence of the vertical component. I went "Eeek" when it was drawn to my attention. Discovering that you could get away with that, figuring out how to do it, and taking advantage of its enormous savings in work and expense—all that is part of Steve Benton's series of inventions in holography.

One of his graduate students, Mark Holzbach, explains to a Lab visitor bobbing and weaving in front of a backlit hologram, "It's based on the principle that your eyes are spaced horizontally, and you are always seeing the world from two different vantage points. So what we're doing with the hologram is projecting vantage points. When you put your eyes into those vantage points, you see what you would see if the object were there." If an alien shows up with two or more eyes spaced vertically, Benton's students will cheerfully recompute the images to display vertical parallax instead of horizontal and still win. (If the alien has three eyes spaced in a triangle, the game is up.)

Another part of the invention was making it so it works in "white" light—ordinary, nonlaser light. Benton pulled that off by tuning different parts of the image to different colors, hence the rainbow effect.

The final breakthrough in the early '70s was RCA making holographic images easily printable via embossing on plastic. Benton: "It was clear that being able to stamp these things out for pennies a square inch was going to mean the whole world could be covered with Benton holograms—my mother would be so pleased—but people who are interested in embossed holograms are really interested in cheap holograms, and that could contaminate the whole process. If they start in the wrong place, they're going to wind up in the wrong place." More blinking-Jesus postcards. Nothing wrong with that, but 3D had fallen in so many gutters of bad taste in its time that Benton wanted to aim higher. The circuitous arrival of white-light holograms in the world is an amazing and cautionary tale with something to say about the role of a Media Laboratory with artists in it.

Steve Benton looks like he strayed into his office from a beer commercial—a big, hearty, athletic-looking, humorous guy. He was part of the glory years at Polaroid, a protégé of Edwin Land, the inventor of the instant film and camera. Benton developed the white-light hologram there, and it was patented there, but it was never really put to work by Polaroid.

Benton recalls the timing. "The patent was issued in '72 or '73. In 1968 anybody could start up a company with 'Holo hyphen something' and get $3 million with no more than two or three phone calls. Everybody was reading about holograms that would be as big as your living-room wall, and the *Encyclopaedia Britannica* that would be on a little hologram that would fit in your wallet, and none of this happened. The problems

Professor Stephen A.
Benton, head of Spatial
Imaging (holography)

were really just too difficult. By 1972 the interest in high-tech start-ups just vanished. Crunch into the ground. I got there too late."

Benton shrugged and went on to other work at Polaroid. Then an artist who had done a few laser holograms saw Benton rainbow holograms and told him, "These are really great. Let's make some bigger and more interesting ones." So they did, and the artist started exhibiting the result at museums and colleges. In 1976 Emmet Leith, one of the fathers of laser holography, wrote enthusiastically about the rainbow holograms in *Scientific American.*

Benton: "Later the same year the Museum of Holography opened in New York. Because of the success of those shows, I held two workshops in New York on long weekends—I'd come out of it with some money and the artists would come out of it with some holograms and a lot of knowledge. That's really how it happened; it was strictly subversive. Polaroid didn't have any idea what they had, and I was getting tired of waiting for them to find out. 'This stuff is published,' I told them. 'What if I just show people what to do?' 'Go ahead, kid.'

"Then the leapfrog process started. Some artist would come back, 'Can't you do a black-and-white image?' 'Uhh, I don't think so.' 'Well, it would really be great.' So I'd try something and try something else, and finally I came up with a practical black-and-white image. And they'd say, 'Well, how about color? That would really be great.' "

The Wiesner-Negroponte theory of collaboration with the arts has a champion. "Part of the reason that I buy Jerry's and Nicholas' philosophy here is that I've seen it work. I think the artists represent a kind of experimentation on the fringe of something that is as valid and important as the technical experimenting. They're making a gamble too. Their careers are tied up in it, and they're more disposed to take it on in an obsessive kind of way. 'I want to *do* this,' and they just don't stop."

Even once they were dramatized by artists, white-light holograms took their time achieving commercial reality. They almost bloomed in a big way with Atari, the California video games company, in the late '70s. Thirteen 3D arcade versions of a game called "Cosmos" were poised to hit the home market when Atari hit the wall instead. Everybody left. "But Steve MacGrew, who'd been the holographer on the case, did the entrepreneurial thing and decided that he was going to keep going. When 'E.T.' came out, Reese's Pieces wanted to do a big promotion around the fact that their candy appeared in the movie, so they had little holographic stickers of E.T. that went out in the big packages of the candy. Something like two million of these things went out in 1982. That started people thinking.

"The chairman of American Bank Note, Ed Weitzen, I guess saw the E.T. sticker and said, 'You know, if we could put that on a credit card, it might make it more secure.' It may not actually *be* much more secure, but it would improve people's impression, and it could be an important marketing feature. So Ed Weitzen did an innovative thing, which was go out and buy all these holographic people and their companies and bring them together to make a product for a specific market. He came up with a technique to embed holograms in the surface of credit cards and sold it, first to MasterCard and then to VISA."

(Concerning the security of Bentonized credit cards, I learned from a radio interview with James Bikoff, president of the International Anti-Counterfeiting Coalition, that the rainbow holograms are considered a highly effective anti-counterfeiting technique. They led to the first-ever reduction of credit card counterfeiting when they were introduced.)

Benton: "Then *National Geographic*, whose editor, Wilbur Garrett, had been noodling around with 3D for a long time looking to put 12 million holograms on covers, could go to somebody who could say, 'Yeah, we did 90 million credit cards and we can do all your covers too.' *National Geographic* had 12 million alternate covers in Canada in case they weren't ready—'Nuts, put on cover B and we'll pretend it never happened.' That's how much confidence . . . that's how much money they had. Their rainbow hologram cover of an American eagle came out in March '84, just after the hologram credit cards started appearing.

"That really launched it. That cover said to people that holography was real—it's a working print medium now. It was very important that it was *National Geographic* because of its credibility in the U.S. and overseas. It might as well be on the Bible. Since then there's been an avalanche of interest."

The ten-year lag between the invention and commercial application intrigued me. "What would have happened if you had developed the rainbow hologram at something like the Media Lab?" I asked Benton. As he answered, I realized he was replying to a better question—"Why are you here now?" Two individuals loom as large in his answer and in his career as in the history of optical science—Harold Edgerton, MIT's father of stroboscopic photography, and the legendary Edwin Land of Polaroid, both of them still actively researching.

Benton: "If the rainbow hologram had been developed here, probably some student would have gotten involved and been much better prepared to do it right the first time instead of it floundering around and being bootlegged for ten years. My role model for this is Harold Edgerton. His students founded EG&G because they wanted to go out and make a living doing what they'd learned to do from him. He was a co-founder and a shareholder in a token sort of way. A lot of that happens here.

"So I don't consider making a move toward academia to be any kind of vow of economic chastity. If anything, the options here are more open. In a normal corporation it takes such a committee decision to get anything done that it's pretty stifling. When Land was the buccaneer head of Polaroid, you only had to sell one guy. If you got turned down, you were dead, you couldn't go back for a couple of years. But with thumbs up, boom, anything you wanted was available—money, resources, people, machine shops, knowledge. A lot of the work we did was based on understanding the chemistry a lot better than other people did. If the Media Lab ever becomes a fifth of what Polaroid was in the '50s and '60s, which I feel was its creative peak, it will have far exceeded Jerry's and Nicholas' goals."

"How did you come to work at Polaroid?" I asked, and learned what a coin of intellectual transaction students are in the flux between MIT and industry. "I started working there when I was a sophomore here. I was interested in 3D, and I was working for Edgerton in his lab here when he came in and said, 'Dr. Land just gave another one of his lectures.' That was Land's way of trolling for disciples. He would give these knockout lectures almost every year for the freshmen in their first week. Edgerton said, 'There was a full-color picture on the screen, sharp, no double image. You put a piece of plastic over one eye and the picture became three-dimensional.' That violates some well-known rules of physics—you're supposed to have a filter over each eye, and there's supposed to be a double image without the filters." So Benton called Polaroid and asked how they did that, and got the usual pause. " '. . . I can't really tell you how, because you're not a Polaroid employee.' 'Nigel, I know what to do about that.' So I just went over and showed them some of my 3D experiments, and they said sure and hired me.

"I learned much more science working for Edwin Land than I learned at MIT—more about *doing* science—looking at a problem and figuring out how to format it so you could pick it apart and do experiments and prove what you needed to know and build up an answer and come away understanding a problem—the kind of stuff you can learn only at the arm of a scientist."

What about the Media Lab, I asked him. Benton: "A lot of what holds this place together is that everybody likes each other's stuff. Some of my students come to study holography and they get seduced by David Zeltzer's computer graphics. Then, like most love affairs, that burns out and they come straggling back and bring computer graphics with them. The way the place is set up, students are expected to cross those lines. Also everybody is pulling together to help the Lab cohere and become a full-fledged department."

Where would you like the holography work here to go, I asked. "For the first time people with enough communications theory background are looking at these 3D imaging problems and saying, 'Really, what *is* the problem?' I subscribe to looking at the human visual system for inspirations. If you consider what passes for acceptable video, our visual system seems to be very 'low fi'—it makes massive assumptions about the way the world is tied together. In fact we're giving it much more data than it wants or can use. My instinct is that there's paydirt in that direction."

The entrance to the Spatial Imaging office area on the Lab's fourth floor has a Benton hologram three feet by three feet. How big can these things get? Benton: "Arbitrary, but it would probably have to be seamed every four feet. A big hologram is a different visual experience than a little one. One of the things I'm hoping we can find sponsorship for is theater-size images that we can put together piece by piece."

Much of the Lab's holographic equipment is in the basement of the Wiesner Building because photographing for holograms requires ultra-steady platforms. A few millionths of an inch of vibration and you have problems. Serious holograms at the Lab are made after the subway a block away shuts down. But not all the images are photographic. Many are primarily computational, some completely synthetic with no real-world imaging at all.

It's the computed holograms that appear to have the most immediate and interesting new applications. One project in Spatial Imaging is called "Medical Imaging," where x-ray-like data from CAT scanners and MRI (magnetic resonance imaging) machines are assembled into 3D images of the body. Instead of a slice at a time you get a whole transparent body. You peer *into* a person's abdomen, peeking around a bone or an organ for an anomaly. If you like, edit the bones out. Formerly obscure structures emerge with remarkable clarity.

The response from medical professionals has been interestingly mixed, Benton told me. "X-ray people, radiologists, don't seem to be interested at all, and I think the reasons are very human. They have spent their lifetimes learning how to read flat x-ray pictures and understand the 3D structure, and if somebody comes along and says, 'I'm going to give you the structure for free!' they go, 'Well, maybe, maybe not.' So the reception there has always been lukewarm or worse. But the surgeons love it. We even expect to let them do a kind of 'practice surgery.' "

The principal sponsor of computed holograms at the Media Lab is General Motors. Their interest is in replacing the clay models for cars that now take a couple weeks and tens of thousands of dollars every time, a procedure that leads too easily to design conservatism and delay. When a clay model is that big a commitment, it's harder to scrap it and start over.

Benton: "The GM design staff is beginning to design and engineer its cars on an integrated CAD system—computer-aided design. The way it's normally done, somebody designs the envelope of the car, and then somebody else figures out how to fit an engine and drivetrain into it. These guys want to design the engine and drivetrain and body at the same time, so they don't get into embarrassments like having to suddenly tilt the engine seventeen degrees back because the hood's in the way. Normally what they do is emit a bunch of drawings, and a sculptor hand-carves the clay model—which was an innovation of GM's in its own right fifty years ago—they've had a history of technical leadership in media, and this is just the latest one. They're going to carve in light instead."

I was in England in mid-1986 when I read in the London Times about the world's first projected hologram being shown at MIT. It was Benton's GM project. On my way back through Massachusetts I got to see it and hear Benton's version of what happened. He calls it an "alcove hologram" because the image of the car floats in the middle of a niche half-surrounded by the image-producing film. The Camaro is a glowing green, parked with its left front angled out, about eighteen inches long, with a green Boston skyline behind it. It is made of one thousand component images held in tight register so it stays rock steady as you move around it.

On the big day the GM Design Team visitors were briefed at length and then ushered into the darkened basement laboratory. Benton recalled, "We all held our breath as they circled around the hologram, muttering and squinting. Finally one of them raised his hand and brushed the image, tentatively, and then they were exchanging grins and significant glances and got down to the work of explaining the project in detail. They're urging us to go on to full color and make it as large a size as we can."

Benton figures that in time 3D holograms will be generated and printed at home with personal computers.

☐ ☐ *Talking Heads*

■ A long-standing interest of Negroponte's is what he calls "the transmission of presence." In 1980, before holograms looked revivable, the Architecture Machine Group showed a radical way to pump human presence through telephone wires. The sponsor of the demo was DARPA, the Defense Advanced Research Projects Agency, concerned with how America would actually be run in event of nuclear attack. DARPA decided it wouldn't do to have the five top leaders in the country—the President, the Secretaries of Defense and State, etc.—all go hide under the same mountain in Virginia. The question was, how could they disperse and yet still communicate as if they were together?

Negroponte: "We came up with the idea of projecting onto video screens sculpted like people's faces and also having the screens swivel a bit—so they could nod, shake their head, turn to each other. At each site the order of sitting of the five people would be the same. At my site I'm real and you're plastic and on my right, and at your site you're real and I'm plastic and on your left. If we're talking and looking at each other, and one of the faces across the table interrupts, we would stop and turn toward him."

The important issue in the exercise, naturally dubbed "Talking Heads," was how well you could transmit nuance. If a senior national official is still dubious about a proposal but eager to come to some agreement soon, that's more likely to be expressed in gesture and facial expression than in words. If someone is joking to relieve the tension, you want that to come across clearly, and the amusement of the others has to be registered immediately, or deep misunderstanding could develop—"Who did he mean when he said that?"

By use of head-tracking devices at each site, the motions of each person's head could easily be transmitted, and fixed video cameras would send the images. The television tubes, it turned out, could indeed be molded like life masks to the shape of anyone's face. Negroponte: "It was uncanny. When we rear-projected talking faces, even though the face-shaped surfaces were solid, you swore you saw physical lips moving. It was creepy. Color was easy. On your video tube I would lay a surface of phosphor that had your skin tone—cheeks a little pinker, hair blond, eyes blue—and I would project a monochrome signal that would be the right color. Like what was called 'Mexican color' in the early days of color TV in westerns—it was a technique of taking blue for the sky, brown for the earth, and pasting it over the picture."

It's a spectacular demo, but as far as Negroponte knows, the system was never implemented. It may have been considered too frivolous, including the name "Talking Heads." Negroponte recalls, "At that time we were in the old laboratory, and we had four or five minicomputers that one signed up for on a big board. I noticed that every weekend for about eight hours straight all four machines were being signed up for

Talking Heads, and I thought it was terrific, because this was our biggest project at the time. Lo and behold, six months later out came an album of the rock group 'Talking Heads' with a cover that students in our lab had produced. They had people from the band here on weekends."

It's a fair sign you're doing something interesting when both the Defense Department and artists want it.

6 VIVARIUM

We want to fashion puppets that pull their own strings.

—Ann Marion

The "Computers and Entertainment" area of the Lab is living up to its title for the redheaded lady from *Science* magazine waiting to interview Marvin Minsky.

Only she and an oversized black dog named Silas are motionless and watching in the tiny suite of rooms packed with late-afternoon activity. Silas is sprawled in the middle of the only bit of open floor, being caressed by a young woman with bright yellow hair butch-cut, vermilion glasses, tie-dyed dress, and denim jacket with beaded epaulets and scalps. From adjoining offices float the bent-piano sounds of several computer musicians independently improvising—convincingly tuneful, skilled, and original, and oblivious of each other. Amid a two-foot heap of synthetic fur, graduate student Allison Druin is converting a chair into a large, friendly creature with a lap. Overhead a somewhat saggy seven-foot-long silver blimp rests against the pipes and conduits of the ceiling.

Fussing and muttering over a disemboweled Macintosh computer and scattered pieces of the blimp's miniature cabin and radio-controlled engines is Margaret Minsky, grad student daughter of Marvin. Her father strolls in and accompanies the bemused reporter from *Science* into his office. Stepping over the black dog he observes, "We ought to have some more kinds of animals."

This is Vivarium country, home of the Media Lab's loosest and potentially most ambitious activity. The founder of the project, Alan Kay, is based in Los Angeles along with the bulk of the $2-million-a-year activities funded by Apple Computer. He visits MIT regularly to rev up the Media Lab Vivarium students and see what portions of the grand vision they've filled in.

It's not the first time Kay has presided over a vision. An earlier one called "Dynabook" is credited with leading to much of the best design in personal computers. It began back in 1971, when he was a Principal Scientist at Xerox PARC (Palo Alto Research Center) in California, one of a soon-famous cadre of outstanding computer scientists collected there. In 1972 his Dynabook scheme looked like a pure pipe dream.

In the jargon of those days it was described as a "hand-held stand-alone interactive-graphic computer" that could handle a couple of megabytes of text, could make pictures with a program called "Paintbrush," could animate them, would allow children to do their own design and programming of tools, including games (this was well before "Pong" and the video game explosion), and would link up directly with other Dynabooks or via telephone with the world's libraries. Priced under $500, one could be provided to every school kid out of textbook budgets.

(Kay designs nearly everything he does for and with grade-school-age children—the Dynabook, the Vivarium, the object-oriented computer language he developed called "Smalltalk," which became an artificial intelligence landmark. Working with kids he keeps a fresher mind, and if kids can understand and use the new thing, its design principles are probably sound enough that adults will also.)

Fourteen years later there are still no Dynabooks in the world, but

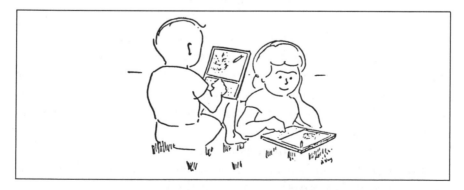

■   Dynabooks in use, as drawn by Alan Kay in 1972

pieces of the fantasy as well as innumerable tools and design ideas developed in its pursuit are everywhere, some still arriving, and Alan Kay is a hot ticket at Future-of-Computers gatherings. The goal of the Vivarium is to do for the next generation of humanizing computer use what the Dynabook did for the first—to be a "forcing function for technology which should have been worked on fifteen years ago."

People often find the genial Alan Kay to be a mental handful. He's a fast talker, and no two paragraphs are about the same discipline. At age ten in 1950 he was a National Quiz Kid on the radio. Once a professional jazz musician, he's now a lover of chamber music and classical pipe organ. Whenever he has a few weeks in Cambridge he signs up for time on the organs at the University Lutheran and Congregational churches. A friend of Kay's for twenty years now, Negroponte was best man at Kay's 1983 wedding to Bonnie MacBird, a Los Angeles screenwriter (her Walt Disney film "Tron" was loosely based on Alan Kay computer practices). Throughout the 1970s, design ideas and people flowed back and forth between Negroponte's Architecture Machine Group at MIT and Alan Kay's teams at Xerox PARC (1971–81) and later Atari (1981–84), where the Vivarium was first conceived. These days one catches Kay between flights—twenty-one in a month is typical—as he carries out his self-defined duties as an Apple Fellow.

□ *Artificial Ecology*
□

■ "I didn't make 'vivarium' up," Kay explained during one of his MIT visits. "It's a real word meaning an enclosed environment for life. The original idea came from Ann Marion when we were at Atari. One of our projects was to try and do intelligent autonomous Warner cartoon characters. You'd send Bugs Bunny and Elmer Fudd into the forest, and they would play out a cartoon as a result of their personalities. Meanwhile Ann Marion was stubbornly trying something else that I couldn't understand for a long time. Her idea was: 'Wouldn't it be great to do something that would be interesting because of its ecological and social communication in an environment?' The example she chose was an aquarium."

Alan C. Kay, Apple
Fellow, founder of the
Vivarium

Ann Marion got her computer-screen aquarium to the point where one animated fish pursued, caught, and ate another fish on its own and settled back in its lair with a satisfied smile, but then Atari itself went belly-up, and the research group dispersed. Two years later Alan Kay, by then at Apple, revived the scheme as a more generalized Vivarium, hired Ann Marion again, and set up two research centers—dividing his time between them. Theoretical research would go on at Negroponte's new Media Laboratory, and the hands-on stuff with kids would take place at an idyllic public school he found in Los Angeles called the Open School.

Mission: create "life." Enable school kids to invent and then unleash realistic organisms in whole "living" computerized ecologies—learn about the universe's creation by doing some of their own. The animals they create would behave, learn, even evolve independently. A Vivarium sounds plausible and interesting. It's also impossible with present computer science.

Alan Kay: "The Vivarium serves different purposes for different factions. I do projects like this to understand more about what children are capable of and to see if there is anything in the computer that can amplify their reach and aesthetic sensibilities. I think from Apple's standpoint they would like to get some spin-offs like we got at Xerox PARC with the Dynabook, which Apple would be smart enough to actually convert to products, unlike Xerox. But there aren't any deliverables in this project. I haven't promised them anything. They're being honest funders of basic research."

In order to work, the Vivarium needs new kinds of animation and robotics, new kinds of artificial intelligence and computer modeling, new kinds of interface with the user, and possibly a whole new computer "architecture." It also needs fresh insight into neurophysiology, animal behavior, ecology, and experimental education. A five-year project at least, in Kay's view, with only medium chances of success. What the Viviarium offers is a way to organize areas of interesting ignorance into a dramatic whole that invites collaborative assault from usually disparate disciplines. Much like the Media Lab itself.

Says Kay, "The hardest thing in design is to get that first good image of the thing, and to get it in a way that is least prejudiced by what you already know. Everything else is relatively easy, because once you have the image, the image tells you what to do. Doing animals is a nice control on the child's sense of quality, whereas doing robots you could get away with almost anything and say that's what a robot does. The representation of an animal has to be finely textured and move and act believably. We have to generate complex behavior from simple modules."

That goal, derived from what's known of animal behavior, becomes a design strategy in its own right. Kay explained to the MIT students, "The rule is, 'Simple things should be simple; complex things should be possible.' One of the ways to design a simple user interface that can really do things is to take the hardest tasks imaginable and try to create convincing scenarios of how they might be done at all. Then the simplest tasks must be considered in the light of the structures postulated for the most complex. The simplest must rule! Force the interaction structures to do *both* without making the simplest and most-done tasks suffer."

So while the MIT students are creating conceptual software tools to make one-celled paramecia and fish, the tools should have the capability of later making squirrels who remember where nuts are buried and the boundaries of their current turf, and who can learn to deal with new predators and unusual weather. In a talk I gave the Vivarium students I described from the scientific literature a sample of well-studied animal behaviors that might lend themselves to computer modeling. For lack of any better organizing principle, I proceeded alphabetically: advertisement (territory-defending display), agonistic behavior (aggression and fear), alarm response, appeasement, appetitive behavior (exploration), avoidance, camouflage, cannibalism, chain responses (behavior sequences), climate, comfort behavior, community, competition, cooperation, copulation, courtship . . . and that's as far as I got in an hour. Elmer Fudd and Bugs Bunny began to look easy in comparison with animals.

In the Vivarium's first exploratory year, student projects probed edges of the problem. Allison Druin's furry creature with a lap, named "Noobie," was designed to be an input device, an alternative to sensually impoverished keyboards, "a warm place where kids can hug their tools and create their fantasies." Squeeze Noobie's nose and a menu of noses is presented on the computer screen in his belly. Likewise with horns, feet, tail, fur (or feathers, scales, etc.). Press Noobie's belly button, and the new animal is created whole, ready to be given behaviors. Druin was able to employ the help of Gwen Gordon from Henson Associates, creator of the Muppets and state-of-the-art soft robots for movies and television, one of the collection of advisors Alan Kay was attracting to the Vivarium. Others are Paul MacReady (designer of human-powered flying craft such as the "Gossamer Condor"), Frank Thomas (Disney animator), Douglas Adams (author of *Hitchhiker's Guide to the Galaxy*), Tim Gallwey (author of *Inner Tennis*), and Koko the Gorilla.

Meanwhile the blimp cadets were using a neuron-like graphic programming language of David Levitt's called "HookUp" to make rudimentary fishy brains and behaviors for the radio-controlled blimps sailing around in the atrium of the Wiesner Building. A preliminary deal was struck with the New England Aquarium in Boston to do something collaborative about modeling fish behavior.

Sea slugs were adopted as the initial organism of choice for working out learning procedures because so much of their neurobiology had been traced by a scientist at nearby Woods Hole Oceanographic Institute. Going back this basic suggests a complete starting over in AI. Alan Kay: "I've been very disappointed in artificial intelligence since 1970, with few exceptions, because people have not been willing to work on the hard problems they were working on in the '60s, like doing learning for real, not trivial learning. This is the high-risk part of this project—the chances are probably one in five that we'll actually have a good idea in AI." Which explains Marvin Minsky's involvement in the Vivarium.

☐
Devil
☐

■ An MIT eminence at fifty-seven, Marvin Minsky is always introduced as a co-founder of artificial intelligence. (The others are his old cohort John McCarthy, now at Stanford, and Herbert Simon and Allan Newell of Carnegie-Mellon University.) Along with Jerome Wiesner he is a major influence on Negroponte and the shape and direction of the Media Lab's research—toward what Minsky also calls "the hard problems."

One noon in the special room the Media Lab has for lunching visiting sponsor groups, Minsky was describing to a collection of Apple Computer vice presidents some virtues of the Vivarium they were funding. A better artificial intelligence computer language was called for, he said, one based on *constraints*. "With constraints like 'Keep the rabbit away from the fox' and 'Keep the fox near the rabbit,' I would like the fox to get smarter and smarter, where he has a mind that can contain a model of the rabbit and will invent rabbit traps."

Minsky drew a box on the whiteboard with complicated messy original things happening in it. "You'd hate to be away from your Vivarium because you might miss something." The young brahmins from Apple nodded. A box you hated to be away from . . . maybe Alan Kay was on to something commercial after all.

Minsky went on to outline the direction of his current thinking, which is indicated by the title of his 1987 book, *The Society of Mind*. He sees mind, whether natural or artificial, as made up of innumerable "agents"—specialized tools and subtools. "You don't know how to walk," he told the vice presidents, and waited for it to sink in. "All complicated things have to be broken up into sections, which are opaque to each other. What people who design Constitutions know is that different parts don't have to handle everything. The part of your brain that walks doesn't want to know whether you're walking home or walking to work."

His *Society of Mind* book, with its one idea per page, seems fragmented at first. "Some people don't like the book because there is no plot." Minsky smiled. "The plot is that there is no plot." It's a crowd of independent capabilities, like mind. The book also seems deceptively simple, concealing the ten years of work that went into it. "Whenever someone asked me what a term meant, I explained what it meant and took it out." The book had countless early readers because Minsky handed out preliminary drafts for years. It was already cited in detail in a dozen books that came out before it did. That process, a product of the book's being a living, adaptable thing in Minsky's computer, he would like to extend—new editions monthly or so as long as the book is useful, with bad ideas lined out amid marginal rude remarks and new ideas inserted along with commentary by readers. This is exactly what electronic publishing will bring.

"I'm for sloppy corrective programming," Minsky told students at a Vivarium meeting. "When you've got a bug, don't fix it. Write another piece of code to recognize that it's about to happen and head it off." He paused. "The biological way of cleaning up code is very cowardly, and you all know what it is: death. Hans Moravec at Carnegie-Mellon is working on how to cure death—trying to figure out how to merge code of immortals without including the bugs. Immortality has this problem: if you live forever, then you get an infinite number of bugs."

Minsky was equipping the students to deal with designing and programming the Vivarium, but along the way, as always, he was equipping them to deal with science. He collects an enthusiastic audience whenever he speaks, often on short notice, always improvisationally, always with humor as dry as lunar dust and a tendency to veer off topic with parentheses that don't close.

He was reestablishing some artificial intelligence basics. "A goal is a description of a desired state—'I would like to have eaten'—plus a feedback device. With Newell and Simon's GPS—the General Problem

Solver, the smartest thing in AI in the '60s—you have something which looks at differences between what you have and what you want. For each difference there's a certain action. I think the GPS is the basis of all robust things, because it has a place to put different things to do when different things go wrong. And it puts priorities on the differences, so you know what should be done first." He looked from the whiteboard to the students. "Look at everything you do as opposing things that are in your way. Being positive is useless."

I interrupted. "When priorities conflict, does that become an occasion to learn something?" Minsky replied, "Tinbergen found that the herring gull has a default rule: if you're out of your nest and you don't see a straw and there isn't one in your mouth, then just wander around aimlessly. What you do when there's nothing special to do always involves activity hoping something will turn up." I wondered if he was talking about how to be a herring gull or how to be a college student. Shortly he was definitely talking about how to be a college student.

"There's always something wrong with a new idea. But you have to be careful of people who say there are no new ideas because they're likely to fool you into never getting any new ideas. 'Those who know history are doomed to repeat it,' someone said." Minsky was inverting Santayana's "Those who cannot remember the past are doomed to repeat it." Minsky looks like a bald eagle, complete with predator's gaze, but his style is devil—Goethe's Mephistopheles in *Faust* or Ambrose Bierce's devil in *The Devil's Dictionary*—a fearless, amused intellect creating the new by teasing taboos. His smile goes from warm to wicked on zero notice, which keeps audiences on their toes.

A student asked if using some ideas from neurophysiology would be helpful. Minsky: "In about fifty years we'll know a lot about that. It's best not to worry your little heads about it now for the following reason: if you work really hard and read papers on neuroscience, I'd say that a cool 85 percent of those papers are wrong, because they're in a very early stage. You don't want to learn a science in its early stages. You'll end up like Harvard, which had one of the first computers. It took it thirty-five years to recover from it and didn't. Learn all the brain science you dare, but realize that almost everything you learn will be wrong in a serious way and that you'll end up knowing less than if you hadn't started.

Professor Marvin Minsky,
co-founder of artificial
intelligence

"You have to think about your own career and your mind as a resource to conserve, and if you fill it up with infantile garbage it might cost you something later. There might be right theories that you will be unable to understand five years later because you have so many misconceptions. You have to form the habit of not wanting to have been right for very long. If I still believe something after five years, I doubt it.

"Anything that you hear about computers or AI should be ignored, because we're in the Dark Ages. We're in the thousand years between no technology and all technology. You can read what your contemporaries think, but you should remember they are ignorant savages."

He returned to the subject at hand by retelling Piaget's discovery that all children at a certain age, regardless of culture, learn to realize that a tall, thin glass with the water from a short, fat glass does not have more water, despite the impressive tallness. "The older child has the same ideas as the younger, but with more bureaucracy—'It looks like more water, but it isn't because it's the same water.' I call that 'Papert's

Principle' because Seymour Papert said that the child's mind had just added more middle managers. This is a plea for bad programming. You're always fixing something. What we're seeking is robustness—independence from conditions. We're used to programs dying in horrible ways with the least change—change one line of code and it just sits there. A dog is different than a program in that a dog will hop on three feet if one foot is hurt. Animals keep going."

A few weeks later I spent a snowy Sunday afternoon at Minsky's rambling brick home in Brookline while he printed out a new version of *Society of Mind* on a laser printer. The rooms were dark-paneled and heaped with books, papers, layers of toys, musical instruments, and bric-a-brac twenty years deep—a museum of the permanent teenage enthusiasms of a family of five. The living room had a jumble of sofas, a trapeze, an electronic piano keyboard, and *three* grand pianos.

"What happened to artificial intelligence?" I asked. "How come thirty years later it's still trying to succeed?" AI was set up as a receding goal, Minsky replied, "a way of asking, 'What are the twenty most important ways the mind works?' 'Intelligence' is a collection of a lot of mysteries. 'Artificial' just means we can make other things than people do them, so we can explore the horizon of unsolved problems in psychology and computer science. Another advantage back then was that psychologists were so repelled by the idea of artificial intelligence that they didn't consider it competition. They would have if we'd called it 'Cognitive Something.' "

"Has any of this cleared up what consciousness is or is for?" I asked. "People have such a small number of memory registers," Minsky said, "that we can't think of much. Everything has to be on automatic. Consciousness is not a window. It's more like a debugging trace you use for reprogramming around problems. Humans are really amazing, considering. Just think of what we must be the next step toward. Imagine having a four-megabit consciousness chip in your head."

Me: "Do you have a standard timeline for when machine intelligence catches up with human intelligence and goes rolling on past?"

Minsky: "Yeah. Between 100 and 300 years. Intelligent evolution is unprecedented. Nobody's ever seen one. So in few hundred years it could do trillions of years of ordinary slow evolution." Me: "And make enormous mistakes." Minsky: "That's the trouble. There's no time to iron out the bugs. It might fill up the universe with styrofoam or something because it had some wrong theory about how the cosmos needs a shock absorber." Suddenly I saw a Vivarium as a swell place to work out some of those problems, rather than in the world.

By now Minsky was pacing restlessly around the room, crunching sugar cubes and smoking a cigarette every half hour. Like everyone I met at MIT, Minsky loves gadgets. As the winter afternoon got later and darker, the living room light kept turning itself off after seven minutes and had to be revived with a shout or a handclap. At least it wasn't filling the room with styrofoam.

I asked Minsky what he meant by the "hard problems" that the Media Lab ought to be addressing. He paced faster. "I'm trying to help Nicholas filter the activities of the Media Lab so that in each case there's a chance for some new theory to grow and lead to really new things, instead of just helping people along a little bit in their craft. Even shallow cognitive ideas can lead to deep engineering. Computers are not a new idea now, and there are millions of people out there who are very smart and are doing all the easy things. So if there is a place for the Lab, it's going to have to be better than a toy company, and that's hard to do, because the toy companies are so good."

He said he was trying to attract people to the Lab interested in working on constraint languages, or at least attract hackers who might grow into it, "But I don't know whether it's possible anymore, because good hackers are very quickly aware of their hundred-thousand-dollar value making products for people. I look for selfish people who don't give a damn what happens in the outer world for five years. At some point you need a hero who will actually work for himself rather than make it easier for others to work. All the people who have short-range goals will be forgotten."

All of Minsky's examples of hard problems seemed to circle back on semantic questions, problems of meaning and cognition rather than just signal processing. "As far as I'm concerned," he said, "the heuristic for making discoveries is: start with a distinction that people make and argue that there are three ways rather than two. Probably all good ideas start by making a distinction, and then they usually die by stopping there and dividing everything up into those two. Information theory is interested in signal and noise. Maybe we should make a *tri*-stinction—signal, noise, and meaning."

After a dinner of take-out dim sum, Minsky, who had been reading the Koran with some dismay at its violent inquiry-blunting formulae, sermonized, "Religion is a teaching machine—a little deadly loop for putting itself in your mind and keeping it there. The main concern of a religion is to stop thinking, to suppress doubt. It's interested in solving deep problems, not in understanding them. And it's correct in a sense, because the problems it deals with don't have solutions, because they're loops. 'Who made the world?' 'God.' You're not allowed to ask, 'Who made God?' "

I said, "Science feels and acts like a kind of religion a lot of the time." Minsky had heard that one before: "Everything is similar if you're willing to look that far out of focus. I'd watch that. Then you'll find that black is white. Look for differences! You're looking for similarities again. That way lies mind rot." That lively loop has been cycling in my mind ever since.

☐
☐ *Player Pianos of the Future*

■ In the basement of the Media Lab is the world's finest player piano. It's a Bösendorfer Concert Series grand, wired to record every imaginable nuance of the masters that are invited to play it. They go, their performance remains. The Bösendorfer is a signal-and-noise approach to music. Minsky and Kay and some of the rest of the Vivarium researchers are intent on extending music research with computers to include meaning— what they call "music cognition."

Somewhat cognitive is Barry Vercoe's robot accompanist, which reads the same music you do and follows your live tempo, playing a superbly adaptive piano to your violin, for instance. Somewhat cognitive is David Levitt's music program, which can "learn" by imitating. Levitt observes, "It should be easy to say, 'Use the melodic/harmonic outline of this Bach motet, but resynchronize the voices with swing and syncopation, like this New Orleans dixieland polyphony'—to see if it delights an audience acquainted with both genres."

I got a better idea of what music cognition might mean talking to Tod Machover, a cheery young composer fresh from France's celebrated computer music center IRCAM (Institut de Recherche et de Coordination Acoustique-Musique), which is directed by the conductor-composer Pierre Boulez. At thirty-four, Machover has an international reputation as an innovative composer of exceptional talent.

Machover wants to try embodying Minsky's Society of Mind in music. "One of my dreams for a long time has been to have compositions which are like living organisms." Machover would do this Vivarium-sounding task by devising "musical agents, primitives, each of them a musical tendency, a melodic shape or harmonic progression or tone color. The trick would be to set up an environment with some kind of constraint

Assistant Professor Tod Machover, co-head of Music Research

language where you could put those things in motion. You might just push a button and watch it behave, or it might be a performance system—you could interact with this structure at any level of detail you wanted. Somewhere between improvisation and composition, it would be a very powerful way of using a computer to allow amateurs to participate in the musical process in a way they've never been able to before."

Machover began sculpting the air with symmetrical hand motions. "I imagine an instrument something like a potter's wheel. There would be this undulating surface. I could mold my sound and in real time I could hear those partials arrive and disappear."

Concert halls, he pointed out, need this kind of technology to head off the prohibitive economics of the business. A symphony can no longer be afforded when there are eighty musicians in a symphony orchestra, each getting $40,000 a year. Doing a program a week, with twenty hours for rehearsals, five hours per piece, they can't afford to try new music. In five hours of rehearsal you can't even get the notes right for a new twenty-five-minute composition. No wonder movie and television scores are now composed and performed on computers by lone musicians like Vangelis or Jan Hammer.

Interactive music might help cure the passivity that music-reproduction technology has brought. Machover: "Music shouldn't be a spectator sport, but it's become completely passive. Most of us now experience music not even by going to concerts but by putting on a record or CD. In previous centuries most people played piano. When something new came out, you'd get the sheet music and play through it. You got your hands on it. You can't play a new Frank Zappa or Boulez piece on the piano, even if you're Pierre Boulez. I think we've lost something major."

Since my time at the Media Lab, Tod Machover has emerged from the shadow of the Vivarium project and is setting in motion a very strong music reseach center at the Lab. Among other things it is arranging public performances in a cavernous five-story space in the middle of the Wiesner Building called the Experimental Media Facility, which Machover now directs.

□ Animating Virtual Reality
□

■   Alan Kay had an exhilarating demo for the Vivarium group one week, the product of one off-hours weekend session at a firm called Evans & Sutherland in Utah, working with their next-generation flight simulator. "With their CT-6," Kay explained, "you can fly over featured terrain at 3,000 mph in real time. It can handle six or more viewpoints simultaneously and thirty-two coordinate systems at once—it can give you complex aerial dogfights or points of view from rapidly rotating helicopters—all at sixty frames per second. A $2.5-million machine. It worked perfectly." Kay was considering committing to the CT-6 as the development technology for the Vivarium, employing the Defense Department's newest, fiercest state-of-the-art simulator for grade-school kids.

He took with him to Utah Ann Marion, Glen Keene, who was Disney's animator on "The Fox and the Hound," and Mark Vickers, "the major 3D-graphics guy at Apple." The product of their weekend jiggering Evans & Sutherland's existing software was two environments, "Infinite Coral Reef" and "Infinite Forest," which he recorded on videotape. He cued up the Reef first on the classroom TV monitor.

The hard-to-thrill Vivarium group gasped and wowed at the sight of a gorgeous underwater realm with sunlight shimmering down and two sinister sharks in the distance lazily swimming toward the viewer. Student voice: "This is in real time!?" Kay: "Yeah. You can fly these fish around like they were planes." Another student: "I *want* one." The sharks swam by, the camera panning after them as they headed off on shark business elsewhere. Student: "They're not casting shadows." Kay: "They could. It took nine or ten hours to get the shark. It's too bad there isn't a close-up so you could see the texture on them. Glen Keene even made their eyes cycle back and forth looking around—we pointed a TV camera at the eyes and texture-mapped them onto the shark." The tape segment ended. Chorus: "Play it again!"

Kay played it again, noting that the CT-6 could handle 500,000 polygons, the basic element of 3D computer graphics. "To give you a sense of 500,000 polygons, the entire New York City skyline modeled to within a meter is 270,000 polygons." Then he ran "Infinite Forest," the viewpoint of the camera loping along close to the ground as if the viewer were looking through the eyes of a small animal running through a forest, ducking through bushes and dashing across sunny patches. It wasn't as satisfactory as the reef, the bushes looking two-dimensional and the loping too even-paced. Marvin Minsky remarked dryly from the back of the room, "This is a cruise missile lost in the woods, looking for something to blow up."

Realistic animation in real time is a major goal of the Media Laboratory. Negroponte: "Computer animation is an interesting new medium from which people are very easily derailed. They get captured by the surface problem of rendering. How many times have you seen the martini glass with the olive showing the specular reflection and the distortion of the olive through the glass that has a bit of martini left so the olive is a little bigger there and you can see through the liquid? It's a very seductive challenge that finally doesn't have too much intellectual depth to it."

All the spectacular computer graphics you see on TV, the spinning logos and transmuting cars and zooming shavers, are generated laboriously beforehand. Likewise the dazzling computer-generated movie scenes made by firms such as Industrial Light & Magic, where months of work may go into a single two-minute sequence. They're beautiful, but they're one-way. You can't interact with them. As far as the Lab is concerned, that makes them a problem, not a solution.

And so David Zeltzer was hired. One week at a Vivarium meeting Zeltzer repeated the demo that was responsible for his position at the Lab heading the "Animation Research" activity. On the TV monitor was a carpeted living room set against a background of starfields. Vangelis' "Chariots of Fire" theme music swelled as a skeleton at the living-room door swung its bony arms back and did a standing broad jump toward the viewer, then strolled past. End. That was Zeltzer's 1984 Ph.D. thesis at Ohio State. The skeleton, nicknamed George, was walking into a new era of computer animation that is based on the way living creatures actually function.

The gain is tremendous efficiency and immediacy. Just command, "George, walk," and he walks, right now. For contrast Zeltzer showed the hit MTV video of Mick Jagger's "She's a Hard Woman to Please," a Frankie-and-Johnny tale of computer-articulated figures going through the agonies of attraction and rejection, a landmark music video appropriately regarded as awesome. Zeltzer: "It probably took two people at Digital Productions in L.A. a couple of months on a Cray supercomputer to make that."

The difference is that George is not just bits mapped on a screen. "He" is a bundle of computer knowledge, of knowledges actually, about how humans move. His leg bone knows it's connected to his hipbone, and it knows the range of movement possible at that joint. His legs know about "stance phase" and "swing phase" in walking, and how to adapt to uneven terrain. A student asked, "Can you make George be tired?" Zeltzer: "Not yet, but he can limp." I thought of Minsky's dog with the hurt foot hopping on three feet.

An energetic thirty-seven-year-old, David Zeltzer has infectious enthusiasm about the acts of re-creation his group is attempting. At the whiteboard he illustrated his debt to two decades of robot research. "Up to the point of moving a physical hunk of metal, robotics and this kind of computer animation have to solve the same category of problems. What the robotics people are looking for is task-level robot control. They want to tell the robot, 'Here's a screwdriver and hammer and parts and a blueprint of the thing. Go ahead and make it.' One wants to be able to describe the operation of the robot in terms of a series of events and relationships, constraints on objects and the task, and perhaps some specification on the time constraints. Well, we're after the same thing in animation. We want to be able to type in a Shakespeare play and have the computer act it out for us automatically.

"We want to make computer animation a medium for flights of fancy as well as for simulating the reality around us. So first we're going to try to learn how to walk, and then we'll learn how to put on wax and feathered wings and fly. At some point we'll have a library of motions that have been simulated well enough that people can use them to assemble other kinds of animation. We're at the point now of trying to identify what the components have to be."

Zeltzer noted that making a "virtual reality" takes a *lot* of comput-

Assistant Professor
David L. Zeltzer, head of
Animation Research

erized commonsense knowledge—that solid things aren't supposed to interpenetrate, that when you let go of something, it falls away. "*We* learned all these 'obvious' facts banging our heads in our playpens. Now we've got to get this knowledge into the machine. Animation research is relearning basics, really relearning them."

The term "virtual reality" tickled a different giggle in me every time I heard it. I began to realize why artificial intelligence and robotics and animation have become such fundamental science. The researchers are reinventing the world from scratch, at least pieces of the world, but whole enough pieces that when anything basic is left out or gotten wrong, the model fails horribly. The connection of kids and animals and Disney-type animation, even Minsky's devilish bent, was starting to make sense. We are banging our heads in the playpens of another level of understanding.

Like all computer animators, Zeltzer practically venerates the "Nine Old Men" of Disney Studios, especially Frank Thomas, who co-authored the classic text *Disney Animation: The Illusion of Life.* At Zeltzer's invitation Frank Thomas gave a well-attended talk at the Lab a few months after I left. Zeltzer: "The Disney animators before they did 'Snow White' watched reels of film of animals and people. They went to zoos, they held special motion workshops, because they found that they couldn't do the kind of animation they wanted to do unless they understood animal motion and human motion very well. They spent a long time learning calculus—if you want to do a bouncing ball, you don't want to space the ball equally, because balls don't bounce like that. You want more frames up here and less frames down here as the ball speeds up descending. They learned how to suggest that the ball was flattening out at the bottom of the bounce and how to suggest that it was stretching the other way as it moved up. They wanted to exaggerate and caricature motion in particular ways, and they wanted to hide everything else."

At the Media Lab one direct but clever form of animation was being pursued in the body-tracking room. Negroponte had told me, "Instead of trying to describe a motion to the computer with a script, you just do it by enactment, and the instrumented suit follows you. To tell it how to curtsy to Queen Elizabeth or bow to the Prime Minister of Japan, you just do your curtsy or bow." One of the Lab demo tapes showed Negroponte looking ultra-punk in the leather-and-studs body-tracking suit, firmly making a sweeping gesture with his arm. On a monitor behind him an animated stick figure made the identical sweeping motion in perfect synch.

But Zeltzer was looking deeper. "A task-level animation system needs to be based—at least in part—on the kinds of control structures we find in human and animal nervous systems. We know animal behavior is organized hierarchically, from the lowest levels of the nervous system on up. For example, walking isn't controlled directly by the brain. There are just too many muscle movements for the brain to direct them all. Instead, walking is controlled by centers in the spinal cord. The brain decides where, how fast, and so on, and leaves it up to the lower centers to fill in the details. You can't explain to me how it is that you can walk, because you don't know. All that is handled for you automatically by systems that aren't wired up to the cognitive portions of your brain.

That's why we can do so many routine movements without needing to think about them.

"Biological systems try to solve problems at as low a level as they can."

But there's more to animation than biology. One of Zeltzer's students, Carl Feynmann, was doing his master's thesis on the physics of clothing, which could be added to the computer's library of understandings. I sat down in the Terminal Garden with him one day to see his shower curtain demo and told him his efforts reminded me of the classical Greek sculptors. He had a different era in mind: "I like to think of myself as being somewhere in the fourteenth century. There was this period where the human figures were still stiffly posed, side-view, Medieval-looking people, but they had this wonderful clothing full of folds and billows and piled up. Someone had figured out how to do that, and it caught on. The same thing is happening here. People are extremely hard to animate correctly, and clothing is only medium hard."

Feynmann was wearing black running shoes, black jeans, and a black-on-black-striped shirt on his slender frame. He began his fabric research by going down to Dollar-a-Pound for samples, but soon found "there are multi-volume *tomes* on the mechanics of fabric from the garment industry. I was completely amazed when I found them." Zeltzer's view of Feynmann's project: "Clothing is a very complicated higher order surface. It's a tough one to tackle." Feynmann's view: "Skin is not a loose membrane, it's the top of muscle, which is three-dimensional and complicated. You can cover up a lot of things with cloth."

At the adjoining workstation Steve Strassmann was muttering in frustration at the image his *sumi-e* ink program was drawing. It wasn't "anti-aliasing" (blurring smooth) the edges properly. I teased him that real *sumi-e* people didn't have that problem. He gritted, "They have naturally anti-aliased materials to work with. Computers are a lot worse than real life. You just have to be hit over the head with that before you realize how true it is."

"Why bother, then?" I asked. "Why not stick with real life?" Strassmann didn't hesitate: "Because you can't automate real life. I can't get this shrimp to swim if I draw it on real paper with a real brush."

Junior deities, we want to be. Reality is mostly given. Virtual reality is creatable.

Old hand Alan Kay is well aware of hubris problems around computers, so he's made sure that the school end of the Vivarium project is firmly rooted in the life and behavior of real animals. The Open School has a working vegetable garden, and the curricula being developed there to work with the Vivarium tools emphasize building and observing a pond at the school, husbanding sundry resident mammals, field trips to tide pools, public aquariums, etc. For the MIT end, he also knows how to exploit computer hubris—i.e., unleash it and see where it goes.

☐ *Flexoids*
☐

■ Marvin Minsky, the Media Lab's master of hubris, translated the Vivarium project into terms attractive to the Defense Advanced Research Projects Agency (DARPA) with an ambitious proposal to build a "workstation for simulating reality." It would be a "sensory-complete and physics-approximate simulation environment for the design of autonomous robots and other automatic equipment." The bait he dangled took note of the military's increasing reliance on robotic equipment and the huge costs of prototyping and testing such things: "Very large robots or robots used to move or to construct large objects are precluded from most experimentation. Similarly, extremely small and intelligent vehicles, as might be used by the intelligence community, are rarely considered. The workstation proposed would allow the design and testing of previously inconceivable robots."

No talk of rabbits and foxes here. He does mention the identical design regime, in the simulator, of building and testing an all-terrain vehicle or a dog. The thrilling element of the proposal is the rich physical environment envisioned: "I believe that it should be feasible to compute, incrementally, in real time, the solid mechanics for many thousands of small elastic bodies." Such computation assumes either dedicated VLSI (very large scale integration) chips or the massively parallel computer called The Connection Machine (see Chapter 10) or both.

For the proposal Minsky invented the term "flexoid" for the fundamental objects in this universe. Each would have a known "resting shape," mass and center of mass, elasticity, and linkages to other flexoids. On the screen of such a workstation you might drop a flexoid teacup on a flexoid table, and, depending on the height of the drop, the hardness of the table, the brittleness of the cup, and the point of impact, the cup, in real time, would shatter into appropriate smithereens, and the workstation speaker would deliver the appropriate crash.

Minsky notes that users of the workstation could also model themselves into the simulated reality.

7 HENNIGAN SCHOOL

Love is a better teacher than duty.

—Albert Einstein

"A grade school. That's nice. Why is a grade school connected to a media laboratory?" It's a common question among visitors, but one that Negroponte doesn't bother to be defensive about. His view is that a grade school is the perfect place to design and test computer-enriched environments which empower the individual. And by carrying further Seymour Papert's noted work with computers in schools, the Media Lab gets the benefit of seventeen years of research momentum.

Since his collaboration with Seymour Papert in France in 1981 on international computer-and-education projects, Negroponte has become passionate on the subject: "There are children who are registered as 'learning-disabled' who are in no sense learning-disabled at all. Their cognitive style just doesn't fit the method of teaching or the way schools are run. It's tragic, because some very creative children are then literally disabled for the rest of their lives."

In the fall of 1985 Papert, working out of the Media Lab, opened a project at an inner-city Boston grade school, Hennigan School in Jamaica Plain, to explore what could be accomplished in an ordinary educational setting if for once there were enough computers—effectively, one per student. Despite over a decade of interest in computers in schools, such an experiment had never been attempted before.

According to Negroponte, "Hennigan is probably the most profound educational experiment K (kindergarten) through sixth that's going on. It's a $1.5-million-a-year effort, twenty-five people from the Media Lab, fifteen from the city of Boston. If it's successful and influential, I think you'll see two things change. One is, we won't be murderously short-changing the entire right-brained population of this world. The other is, we'll find that curricula become much more complex, and they'll be more driven by the child than by the topic." ("Right-brained" usually means the more pattern-oriented, artistic of us, versus the more language-driven linear qualities of the "left-brained.")

"You can take any six-year-old from anywhere in the world," Negroponte went on, "and plunk them down in Paris to live for a year, and they'll learn French—whether they have a 'propensity for languages' or not, whether they even consider themselves capable of learning a language. Seymour's initial idea, dating back to 1968, was, could you build a fictitious country called Mathland which you could drop a child into and the child would learn math? The idea was so strikingly different in that time of drill and practice. It was too powerful for its time, because it needed personal computers. It needed to let the child take over the technology."

Papert did two things with his idea. Starting in 1968, when he was co-director with Marvin Minsky of MIT's Artificial Intelligence Laboratory, he began developing a computer programming language meant to be used by children, called "Logo." Then in 1980 he published a book based on ten years of work with Logo, titled *Mindstorms: Children, Computers and Powerful Ideas*. The book has become a classic, translated into nine languages; no one else is perceived as having as clear and benevolent ideas about how to use computers in schools.

□ *One Student, One Computer*
□

■ I visited Hennigan School in early 1986, only five months after the project had begun. It's the kind of place that's easy to find parking near, a random-feeling, freeway-bruised, non-neighborhood. The concrete-slab walls of the school, built in 1972, are covered with faded graffiti. The spacious common areas inside have signs in Spanish as well as English. One of the reasons the school was selected was because of its racial makeup: 40 percent black, 40 percent Hispanic, 18 percent white, 2 percent Asian. Many of the kids are from single-parent, illiterate homes. Of the 600 children in the school, 220 are involved in the computer project.

Hennigan had the usual loud, busy feel of any school, but it had almost none of the usual "SIT DOWN AND SHUT UP" tenseness from the teachers. The kids seemed to be too interested in learning to hassle the system. I found the place so gleeful to be around that I went back a couple of more times later just for the pleasure of it.

I strolled through two computer common areas, each with two large circles of IBM PCjr personal computers facing outward, thirteen in each circle, classrooms fanning out all around. Scattered around the circles were kids at the keyboards messing around. Apparently a new spelling game had just turned up, so many were exploring what it had to offer.

On the walls were signs with the main Logo commands—PD (pen down), PU (pen up), HT (hide turtle), FD (forward), etc.—and pinned-up word-processed stories ("MI CARRO ES ROJO. MI PAPA TIENE UN CARRO ROJO . . ."). The kids evidently treated visiting grownups with aplomb, so I sat down next to one Rachel, fifth-grader, who was using Logo to animate a story. She typed "SETBG1." The screen responded, "I DON'T KNOW HOW TO SETBG1." Rachel shrugged and corrected, "SET BG1." The screen background obligingly turned blue, and she ran the end of the story. A flashing-color snowflake tumbled down a slope as words appeared:

> ALL OF A SUDDEN
>
> OCCY TRIPED. HE
>
> ROLLED AND
>
> ROLLED
>
> AND ROLLED.

At the next console Mike Travers from the Vivarium group was watching a boy of light-brown complexion and intent demeanor making a stick figure walk on his screen. Travers' eyebrows were up: "He's discovered transformational geometry." A bell, classes changed, and the number of kids in the circle went from three to ten, picking up projects on the computers where they'd left off. They were on their own time.

Before visiting Hennigan I had talked with Papert in his office at the Media Lab about why the density of computers might matter. He's a soulful man—warm brown eyes always seeming about to smile, eyebrows canted up at the outside, gentle cottony voice with a British colonial accent from his South African origins overlaid with a French flavor from his five years working with Jean Piaget on child development in Geneva. His beard blurring grayly down and his hair grayly up, he seems devoid of hard edges.

"There are a million computers in American schools," he told me, "and 50 million students. What do you do with one-fiftieth of a computer? Boston has the highest ratio of large American cities, a computer for every eighteen students. Each one gets about an hour a week. It's like having one pencil for every eighteen students. At Hennigan there's about 100 computers for 220 students—enough for the kids always to be able to get at one. They can get an hour or two of computer time a day.

"It's too soon to know what real difference that will make, but you can see some things. At Hennigan the girls play with computers *just* as much as the boys, unlike most schools, where computers are competed for, and the girls drop out of that game."

Professor Seymour A. Papert, head of the Epistemology and Learning Group

"Kids like computers?" I asked. Papert: "It's a total love affair between kids and computers." "Why?" I wondered.

Papert: "I think it corresponds to <u>children wanting to be able to control an important part of the world.</u> They're always reaching out to grab what is perceived as important in the adult world. They grab a pencil and scribble with it. They can feel the flexibility of the computer and its power. They can find a rich intellectual activity with which to fall in love. It's through these intellectual love affairs that people acquire a taste for rigor and creativity." Me: "And they see games right away that are fun to play." Papert: "And they see games right away that are fun to play."

Part of the attraction of Logo is that it has lived up to its original design principle: "low threshold and no ceiling." Anybody can get into it and quickly start being amused by doing things, and in time they can use it for anything a computer can do—drawing, writing, doing math, making music. From the very start they are programming the computer rather than being programmed by it. Since the child is alone with the utterly nonjudgmental machine, activities like guessing, playing, imitating, inventing, all come easily—exactly the real-world learning behavior that is cramped or suppressed in most classroom settings.

They're not quite alone with the computer, actually. Kids naturally help each other and show each other things they've made and peek at each other's work, and the teachers soon catch on it's better to let that happen. It's not cheating. It's the kind of joint exploration that is group learning at its best. Teachers who are too committed to being the imparters and arbiters of all knowledge in the classroom can have a tough time making the switch.

Hennigan is a classic Media Lab situation. With sufficiently personalized technology, power shifts toward the no-longer-passive individual.

Music amid the computers at Hennigan is an interesting case. Papert: "Almost all the fourth- and fifth-grade children know music notation—that's considered impossible in most music teaching—and they're all writing music. Some are writing some extremely beautiful things that you'd admire. In our society music creativity is poorly represented. At school you don't learn to compose, you learn to sing in tune and play the piano. Composition is only for specialists, and there's no reason it should be. Everybody draws, everybody writes, everybody talks, everybody does theater. I think one reason is that you need too much performance skill with music to be able to listen to your piece. With a computer as a musical instrument it becomes possible to create a piece of music and hear it independently of your performance skill."

And the kids do, but the computer angle is so blended in you hardly notice it. A Hennigan music class that I watched consisted mostly of singing and "body movement"—fiercely inventive dancing led by the black students—along with enthusiastic improvisation on traditional instruments and homemade ones. I saw an upright piano, slide whistles, bottle-cap rattlers, and a toy xylophone in use as well as an Apple IIe computer and a Yamaha keyboard and attached computer. Discussion with the teacher between pieces was of chords and harmonies, tempo and composition.

Before at Hennigan, Papert recalled, "music was the most hated subject. It was hated worse than math, even worse than punishment." The change has affected the teachers as much as anyone. "The other day one of the teachers was sitting on the floor with the children making bird sounds. Six months ago that would have been unthinkable. If we'd told them at the beginning that would be expected, they would have said, 'Do your experiments somewhere else.' "

□
□ *LEGO/Logo*

■ A major investigation going on at Hennigan extends Logo further into the physical world by tying it to one of the most popular of all toys, the LEGO system of blocks. What started out years ago in Europe as a set of dimpled plastic bricks has become a constructionist universe that surpassed Tinkertoys and Erector Sets. Now a team at Hennigan led by Steve Ocko has hooked all that to an Apple IIe with an interface soon destined to be a commercial product. The interface box connects to a variety of LEGO-compatible motors, touch sensors, infrared sensors, and light sensors—basic robot equipment. LEGO blocks are seen as a brilliantly intuitive programming language in their own right, and now they are linked directly to the power of Logo.

When I visited the LEGO/Logo room one day, Ocko was introducing a solemn handful of Hispanic first- to third-graders to the system. A yellow-and-blue LEGO "turtle" on the floor was hooked up to the Apple computer. He typed "TFD 20" (turtle forward 20), and the kids' teacher explained in Spanish what he did, ending "¿Cuánto?" "Veinte," murmured the kids. Ocko hit "return" and the turtle graphic on the screen and the toy on the floor both marched forward a couple inches. "Do they know 'repeat'?" Ocko asked the teacher. They did, so he instructed the turtle to drive around in a square, the kids helping him figure out the single command for it ("REPEAT 4 [TFD 20 TRT 90]").

I wandered around. Scattered about in conditions of assembly and disassembly were LEGO pop-up toasters, ovens, garages, assembly lines, carnival rides, and ferocious-looking vehicles. On a wall were posted xeroxes of the original patents for barbed wire and the airplane ("O. and W. Wright, May 22, 1906"). Underneath were more recent patent reports by the kids. One booklet, invitingly titled "TOP SECRET KEEP OUT," showed a drawing of a car with features labeled "front wheels; sensor; motor; back wheels; wind resistance; machine gun," and was signed "Sean M."

"LEGO is just grabbed by kids," Papert explained later. "Steve Ocko started one group with a sort of soapbox derby"—Papert pronounced it "darby"—"running different cars down a track and then measuring how far they went. They recapitulated physics. They discovered friction—an axle through too many holes wouldn't work very well. They found out about measuring—you could measure with anything, book lengths or string. They discovered averaging, because the same car would go different distances different times. There were philosophical arguments—a simple pair of big wheels won every time, but was it a car?

"When they hooked up the computer and the motors and started working with gears, they discovered about trade-offs—such as speed versus power. To boys, giving up speed just seems perverse. Girls find it easier, and they learn about gears quicker." To some extent this kind of learning goes on with toys anywhere, but the combination of the school setting, interested, non-pushy teachers, and having to make things terribly explicit for the computer pushed it over into amateur science.

Everybody who's been to Hennigan has anecdotes to tell. Negroponte's favorite concerns a six-year-old who had been classified as learning-disabled: "He put a motor on a clump of LEGO blocks, and the vibrating made the thing sort of oscillate around on the table. What he did then is install an eccentric propeller—I don't know if the eccentricity was purposeful, but at any rate the shaft was not in the center of the propeller. When you started up the motor it vibrated even more, it shook all over the table. Then the child made a very fundamental observation: when he told it to start, the blade jerked the whole collection of LEGOS to the right. If he typed RD—'reverse direction'—the blade jerked the whole thing over to the left and then went into random motion.

"At this point the boy put two photocells on the bottom of this thing, drew a line on the table, and wrote a program so that when the right photocell saw the black line, it had the propeller rotate clockwise and jerk the clump back to the right, and vice-versa for the left photocell, and so this thing vibrated along, following the line. It was a brilliant series of steps to build an effectively one-legged walking machine that doesn't hop that could be of significant interest to the Department of Defense as far as I'm concerned. Then he became a sort of class hero, and then he felt good about himself, and he felt good about school, and that led to . . . you can guess the rest. A heartwarming tale."

☐ ☐ *Bug Appreciation*

■ The success of Logo and the beginning success at Hennigan School have their basis in a philosophy of intellectual process that is shared by Papert, Negroponte, Minsky, and Alan Kay, and has become an underlying philosophy of the Media Lab. Papert may be the most explicit of all of them about it.

In *Mindstorms* he wrote:

Many children are held back in their learning because they have a model of learning in which you have either "got it" or "got it wrong."

But when you program a computer you almost never get it right the first time. Learning to be a master programmer is learning to become highly skilled at isolating and correcting "bugs," the parts that keep the program from working. The question to ask about the program is not whether it is right or wrong, but if it is fixable. If this way of looking at intellectual products were generalized to how the larger culture thinks about knowledge and its acquisition, we all might be less intimidated by our fears about "being wrong."

And that, Papert adds, "presupposes a massive penetration of powerful computers into people's lives. That this will happen there can be no doubt." Much of learning to work with Logo, and much of his book, is devoted to strategies of debugging, such as developing separate subprocedures so that bugs can be easily isolated and fixed. The priceless by-product of learning these skills is a new attitude about errors. Papert: "Errors benefit us because they lead us to study what happened, to understand what went wrong, and, through understanding, to fix it. Experience with computer programming leads children more effectively than any other activity to 'believe in' debugging."

Some people worry that this kind of approach in school, or in life, can lead to loss of rigor and discipline, and indeed there are lots of fraudulent forms of interactivity that can relax into a self-perpetuating sloppiness. But when teacher and student, or anyone, stick with the drive to make an actual connection, an actual program actually run (in a computer or in life), then rigor grows. Discipline flips from the external and oppressing "get it right" to the internal and intellectual "make it work."

An adult example of the difference between working with and without interactivity and debugging is the difference between what happened with Logo in schools and New Math in schools. Logo has been sifting adaptively into schools for decades, riding in with the arrival of personal computers, being grabbed by enthusiastic individual instructors. Experience in the schools fed back into later versions of Logo and approaches to teaching with it. That interplay has a long way to go yet.

New Math, you recall, was the notion that set theory, since it was fundamental to mathematicians, should be taught at the very beginning of math instruction in schools, and then everything would be built on it. Suddenly in the '60s all over the country parents were unable to help their kids with their math homework.

Sitting in the library at Hennigan School, I asked Papert what happened with New Math and why it died so ignominiously. He leaned into the question: "Some people sat in conference rooms and planned a new curriculum and how it was going to be imposed, and even a time-table. The research mathematics community at that time happened to be in a certain phase where a group of French mathematicians called 'Bourbaki' were extremely influential. There was a convergence of what mathematicians were seeing as the big issues at the time with what psychologists on certain readings of Piaget were seeing as big issues. New Math made its environment among these academics, but it had no basis in the school and it had no basis in the general culture. So that's one reason why it didn't work, because it was imposed from on top. Another reason why it didn't work—not only didn't it have roots in the culture, it went against it. Already mathematics in our culture is a very alienated thing. Generally people don't like it, and don't quite see the point of it, although they see certain pieces of it are sometimes useful. The New Math people took something alienated and moved it in a direction that made it even more alienated. It's a very interesting case study because here was one of the largest-scale deliberate attempts to change the way people think on a planetary scale. There were tremendous resources, in terms of monies. They could mobilize the school systems of the world, and did."

"It was really worldwide?" I asked.

"Pretty nearly. All the European countries. I ran into it in Africa, the 'African Mathematics Project,' at a conference about it in Ghana in 1959. I didn't like it. But what I got from that conference . . . well, let me tell you the story. At a certain point the Nigerian delegation stood up and walked out. It was quite dramatic—they were dressed in beautiful African robes. Then the meeting broke up and I had this conversation with one of the people from the Nigerian delegation who went by. 'Why did you walk out, what's going on?' 'I can't talk to these Americans.' (Nobody thought of me as an American.) 'Why not?' 'Because they say what they mean.'

"We're so brought up with the idea that communication fails when people don't say what they mean. The man explained, 'When two Americans have a conversation, each one says what he thinks, and then there's a confrontation—one's going to be right and the other one's going to be wrong. We don't do it like that. We sit around under the tree, and somebody says something, and somebody else does, and we talk, and nobody has a position. It goes on for a long time, and maybe tomorrow, or eventually, everybody agrees on a position. Then everyone is right and there isn't anybody's point of view left out.'

"That had a huge influence on me. There's a negotiational approach to learning and to knowledge, to doing anything. How could we make a more negotiational approach to mathematics? The way we teach math is incredibly confrontational—'This is the theorem, this is the truth, and now I'm going to prove it, and you're going to have to agree with me.' In American supermarkets the price is the price and that's that. In the rest of the world, bargaining the price is part of the fabric of life. It's the difference between dislikers of ambiguity and dislikers of confrontation.

"You see the same thing in students, especially working with computers. One striking category difference you will immediately recognize are those who like to plan versus those who like to tinker. Planners like to sit down, know what's going to happen, think it through, plan it out, use diagrams, and they get tremendous pleasure from that. The others like a more negotiational approach. They just start, and once they get it going they will elaborate it and add on and see how it improves and understand it and maybe scrap it and start again, and so it grows. It might grow into something extremely structured and complex."

I commented, "It sounds like you have preference for the tinkerers over the planners."

Papert: "Certainly I see more need to argue for the tinkerers. In the school system the planners are the ones who are treated clearly. Maybe not in the art class, but in the math class. Schools don't yet tolerate intellectual negotiations. Though ever since Thomas Kuhn's *The Structure of Scientific Revolutions* we've known that science is negotiational and not so rational."

I asked, "Do you think this high here at Hennigan will last?" Papert considered the question a while, then: "Six months into it there's no wearing off. On the contrary. A measure: a month ago I invited the fifth-grade kids to come in on a Saturday morning to introduce a new version of Logo—it was seen by them as more of the same. All forty-six came, except for three whose parents had made other plans."

Papert likes to connect school doings to the rest of life, via LEGO toys, odd scheduling, anything he can think of. "People know a lot," he told me, "and the important kind of learning is bringing out what they know so you can make another step further from there. To do this we have to break down the barriers between school knowledge and ordinary life out there. Even a small child knows how to walk around and find his way through the complexities of three-dimensional space and argue with people."

"That's what I like," I said, "about people with backgrounds in artificial intelligence and robots. You have respect for kid abilities like getting around and picking things up and putting them down."

"Imagine if you tried to teach those abilities in a school with a curriculum," Papert said.

8 THE ROOM WHO WILL GIGGLE

MARRIED CONVERSATION:

"Okay, where did you hide it?"
"Hide what?"
"You know."
"Where do you think?"
"Oh."

—Nicholas Negroponte

Jerome Wiesner is MIT's man for all seasons. Like the Sir Thomas More portrayed in the movie "A Man for All Seasons," he is a man of principle who has held high offices successfully, charmed multitudes, and been creative across a wealth of disciplines and public activities. As an electrical engineer in 1940 he collected folksongs in the Southwest with folklorist Alan Lomax and two years later was at MIT's brand new "Rad Lab" helping design radar for the war effort. His subsequent work with airborne radar led to the present AWAC systems. In national life he is best known for serving as Science Advisor to Presidents Kennedy and Johnson (1961–64), but he worked for several years as a member of President Eisenhower's Science Advisory Committee and has had an even larger, though quieter, public service role in limiting nuclear arms—participating in a major way in the banning of atmospheric nuclear tests and the limiting of antiballistic missile systems. He's promoted the arts worldwide, worked for civil rights, and (I admire this most, considering his workload) served on his town's School Committee.

Wiesner's countless awards and honors include the President's Certificate of Merit (1948, America's second-highest civilian award) and the First Class of the Order of the Sacred Treasure (Japan's highest decoration to a foreigner, given by the Emperor, 1983). At MIT he was Dean of Science (from 1964), then Provost (from 1966), then President (1971–80). A typical caption at the MIT Museum says he "strengthened the Institute's teaching and research programs in the social sciences, in the humanities, and in the fine arts"—in other words he broadened the place.

He has shone particularly as an organizer and sponsor of research at MIT. Negroponte asserts, "Wiesner amplified the creativity of other people more than anybody before or since." Since 1980 Wiesner has devoted much of his MIT time to helping Negroponte create the Media Laboratory, serving as his partner and mentor.

I figured that talking to Wiesner, who was in on the founding of communication science, would be my best shot at finding out how the Media Lab fit into everything, so we spent an hour on the subject one day in his corner office at the Lab. "This looks like the most challenging intellectual activity I've seen in thirty years," Wiesner said of the Lab's research. "My romantic vision is that in the information revolution we're reliving evolution. It'll probably be just as random as the first evolution." Wiesner murmurs like a cello reflectively tuning up, all deep vocal cords, very little air moving, with a pipe smoker's long pauses. You lean close to hear him. His face is noble and homely, with a lopsided, close-lipped smile and steady glance that pins the listener.

I asked him what he meant about reliving evolution. "In building these thinking machines and robots using electrical signals," he said, "we're going through the same cycle again, aren't we?" "You mean we're refolding the cerebral cortex or reinventing the spinal cord?" I asked.

Wiesner relit his pipe. "Maybe both. An airplane already has both. There are many places in an airplane where there are little microprocessors that control function, and then there's a centralized computer that controls them all. Why does your spinal cord manage your leg reflexes? Because once you've learned the process there's no need to control them from the brain.

"I'm not arrogant enough to think that we're going to develop real thinking machines in a short time. But nerve signals travel at 300 meters a second. Electrical signals travel at, um—" he muttered, deriving out loud, "3 times 10 to the 8th, that right?—300 million meters a second.

Professor Jerome B.
Wiesner, former
President of MIT

Also the components we make are much more reliable than neurons. Now, maybe after a computer reaches a certain size it becomes important that the components not be reliable and forget. It's conceivable that you can get painted into an impossible corner if you acquire too much information and try to manipulate it in a system, but so far we haven't come anywhere near that in a computer. The higher degree of reliability of the components and the very much higher degree of speed of the impulses means to me you ought to be able to make machines that are just a hell of a lot better than the brain, if you knew how to do it." "You expect that?" I asked.

Wiesner: "Yeah, not necessarily in my lifetime. No one has given a reason why it can't be done. They make all kinds of crazy arguments— 'A computer doesn't have a soul.' How do we know that it won't have the same soul that we do? After all, humans will program it. I don't think questions about identity are very interesting." My cue: "What questions are interesting?"

Wiesner: "Why do you light up when you recognize something? What is recognition? What is analogy? Why does the brain recognize both verbal and visual analogy and even the link between them?"

I asked about the sequence of events that led to Wiesner's being so involved in the Media Lab. He said it began back at the University of Michigan in the late '30s when he was working with radio, high-speed photography, music, and speech therapy: "I began more and more to think of communications as one big set of things."

In 1952 Wiesner took over as Director of MIT's first interdepartmental lab, the RLE—Research Laboratory of Electronics—which was building on the spectacular wartime success of the Rad Lab. MIT mathematician Norbert Wiener at that time was founding and naming the science of cybernetics—"communication and control in animal and machine"—and Wiesner used the "interdisciplinary" (new term then) attractiveness of Wiener's ideas and work style to draw an extraordinary collection of talent to the RLE.

□
□ *The Golden Age of Communication Science*
■ "The Research Laboratory of Electronics," Wiesner told me, "was probably the most exciting place in the world for anyone interested in communications. We were doing research on neurophysiology, we were studying electrical noise problems, we were doing coding, we were following Shannon's work on information theory, we were even thinking about computers. Out of this I acquired the idea from Norbert Wiener that we would understand both living system communications and machines better if we worked on them not necessarily together but in the same environment." I commented, "That's held up surprisingly well."

Wiesner: "I think we were overly optimistic, and there were a lot of claims made for cybernetics that would make you cringe—for example that the brain was organized like a computer, which I never believed. In one of Norbert's books he says, 'Without communications there would be no life,' and that's true at every level, from the simplest gene to the most complicated society. At one stage we had twelve different fields represented in the laboratory. The Linguistics and Psychology departments grew out of groups that were started in the lab. At its peak from 1950 to 1960 it was attracting the best people from all over the world."

Wiesner wrote in a 1966 essay that the communication engineers at the RLE were joined by "neurophysiologists and other biologists, linguists, economists, social scientists, and psychologists of the various persuasions. . . . For all of them, the concepts of information theory, coding, feedback, prediction, and filtering provided new pathways to explore, pathways that seemed to wind unendingly. . . . They explored each other's fields and slowly began to comprehend each other's lingo and exhibit that spirit of mental intoxication that characterizes the pursuit of an exciting new idea. . . . The two decades of RLE were like an instantaneous explosion of knowledge."

News of the intoxication even reached the West Coast and bent my undergraduate mind at Stanford in the late '50s. The terms of reference of my wondering about things, which still serve me, were set by the writings of MIT stars like cyberneticians Norbert Wiener and Warren McCulloch, biologists Jerome Lettvin and Walter Rosenblith, psychologists George Miller and Alex Bavelas, information theorists Claude Shannon and Robert Fano.

As the RLE had built on the Rad Lab's success, Wiesner wanted to build on RLE's success and create a Communications Sciences Center. MIT's president promised him $10 million to start it, but then Wiesner learned the money had gone into faculty salaries instead. That upset him enough that when Jack Kennedy invited him away to Washington to be Science Advisor, he went.

"What happened when you came back to MIT?" I asked. Wiesner said that by that time there was a Psychology Department, a Linguistics Department, and so on: "I decided the whole of MIT was a computer lab." Nevertheless, listening to him, I had the feeling that even though he denies it, his blunted ambition for a Communications Sciences Center had something to do with his efforts to help create a Media Laboratory which might regather scattered intellectual threads and generate a new intoxication.

One of the landmark products of the RLE was computer time-sharing, which soon became an institution of its own. Wiesner recalled that with Walter Rosenblith he discussed having a large central computer in the new building. Shortly afterward he bumped into Marvin Minsky and John McCarthy and asked them how hard it would be to have one central computer and then consoles "all over the place" that could simultaneously use the big machine. "They came back in a couple days and said, 'Easy.' " By 1962 the Pentagon was funding something called "Project MAC," which stood for Multiple Access Computer *and* Machine-Aided Cognition, headed by Robert Fano.

It was a breakthrough technology which vastly increased the efficiency of computer use, but, more important, it put humans one-on-one with powerful computers for the first time. The first hackers showed up at the back door late at night, were quietly let in, and soon were half dominating the place. The democratization of powerful computers that has dominated the last twenty-five years began at Project MAC.

Within Project MAC, but separate, was an even more radical undertaking, the beginning of Artificial Intelligence. Marvin Minsky recalls, "There were no proposals. I met Wiesner in the hall in 1959, and he said, 'Do you have enough money to do what you want?' I said, 'Well, we'd like a room and a couple of students.' He said okay, and the next Monday we had this room and enough money for a couple of students in the basement of Building 26. We got two kinds of students. We had the hackers, who appeared because we had some of the first computers, and some were very talented at building hardware. Some of them came from the famous MIT Model Railroad Club, which was beginning to think of making computers to control its trains. And we had people from the Math Department getting doctoral degrees. We had the best students at MIT getting interested. Then Licklider, my old professor from Harvard, started mailing a million dollars a year to Project MAC from Washington."

In 1963 Minsky's partner John McCarthy went to Stanford, and Seymour Papert became co-director of the Artificial Intelligence Lab. By 1970 the AI Lab was separate from Project MAC, which had become the Laboratory for Computer Science. The momentous career of AI since then is an oft-told tale which I won't repeat, except to note that the old AI Lab is still alive and well at MIT on the seventh and eighth floors of Tech Square. One afternoon in late 1986 AI students were giving presentations on projects with titles such as: "A Robot with an Appetite," "Leaning on the World," "Pengi, the Politically Correct Penguin," "Artificial Infancy: The Implementation," and "The Construction of Reality in the Computer."

Some students around the Media Lab think (hope) that the Media Lab will be to the AI Lab as AI was to Project MAC and Project MAC was to computer stuff before it: the next hairier thing. What drove the next hairier thing each time was exploring wilder *uses* of the new technology rather than just the technology itself.

But the Media Lab also has its own core history. The largest of the half-dozen groups that came together in the Media Lab was Negroponte's Arch Mac, whose history goes back to 1967.

☐☐ Architecture Machine Group

■ So far as I know, the only thing resembling an architecture machine ever publicly demoed by Negroponte's Architecture Machine Group involved gerbils as the architects. It was in fall 1970 at the Jewish Museum in New York. A large glass case containing 500 two-inch metallized blocks and a colony of gerbils was watched over by a computer-driven straightening machine. As the restless gerbils went about their business, they knocked the light blocks around a bit by their traffic.

"A block slightly askew," Negroponte wrote, "would be realigned. One substantially dislocated would be placed (straight, of course) in the new position, on the assumption that the gerbils wanted it there. The outcome was a constantly changing architecture that reflected the way the little animals used the place."

The history of the Architecture Machine Group is a classic case of a phenomenon that Minsky often refers to as the tyranny of subgoals: "The topmost goal in the intentional model has the lowest priority in the behavioral model." Starting in 1964, architecture student Negroponte wanted to have a machine that would help architects do better architecture. For such a device to be truly helpful, he decided, it would have to be intensely interactive with the human user. Twenty-three years later he's still working on that part of the problem.

Along the way, the Architecture Machine Group he founded in 1967 achieved some impressive subgoals. Some of its early work (1969) helped lead to the now quite commercial world of CAD —computer-aided design. A body of theory and demos called the "Spatial Data Management System" (1977) became embodied in the "desktop" metaphor of personal computer screens. And projects such as the Aspen Movie Map (1978) and a voice-directed screen called "Put That There" (1979) showed a generation how intuitional and productive conversation with a computer could be. The influence of the group's work was quiet, deep, and very wide.

The scheme of computerized "spatial data management" came from two sources. One was "the notion of motor-memory reinforcement, as the psychologists call it," Negroponte told me. "I take this book and I go over to the shelf and stretch up on my tippy-toes to put it on the top shelf, and I've done this with my left hand. That helps me remember, when asked later, that it's on the top shelf on the left." He and co-researcher Richard Bolt noted in their book on spatial data management, "Two individuals, arguing a topic in front of a blackboard, will refer each other to diagrams, equations, and terms on the basis of where they had been written, even long after they have been erased."

The other source was from Negroponte's Greek background. Negroponte and Bolt wrote, "Simonides was a poet of ancient Greece famous for his ability to give long recitations entirely from memory. His secret was to tie each successive part of a to-be-remembered poem or speech to a specific locale within the mental floor plan of either an actual or imagined temple. . . . For each successive subsection of the talk to be given, the orator would mentally walk from place to place within the temple, rehearsing the appropriate material before some specific piece of statuary." By the time of the Renaissance every Mediterranean intellectual had a "memory palace" where he kept everything, an early version of "virtual reality." In 1596 the Jesuit missionary Matteo Ricci won over the nobility of China with his spectacular feats of memorization using a Simonides memory palace, a technique he then taught in exchange for permission to stay and proselytize.

In 1976 Negroponte won over the Defense Advanced Research Projects Agency (DARPA), who funded the group's effort to computerize

Simonides. Instead of a palace or temple, the group focused on what was right in front of them, the desktop. Negroponte and Bolt wrote, "The appointment book is up and to the right; the telephone is in the lower right corner; high-priority memos are kept in an 'in' box immediately to the left of the desk blotter. . . . Perhaps some well-meaning soul tries to tidy up. . . . The now 'well-organized' desk is for us an organizational disaster."

It would be likewise if someone were to tidy up the array of "icons" on the "desktop" of the screen of the Macintosh on which this book was written. The Macintosh screen is the grandchild of Arch Mac's desktop metaphor, via Xerox PARC and Apple Computer. "Icons" are the little images of folders, programs (tiny text page for a word processor, etc.), and so on that serve as reminders when you see them and commands when you invoke them. They can be parked anywhere on the screen, just as on a desk.

The problem with computer screens is that they're so much smaller than real desks. The Architecture Machine Group went the other way: their screen/desk was the rear-projected wall of a room dubbed the "Media Room." In the middle of the room was a luxurious Eames chair—its style "rebuts the premise that system users must live in severe, ascetic settings," wrote the researchers. Effectively, it was a room-sized personal computer where your body was the cursor-director and your voice the keyboard. In a demo entitled "Put That There" you sat in the chair, pointed at the wall with your arm, and issued voice commands. Pointing (a big cross on the screen following wherever you pointed, your arm being body tracked), you might say, "Put *that* . . ." (a yellow ship on the map of the Caribbean would illuminate with the cursor on it, and the wall would prompt aloud, "WHERE?" and you would swing the cursor to another part of the map) ". . . *there*," and the yellow ship would vanish from its previous spot and reappear where you were now pointing.

(Such rooms still exist, but they've become head-sized. The military is experimenting with pilot's helmets that display a computer-enhanced real-time landscape on the visor, with the pilot, in real or simulated flight, issuing voice commands like "select," "zoom," "god's eye," "fire." Instead of arm for pointer, the pilot points with his eyes. "Fire": the definitive piercing glance.)

Everything Arch Mac touched had to be graphically rich. In one
of their proposals they quoted Suzanne Langer's *Philosophy in a New Key*:

> Visual forms—lines, colors, proportions, etc.—are just as capable
> of *articulation*, i.e. of complex combination, as words. But the laws
> that govern this sort of articulation are altogether different from the
> laws of syntax that govern language. The most radical difference is
> that *visual forms are not discursive.* They do not present their con-
> stituents successively, but simultaneously, so the relations deter-
> mining a visual structure are grasped in one act of vision. Their
> complexity, consequently, is not limited, as the complexity of dis-
> course is limited, by what the mind can retain from the beginning
> of an apperceptive act to the end of it.

By the late '70s the Architecture Machine Group was accumulating
some design principles that still live on in the Media Lab. One was:
"Never either/or, but both/and." If there was an argument about whether
something should be a data tablet, a light pen, a mouse, or a touch
screen, the directive was it should have the advantages of all of those
and don't stop. The effect of trade-off situations, instead of forcing choice,
was to force further imagination.

Another discipline came from a kindly assumption about the users.
Walter Bender, the keeper of the Terminal Garden, put it this way: "We
have this party line: if the reward is great enough, you'll learn how to
do something no matter how hard it is. Everybody learns how to drive.
It's hard, a pain in the ass, expensive, but everybody learns how to do
it because it's so damn useful. But we figure our customer base is people
who don't have to use our products. They don't have to pick up the
electronic newspaper. They don't have to pick up the Movie Map or the
Conversational Desktop. It's got to be inviting, there's got to be some
sort of entertainment value in it. We used to say, we cater to kindergarten
children and admirals—people with very short attention spans: 'What I
want, I want now.' "

Designing the human-computer interface, the rule was: do what's
good for humans, modeled on how humans already do things; ignore
what's convenient for computers.

The Aspen Movie Map, done in 1978–79, was a feat of virtuosity exploring the then brand-new technology of videodisk. It was a byproduct of Pentagon interest in the Entebbe hostage-freeing raid of 1973, where the Israeli commandos made a mockup of the airport in the desert and practiced there before trying the real thing. Could such "experiential mapping" be done with computers? An Arch Mac undergraduate named Peter Clay did a term project being scooted around the corridors of MIT in a wheelchair with a movie camera. Soon Negroponte and cohorts were scouting for a town to do that to. They selected Aspen, Colorado, for its street-grid form, doable size, and visual charisma.

" 'Aspen' wasn't a travelogue," Walter Bender recalls. "It was the whole town. It let you drive through the place yourself, having a conversation with the chauffeur." There was a season knob—any street you were driving down, any building you were examining could be seen Winter-Spring-Summer-Fall. Many buildings you could go into. Some, like restaurants, you could go in and read the menu. Some had "micro-documentaries"—brief interviews—inside. Some had a time knob—you could see historical pictures of the building. And much more.

"Aspen" shook people. Scales fell from eyes at conferences where it was demoed about what computers could do, about what videodisk could be, about how *un-authored* a creative work could become. For the first time the viewer could be thought of as an animal instead of a vegetable, active and curious instead of passive and critical.

Senator William Proxmire tried to give a "Golden Fleece" Award to the Aspen project, implying there were generals frolicking amid the snowbunnies in Colorado. It's time someone did a retrospective critique of Proxmire's awards. I've found him as routinely crippling of genuine creativity as unions or building codes. "Aspen" cost about $300,000 from DARPA, a bargain.

Another authorless work was Arch Mac's "movie manual," the videodisk-based manual on transmissions mentioned in Chapter 1 as sometimes boggling. Andy Lippman, who directed the project, mused about it during a demo one day: "It's a book that's sort of written as you read it, by your finger when you touch the screen. So it's different from a normal book not only because it has sound and light, but also because it's got more than any book would have. And in addition you read it by interacting with an agent who knows something about what's in the book."

Designing an "Aspen" or "Movie Manual" isn't authorship, it's a work of virtuoso cartography. The customer explores the product the way a good map is explored, or the world is explored. A book that inspired Negroponte and the Architecture Machine Group was called *Architecture Without Architects*, a provocative collection of photographs of beautiful vernacular—native—buildings from all over the world. Negroponte wanted that kind of giddy originality, adaptability, and local discipline to be machine enhanceable. It turned out the really operative word in "architecture without architects" was "without." Arch Mac was following that thread wherever it might lead—books without authors, films without scripts or directors. A grander scale of research, something like a Media Laboratory, seemed worth attempting, and Negroponte teamed up with Wiesner to fund it.

Then Negroponte took a side trip. The French publisher Jean Jacques Servan-Schreiber had written a book in 1979 called *The World Challenge* that inspired Mitterrand to establish a World Center for Personal Computation and Human Development in Paris to help the Third World make a shortcut into the Information Age. Seymour Papert and Alan Kay had been in on the design of the thing. Nicholas Negroponte, who spoke French fluently from his Swiss childhood, was invited to be its first executive director. With fund-raising to build the Media Lab behind him, and weary of academic politics at MIT, Negroponte accepted a two-year tour of duty. Seymour Papert also accepted the position of Chief Scientist and ran a number of ambitious projects for social use of computers in French cities and in Senegal, Africa.

Fourteen months later they were both back at MIT, scarred from French political infighting, disgusted with the French-chauvinist, commercial turn the whole altruistic enterprise had taken. They were ready to continue where they had left off, in an environment they could somewhat trust. Nobody much liked the name "Media Laboratory," but as Minsky later remarked, "Can you imagine any MIT department saying, 'They can't have a media laboratory. That's what *we* do.' "

It took shape, true to its origins, administratively within the School

The Media Laboratory

Massachusetts Institute
of Technology

MIT's Media Laboratory is
housed in this new building
(1985) specially designed by
I.M. Pei for advanced communication research. Named the
Wiesner Building in honor of the
13th president of MIT and co-
founder of the Media Lab, Dr.
Jerome B. Wiesner, the building
also provides extensive
exhibition space for the arts.

A past "future" of the Media Lab, a white-light hologram of an early model of the building, was positioned against the real site. The sun was not quite at the right angle, so the model appears to float above the ground.

Much of the visual appeal of the Wiesner Building was achieved by close collaboration between architect I.M. Pei and artists Kenneth Noland, Richard Fleischner, and Scott Burton. Particularly impressive is Ken Noland's Mondrian-like mural covering an entire wall of the five-story atrium and wrapping around to part of the outside of the building. *(above)*

Kenneth Noland's mural has become the Media Lab's graphic motif for everything from business cards to publications such as this videodisk cover. Every year or so the Lab prepares a new videodisk "catalog" of its current demonstrations—dynamic versions of the kind of thing you see in the following pages. *(left)*

The Visible Language Workshop (VLW), where designers, photographers, and musicians mix previously separate media forms, has its own "garden" on the 4th floor adjacent to black & white as well as color processing studios. Like its counterpart on the 3rd floor, the VLW rarely rests, open 24 hours a day, 365 days a year. *(right)*

Many of the Media Lab's computer-intensive projects intersect in the "Terminal Garden", itself a gateway to the most powerful computers in the building which are in use 24 hours a day. The Garden never sleeps. *(below)*

The Media Lab's holography apparatus, set in the basement to reduce the effects of vibration, has a direct connection to the Lab's most powerful computer systems. Even in the basement, the nearby Red Line (a subway connecting downtown Boston with MIT and Harvard) still restricts laser work to the early hours of the morning. Atop these tables, computer-generated graphics are assembled into holographic images via a liquid crystal video projector. *(right)*

In the middle of the Wiesner Building is the four-story-high cubical Experimental Media Facility or Villers space (named for entrepreneur Philippe Villers). Designed on a "naval shipyard metaphor," it is for large scale experiments in visual display, holography, acoustics, robotics, and performance research. Pictured here *(right)* is the cube emptied of all but the Bösendorfer piano, and *(bottom)* the first artistic use of the "cube", a performance called "Radio Interference" created for the space by the Lab's Film/Video Group and the Antenna Theater group of California.

The Media Lab's Bösendorfer Imperial Grand piano is considered by some to be the world's finest recording instrument. Every nuance of a performance is computer-recorded in the piano where the hammers meet the strings. Artists who have recorded on it include Oscar Peterson and Pierre Boulez. *(center)*

The *Aspen Movie Map* videodisk project (1978) allowed the user to visit Aspen by "driving" through it as if literally behind the wheel, deciding at every corner which way to turn. One could also stop, enter buildings and meet people, change seasons, or look at electronic maps. "Aspen" achieved considerable fame as a demonstration of an intensely interactive electronic medium, and it introduced the idea of "surrogate travel."

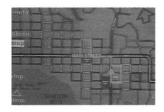

The *Movie Manual* was an early application (1978) of videodisks to training. The voluminous electronic book was like having a conversation with an expert transmission mechanic. The system was fully interactive and audio-visually rich; people would gasp when they saw a color illustration turn into a movie with sound. *(above)*

The front page of *NewsPeek,* an
ultra-personalized newspaper, *IS*
the newspaper. All further material is found "behind" this image,
like opening an advent calendar.
Highlighted words can be
touched to get further information. Such queries are watched
by the system to build itself a
model of the user's tastes and
interests.

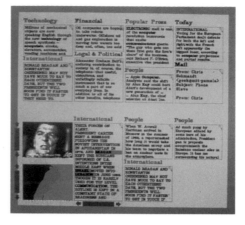

Stories in *NewsPeek* are culled
from the full range of television,
wire service, and photographic
media. Color illustrations come
to life—here a sequence captured from the ABC Evening
News with Peter Jennings.

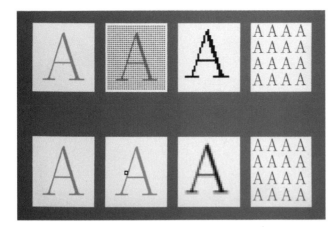

The counter-intuitive use of blurring, called anti-aliasing or Fuzzy Fonts, makes text more readable on computer screens. The technique was pioneered in 1972 at the Architecture Machine Group (a predecessor of the Media Lab) but ignored by industry until 1987. You lose sharpness by introducing shades of grey instead of sticking with strict black & white, but you gain resolution. It is dramatically less tiring to read Fuzzy Font text.

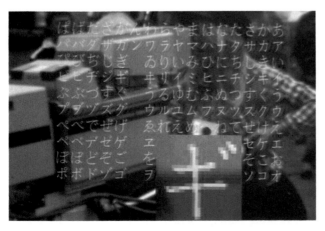

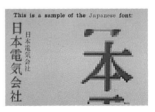

Anti-aliasing of Japanese kanji (here the relatively simple character for "root") is even more effective than with Roman lettering because of the complexity of many ideographic symbols and the number of their horizontal elements, which are often poorly displayed on horizontally-scanned screens. (above)

Anti-aliasing text on top of a complex color scene like this requires point-by-point comparison of the line with its background. This use of computer intelligence to improve images can result in far more attractive, readable, and economic display techniques for television, computers, and even movies.

One project of the *Movies of the Future* program is *Paperback Movies* — an effort to deliver high definition full-length films via compact audio discs or eventually standard telephone lines. If successful, you could move Monday night's movie of choice from a database downtown through a modem into your home computer's storage device and then display it on your television receiver.

The frames in this sequence of Yankee center fielder Ricky Henderson sliding into second base and then moving to third base are constructed from digital information stored on a compact disk. The bases, stadium, Henderson, etc. are "1's" or "0's" in a binary language. To achieve the necessary data compression, the computer analyzes all of the frames in the sequence at once and provides binary codes for the features that are most noticeable.

The *Spatial Data Management System (SDMS)* drew upon the uncanny human ability to remember where one physically left something using spatial clues. A key idea in *SDMS* (1978) was the concept and display of "Dataland," an information display world built by the user, with neighborhoods of data which could be browsed. The re-enactment of spatial clues with computers ("I left that file on the lower left of the screen where I always put the urgent stuff.") was unexplored at the time and remains only partially used today.

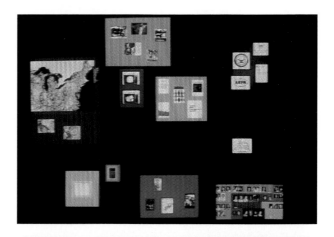

The *SDMS* screen displayed a working calculator, calendar, and telephone. At the time they were ridiculed, but such "desktop utilities" are now commonplace on personal computers.

In this 1980 project, called *Put That There,* Principal Research Scientist Christopher Schmandt demonstrates the enormous advantages gained by using parallel channels (speech and gesture) of communication. A position-indicator on his wrist tells the computer where on the wall-size screen he is pointing, so when he says aloud, "Put that . . . ," the computer knows what he is talking about. He can then point at another spot on the screen and finish the command, ". . . there," and the computer moves the object he was pointing at to the new spot. Currently the Lab is working feverishly to add yet another parallel channel—eyes. *(right)*

These sixteen lip positions are all that are required to simulate lip synchronized English speech. When selected one-by-one, ordered properly, and displayed thirty times per second, they can be made to talk with visual realism. *(right)*

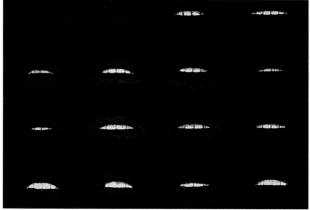

The *Conversational Desktop* emulates a human receptionist with unnerving success. It can recognize who is calling, query the caller for specific information, pass on complex spoken messages, schedule appointments via other "conversational desktops" and even identify individuals as welcomed or unwelcomed and act accordingly. *(left)*

The *Phonetic Dictionary,* created by Media Lab graduate student Jim Davis, inverts the normal path followed by speech-recognition hardware. The user can type phonetic approximations of a word and get the correctly spelled word. Type in "numonia" and the machine instantly provides the always elusive "pneumonia." This work by a speech researcher evolved in the context of the Hennigan School project, from a body of thought in developmental psychology known as "invented spelling"—a typical case of disciplinary overlap at the Media Lab. *(above)*

The *Talking Heads* teleconferencing system projects the video image of the person onto a translucent mask formed from a plastic mold made of the speaker's face. Above is the idea in an early sketch. Below, in the final implementation, Media Lab director Nicholas Negroponte is talking to Japanese TV star Kazuki Kozakai, who would be seeing a similar image of Professor Negroponte at the other end, projected onto a similarly derived video screen. *(right)*

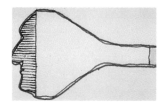

The original "Talking Head," circa 1979, had gimbals to replicate head movement. It would enable five people, in widely separated locations, to meet around a highly intimate "virtual" conference table. At each of the five locations there would be one real person and four video faces representing real people, glancing at each other, nodding or shaking their head, able to converse with a high degree of nuance. *(above)*

Eyes can be separately transmitted in a teleconference and projected onto a static image, mimicking the speaker's expressions with surprising persuasiveness. This was accomplished at a great savings in bandwidth efficiency—the greatest limiting factor in communication technology. *(below)*

This spectacularly inexpensive teleconferencing system was devised in 1981. The display device, here showing former MIT president Dr. Jerome B. Wiesner, cost only a few dollars. All it did was "wiggle" a lenticular photograph in which the only real facial movement was in the lips. From the correct vantage point, the face appeared to talk in lip synch with Dr. Wiesner's voice on the telephone. *(above)*

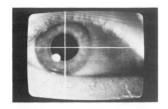

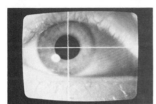

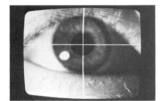

In the Lab's vision of eye-tracking technology, the user can be looking at a word in a text and request aloud, "What does that mean?". The computer would recognize the intersection of parallel channels, eyes, and speech, and know which word to look up in its dictionary and display for the user. If the computer were explaining what was going on in a picture the user was examining, the explanation might vary depending on where the user was looking. One such system allowed the computer to "focus" the picture only where the viewer looked, thus saving large amounts of wasted bandwidth. *(center)* An earlier eye-tracking device included these glasses, here worn by Principal Research Scientist Walter Bender. It was considered too invasive and cumbersome for the user. *(below)*

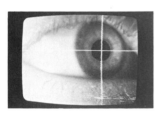

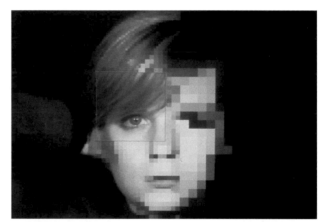

The eyes as seen and tracked by a computer. *(Photographs compliments of ISCAN Inc.)*

The hand is one of the most versatile of human instruments, but so far computers are blind to its expressiveness. One of the goals at the Media Lab is to make computers sensitive to the nuances of human gesture. Infrared LED's (light-emitting diodes) in this glove permit optical tracking. Just as a "mouse" is used to move a cursor around on a personal computer screen, this technique could provide a multiply-articulated "mouse" in three dimensions.

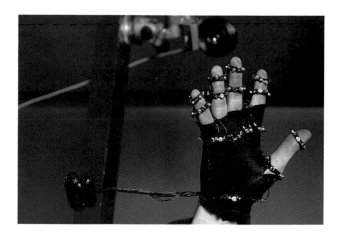

With the full body optical-tracking suit, a computer can be taught how humans move, permitting highly realistic and efficient animation techniques. Likewise, a computer can reflect or interpret a person's movements as they are made—"dance as command." In the picture above, director Nicholas Negroponte makes a sweeping arm gesture which is picked up by the computer and echoed in an animated figure on a screen nearby. The picture to the right shows graduate student Marc LoCascio in the full suit watching his own movements repeated on the computer screen. The process is referred to as "animation-by-enactment."

By sensing the pressure exerted on the screen, this demonstration allowed the user to literally feel data. Pressing hard or lightly against the screen is interpreted differently by the computer. As demonstrated above, moving a "heavy" object on the screen, for example, requires greater pressure by the user's finger.

"Force feedback" permits computer simulation of almost any physical interaction. This joystick is fighting student Mike Halle's hand as if there were a strong fish on the other end. *(above)*

A pressure-sensitive keyboard is a way of measuring the typing equivalent of "tone." Your fingers can whisper or shout, emphasize or insinuate. The technique can also be a method of identifying users by their unique typing styles. The red readout here is showing the impact of each of graduate student Jim Puccio's keystrokes. *(right)*

Research Affiliate Steven Haflich here conducts three musicians, violinist Chung-Pei Ma, flautist Ellen Sebring, and a computer (playing the keyboard in the foreground). The program by Professor Barry Vercoe, called the *Synthetic Performer*, hopes to be the perfect accompanist, able to follow and learn by reading the score and understanding the visual cues of the conductor while listening to the actual performance of the other musicians. The program is a quick study, proven capable of learning rapidly from experience with the musicians and score. *(left)*

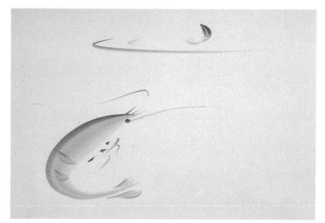

These two sumi-e ink drawings were done on a computer using graduate student Steve Strassmann's *Hairy Brushes* program. The user, like a sumi-e artist, can dip the "brush" in different sorts of ink, can draw quickly or slowly for different effects, can make a splatter effect, can have the brush dry out during the stroke. The technique achieves a degree of graphic subtlety never seen before on computers. The above drawing was subsequently animated into a film, showing the leaf settling into the water as the shrimp swims toward the surface to meet it.

Computer "paint" programs
have come a long way since
their origin in 1972. This remarkable program, designed by then
freshman Bob Sabiston in the
Visible Language Workshop,
offers rich color tables (bottom
of screen) and twenty-five
immediately available graphic
tools, all reconfigurable by the
user. On the right of the screen is
a catalog of completed images.

These other five are images made with this program, including a "painting" of rock musician Peter Gabriel which was done while he watched, working from a live digitized image of his face.

Artists (clockwise from upper right): Ronald MacNeil, Christopher Crowley, Bob Sabiston, Alkae Badshah, Anne Russell.

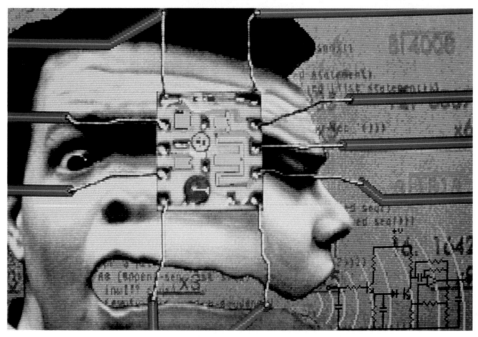

3D rendering problems include understanding light, color, and texture. For example, a simple red sphere can be made to glisten like a billiard ball or reflect dully like the rubber surface of a handball. *(center)*

Raining Polyhedra, developed by graduate student Karl Sims, portrays properties well beyond the visual, such as elasticity and mass. The objects bounce according to how they hit the surface. This research is leading toward computer "flexoids," which will have even more realistic qualities, such as sound. Tap a flexoid glass, and it goes "ting." Tap it harder and it shatters. *(bottom)*

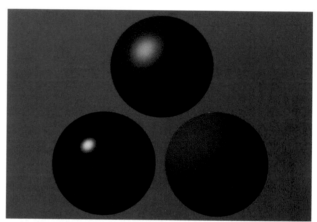

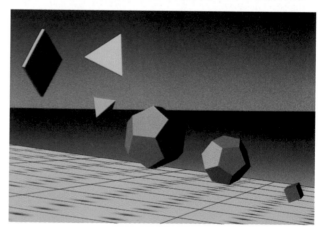

Up until now, rapid real-time 3D computer animation has been limited to military and commercial flight simulation applications such as these scenes from a Swiss database running on the Lab's special purpose Trillium computer. The Media Lab is working to make such graphic capabilities a common component in the personal computers of tomorrow. *(above)*

Tell Karl Sims' "intelligent worms" where to go and they'll figure out their own way to get there. This is part of developing an "intention language" for computer animation, which will allow simple commands to initiate complex behavior in computer generated environments.

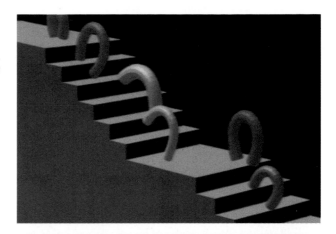

These abstract animated three-gaited creatures (referred to as "coffee tables") explore their computer landscape in real time, their joints and stride adjusting to the uneven terrain. Eventually they will be fleshed out by Karl Sims to look like realistic animals. *(above)*

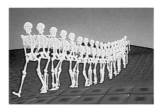

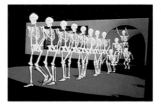

"George," a walking, jumping skeleton, was developed by Assistant Professor David Zeltzer at Ohio State before he joined the MIT faculty to take charge of computer animation research at the Media Lab. Animation can be much more realistic and efficient when the animated figures have their own kinematic knowledge. "George," for example, "knows" how to walk over uneven terrain and jump when necessary. *(left)*

A highly practical way to get 3D video output is with a liquid crystal "shutter" which rotates the polarization of the screen in front of the computer display thirty times a second, so that each eye of the observer wearing polarized glasses sees a different image, permitting dramatic depth of view. This process, developed by Polaroid's K.C. Chang, has become a routine tool for testing the Media Lab's 3D images.

In an early 3D project by the Architecture Machine Group, a vibrating mirror stretched over a drum combined with a field sequential color display provided a 3D image which did not require glasses to see–real 3D! *(above)*

Text, a stylized brain, and a Da Vinci sketch are all seen floating in the same space. This three-foot-square multi-color synthetic hologram, the world's first, was a joint project between the Media Lab and Polaroid Corporation. It was displayed in the American Pavilion at Expo '85 in Tsukuba, Japan. *(left)*

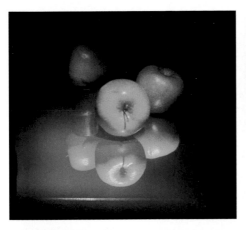 

A holographic representation of time. As the viewer moves from right to left, the apples are progressively eaten to their core. This time parallax is accomplished by recording many animated views of the apple side-by-side in a single hologram. *(top)*

 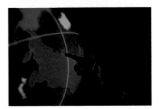

This is the world's first projected hologram. The Camaro appears to be parked in mid-air, shown on the hand of inventor Professor Stephen Benton, with the Boston skyline in the background. This image is produced by a synthetic hologram, which was computed from a database rather than photographed with lasers. The research was sponsored by General Motors Corporation, who expects to use synthetic holograms to supplement clay models of automobile design, cutting perhaps a month out of the design process. Holograms at the Media Lab are being developed up to theatrical scale; soon the car will be life-size. *(center)*

Holographic images generated from medical data such as X-rays, CAT scans, and MRI (magnetic resonance imaging) scans show significant diagnostic promise. In this case, a Media Lab hologram generated from a CAT scan by Dr. Peter Kijewsky of the Harvard Medical School of a woman's hip socket shows exactly how her hip joint implant is failing—information that would be extremely hard to get from flat images. *(above)*

This touch-sensitive world globe, under development in the Lab's Spatial Imaging Group, will offer an extremely wide range of geographical display capabilities on its dynamic, interactive surface. *(above)*

The Vivarium is a long-term project supported by Apple Computer, Inc. and initiated by computer visionary Alan Kay to enable school children to create highly realistic animals that come to life in complex computerized ecosystems and proceed to behave on their own. The task cannot be done with present artificial intellience capabilities. Part of the Media Lab's role in the Vivarium project is to make it possible.

In response to the aridity of computer keyboards for children, graduate student Allison Druin built "Noobie," a prototype of a computer interface for the Vivarium with sense-filling texture, scale, and personality. Noobie (for "new beast") is a sort of menu. The child squeezes Noobie's ear, and a series of ears appear on the creature displayed on the computer screen in Noobie's belly. So it proceeds through the mouth, eyes, hands, feet, tail, horns, etc. Later there will be choices of creature emotions, behaviors, and environments for the child to select. *(left)*

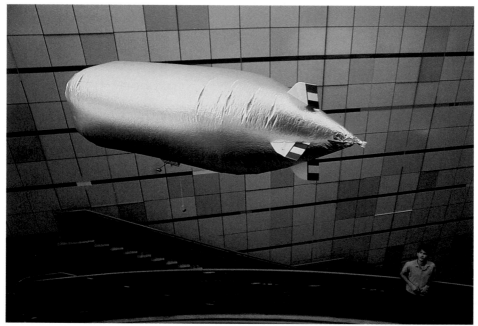

The first creatures created for the Vivarium were radio-and-computer-controlled blimps that pretended to be fish, swimming around in the Media Lab's atrium. The blimps had rudimentary sensors that helped them orient in relation to walls, each other, and "food" (electric-

ity). With the help of some blue light a classroom was spectacularly transformed into an ocean where child and "fish" became collaborators in a shared environment. *(center)*

Using America's most advanced flight simulator at Evans &

Sutherland in Utah, Alan Kay and professional animator Glen Keene created "Infinite Reef," a beautiful underwater world with two animated sharks that can be piloted by the user. In time, they and other Vivarium creatures will swim around according to their own behavioral habits. *(above)*

The *School of the Future* program at the Media Lab is exploring the effects of high density computer use (1:1 student-to-computer ratio) in a public grade school. The James E. Hennigan School, the site of the experiment, is in inner city Boston—its student population is 40% black, 40% Hispanic, 18% white, and 2% Asian. In an environment that is so computer-enriched that every child can get in several hours a day alone with a powerful personal computer, the kids become highly collaborative.

LEGO/Logo at the Hennigan School is about toys to learn with. The Media Lab has developed sensors and actuators for LEGO modules to connect directly to personal computers running Logo. The result is a gleeful invention of vehicles, buildings, toasters, factories, and robots. It all has a rigorous learning element because programming the toys takes a good deal of exploratory trial and error. The children become expert debuggers and designers. *(left)*

Professor Marvin Minsky chal-
lenges computer developers to
show him a machine that can
differentiate a cat from a dog.
When this is accomplished, he
tells his students, everything we
think we know now will have to
be rethought. The Connection
Machine, developed by one of
Professor Minsky's graduate
students, Danny Hillis, leads
a new generation of supercomputers. With its massive number
of parallel processors (64,000),
it can manage enormous complexity at previously unimaginable speeds. The Media Lab's

Connection Machine is being
used for synthetic holography,
animation, electronic publishing,
compressing movies, and as
an artificial ecosystem for the
Vivarium. New machines with
new capabilities draw new talent,
the Media Lab's most treasured
resource.

The dog is Silas.

of Architecture and Planning. By now it had nothing to do with architecture at all.

□
□ *Eyes as Output*
■ My clearest sense of how the Media Lab emerged from the Architecture Machine Group came from a session with Richard Bolt, whose line of research seems to be closest to Negroponte's heart.

You become self-conscious talking to Richard Bolt, head of the Lab's Human Interface activities, creator of the Media Room, not because of his manner but because of his subject. His manner is the gentlest in the Lab, with feathery soft voice and tall, graying, distinguished look. The author of the 1984 text, *The Human Interface*, is a psychologist by training, and the topic of conversation with him is apt to be what you're doing with your eyes.

"I'm really less interested in devices than the actions performed

Richard A. Bolt, head of
Human Interface

by people," he began one afternoon in his office. "The common link between people is the context that they share. If this interview were about Dick Bolt's office and you were looking about, then I would tend to respond to your body language and where you're looking. If I saw you looking broadly at these prints on the wall, my tendency would be to chat about them as a collection—'We bought them at a sale at the Harvard Coop.' But if I saw you devoting most of your attention to the one on the left there, I would talk about that—'It's a Monet.'

"I would modulate my commentary as a function of what I perceive to be the focus and scope of your interest. People are pretty good at tracking the eyes of another person. Even across rooms they can pretty much tell whether they're being directly looked at. It's an extremely valuable cognitive ability that is picked up early on by small children. It's taken on early by humans, and now I'm trying to get it taken on by computers."

I found myself maintaining much warmer eye contact with Bolt than is my style. I also saw Bolt notice that and graciously ignore it. *What did I see?* Negroponte raised a similar question with me later: "Eyes latch on to each other like magnets, and the angles involved are incredibly small. How the hell do they do that? What is the language of eyes?"

Bolt continued, "With a computer, what the conversation is about is what the computer has on its display—the screen is the analog of the room which you and I now share. I think that a whole graphic art will arise concerning 'lookable' graphics—graphics which are concocted and generated with an awareness that they will be looked at."

I asked, "Is this a semantics of display?" "That might do as a quickie label," he replied. "The issues are not the attractiveness of design as such. You want to be able to look at something on the computer screen and say, 'Explain that,' and have that combination of your eye and voice be a command the computer can respond to. The Media Lab is more interested in the perceiving computer, as the AI Lab is more interested in the thinking computer, but these two worlds may be tunneling toward each other. More likely they'll meet at a new level of integration. The problems involved are truly novel."

The technology that makes "eyes as output" conceivable is called eye tracking. A rig can be put on a computer that measures with some precision exactly where you're looking—to within a degree anyway. That's about the angle your little fingernail covers at arm's length. The best current technology is a remote corneal reflection tracker that costs $35,000 to $100,000, but the price would come way down if it became a common consumer item or even a standard research item. You could look at a word on a computer screen and request aloud, "Definition," "Cross-reference," "Synonyms," "Spell."

Interesting: horses and bass and other prey animals don't point with their eyes; they watch everywhere simultaneously. Predators such as humans, hawks, and ocelots look precisely at what they want to eat or think about.

Bolt turned to his desktop PC to show a demo he was working on. The screen filled with: a living-room wall in color, a fireplace with brass andirons, a mantel with brass candlesticks and a ship's model, and two pictures on the wall. Two programs would function with this display, Bolt said, "looker" and "show-er." "Looker" is the trace of the viewer's point of regard as it dashes around examining different parts of the screen's image. "Show-er" will be the computer's verbal response to what "looker" is doing, explaining "It's a Monet" if the viewer concentrates on the left picture, continuing with further explanation, perhaps, if the viewer lingers on the picture, moving on to other topics if the viewer keeps looking around.

Soon "looker" would be replaced with a real eye-tracked human, and "show-er" would be a whole set of remarks about the room in computer-speech. Bolt: "Just as in real conversation, who takes the lead would go back and forth. And pace would vary. If you're kind of laid back, it will not press itself on you. If you're more up and alive, it will be more sparkling. It will know when your attention is wandering and deal with that."

Also the "show-er" would be represented on the screen by a little personage. A blue square face with big eyes appeared on Bolt's screen. It looked around, then gazed straight out, establishing something that felt all too familiar—eye contact. It was fake at this point, since the computer had no eye-tracker, but I could feel the real thing coming— sincere eye contact with a computer.

For Bolt, eye-tracking might lead in a number of directions. Staring at part of a screen could prompt the screen to zoom up more detail of a map, or to give an x-ray view into an object. By tracking point of regard the computer can know when, or if, the viewer has "got" a visual message on the screen. Then there's "addressable resolution." Our sharpest vision is in the foveal area right around where we're looking—computer graphics could run much faster if they just provided high-resolution detail where you're looking and let the rest be sketchy.

In the Media Room, Bolt has experimented with "gaze-orchestrated dynamic windows"—an array of forty simultaneous moving images, some coming and going, with all the sound tracks making a cocktail-party low roar. Wherever the viewer looks steadily, that sound track swells up, and then, if interest persists, the image zooms up to full size. A related proposed idea is called "Multi-Eyes"—the array of moving images is different views of the same subject, much like what a TV editor at a live sports or political event sees, simultaneous feeds from twenty different cameras. In this case, editing would be done by selective looking. Personally I'd like to do that right now, say with two TV sets, one showing the gamut of camera feeds, the other showing full-screen the one I've indicated most interest in currently. If it was a football game, instead of two announcers there might be ten covering different aspects of the game that I also could select among visually.

If a computer can read eyes, why couldn't it read lips? "Forty percent of English is visible in the lips," says Bolt. Considering how limited speech recognition still is, this might offer another avenue to "speech interpretation." Negroponte is interested in pursuing it: "We believe that you can pull signal out of lips, and when the machine is not sure of what the person has said, looking at the lips can help disambiguate. So if I say the word 'lunch' or the word 'punch,' the energy of *l* and *p* are close enough that the speech recognizer might not pick up the difference, and yet the lips are so distinctly different you can tell clearly."

Lips have been fascinating Architecture Machine Group people since they first started trying to manage the "transmission of presence" in projects like "Talking Heads." In order to compress the information of talking faces they explored the lip-reading literature and discovered there are only sixteen lip positions in English. Negroponte told me, "You could cycle through those in whatever order to produce any word." "Gosh," I said. Negroponte continued, "If we want to transmit the word 'gosh,' we just figure out which ones and send the bits. It's four bits per lip position, and you want to send thirty times a second, so it's 120 bits to have 30-hertz lips. You send the lip number and it re-creates it at the other end. And we can photographically store *your* lips—it doesn't have to be little diagrammatic lips. We get you to say, 'I thought you really meant it.' I think that phrase has all sixteen in it. The demo really was very convincing."

All this interest in eyes and lips, and also speech intonation and paraverbals like "uh huh," is part of Negroponte's conviction that communication should take advantage of parallel supporting channels. His standard illustration is of going to a dinner party in a foreign land where you're the only nonspeaker of the language everyone is using. So long as the conversation is "Pass the salt" and "The soup is wonderful," you can sort of cope, but if the topic turns to local politics, you're lost.

Negroponte: "When I say to you in Swedish, 'Please pass the water,' you may not understand even the word 'water' or 'please' or 'pass,' but you know enough about dinner tables, you see me looking at the water pitcher, you see my water glass is empty, and you can put two and two together and pick up the water. If you really don't know what's going on and there's a butter dish in the same line of sight, you might ask and point, 'Butter?' 'No no, water.' What's really happening is that everything in the spoken sentences is right there on the table, unlike local politics. The general principle is, when you're interested in the human interface with computers, you always want to use multiple channels. The combination tends to perform much better than any one alone. Example: if you don't speak a language fluently, you find it very painful to talk to somebody over the telephone, because you've got to get all the message through the acoustic channel."

"We are multi-modal creatures," Bolt told me. "So, what other modalities tempt you," I asked him, "smell, blood chemistry, brain waves?" Bolt leaned back in his chair: "One of the most complex senses is the haptic modality—touch, pressure, temperature—the information we get by handling things. I devised a gadget—it's in pieces in a box over there—for appreciating surface textures—ceramic tiles or rugs or whatever. And a device that would become cold or hot, so you'd know if it was a metal surface or a plastic surface. The device would be below a half-slivered mirror which would be reflecting an overhead TV image of the object you're 'feeling,' so you'd see and feel the virtual image. It would also convey the thing's mass, and you'd hear your finger rubbing it."

I could feel myself slipping into boggle mode again, so I headed back to familiar ground by asking Bolt about the Media Lab in general and got what turned out to be the clue I needed for my deeper question: What holds this place together? The Media Lab, Bolt said, is the pure product of Nicholas Negroponte's energies and outlook, his élan and imagination. "It's the combination of a vision about the possibilities of these machines with a sense of humor, a reservation about what those possibilities might be. It's all there in his book *The Architecture Machine*, from 1968. Many of the ideas and examples in there are still alive today."

□
□ *The Founding Image and the Connecting Idea*
■ Nearly every successful enterprise retains some of the founder's character, even long after the founder is gone, and that becomes an important part of the institution's sense of continuity and therefore of its durability. But trying to figure out how the Media Lab ticks has made me more interested in the sequence of two key events at the founding of an enterprise. One happens in the founder; the other happens to the founder. The first, what I'm calling the "founding image," is that initial motivating glimpse of something better (or less awful, in many cases, since rage is a splendid motivator) that kicks the founder into action.

The connecting idea is the second key event, generated by the attempt to enact or enable the founding image. The original effort works, or doesn't work, or partially works, and in the follow-up, or recovery, or desperate floundering, *something connects*, and current begins to pour through the connection. That new traffic shapes everything it touches, because the world has few defenses against a new idea. Connecting ideas set in motion positive feedbacks by rewarding all the players in the game.

The more everybody does, the more everybody does, until the world detects a potential runaway and sets in motion appropriate negative feedbacks, and everything settles down. The next few generations will see what the world does with the potential runaway of computer intelligence. And that brings us back to the Media Lab.

The architecture machine in *The Architecture Machine* abides as the Media Lab's founding image. The book is a passionate manifesto, brilliant and quirky, and still a provocative read twenty years later. Negroponte later claimed the book was about personal computers ten years before they existed, and that's fairly accurate. He had been bit by those early time-sharing consoles of Project MAC in the mid-'60s, had seen the future, and wanted it for everybody. But the book is more radical than that.

In its "preface to a preface," twenty-six-year-old Negroponte wrote:

You will find that this book is all beginning and no end. . . . The [architect's] design process, considered as evolutionary, can be presented to a machine, also considered as evolutionary, and a mutual training, resilience, and growth can be developed. . . . I shall treat the problem as the intimate association of two dissimilar species (man and machine), two dissimilar processes (design and computation), and two intelligent systems (the architect and the architecture machine). . . . The partnership is not one of master and slave but rather of two associates that have a potential and a desire for self-fulfillment.

To accomplish all this, Negroponte posited a high degree of intelligence in the machine, a high degree of intimacy between machine and user, and a rich dialogue between them. Since people like his friends Minsky and Papert were dealing well with machine intelligence, he took on the other two—intimacy and dialogue.

He wrote:

Imagine a machine that can follow your design methodology and at the same time discern and assimilate your conversational idiosyncrasies. This same machine, after observing your behavior, could build a predictive model of your conversational performance. . . . The dialogue would be so intimate—even exclusive—that only mutual persuasion and compromise would bring about ideas, ideas unrealizable by either conversant alone.

The book surveyed the cutting edges of artificial intelligence and computer graphics of the time, it reported on work Negroponte was doing with an urban environment simulator called URBAN5, and it ended:

We, the Architecture Machine Group at MIT, are embarking on the construction of a machine that can work with missing information. To do this an architecture machine must understand our metaphors, must solicit information on its own, must acquire experiences, must talk to a wide variety of people, must improve over time, and must be intelligent. It must recognize context, particularly changes in goals and meanings brought about by changes in context.

Negroponte, quoting Stanford Anderson, was interested not in "problem-solving" but in adaptive, collaborative "problem-worrying." Machines not able to recognize context or to learn, Negroponte insisted, would operate strictly on "the built-in prejudices and 'default options' of their creators. These would be unethical robots."

The Architecture Machine was dedicated: "To the first machine that can appreciate the gesture."

Pursuing intimacy and dialogue with computers is what became the connecting idea for the Architecture Machine Group. That continues with the Media Laboratory, for the simple reason that neither subgoal—intimacy or dialogue—has been fully achieved yet, but both remain productively tantalizing. Computer intimacy, as expressed in projects like Personal Newspaper, Personal Television, and Conversational Desktop, is a major selling point for the Lab. Negroponte told a large group of potential funders in 1986, "The binding principle at the Media Lab, the primary theme, is personalization."

I disagree slightly. I think the binding principle at the Media Lab, the primary theme, is *conversation*, with computers and through computers. Arch Mac and the Lab have been at their most original, rigorous, and productive when pursuing interactivity, mutual interruptibility, parallel modalities, transmission of presence, the nuances of human conversation, and all the niceties of the computer interface from the desktop screen to high-resolution TV. Personalization is the valuable by-product. With machines as with humans, conversation builds intimacy, not necessarily the reverse.

Is that an important answer to an important question? It would be if it were true of the media laboratory of the world at large—if the binding principle, the dominant theme, of these decades were enhancing conversation, with personalization the valuable by-product.

It's instructive to see what happened to the image of the architecture machine with Negroponte's group. In 1972 he assembled a second book, *Soft Architecture Machines*, which reported on four years' work by the Architecture Machine Group—the sketch recognizer, the plan recognizer, the gerbil village, a community project in Cambridge, and a design philosophy becoming ever more radical. Now instead of aiding the architect, Negroponte was ready to remove the architect:

> The general assumption is that in most cases the architect is an unnecessary and cumbersome (and even detrimental) middleman between individual, constantly changing needs, and the continuous incorporation of these needs into the built environment. The architect's primary functions, I propose, will be served well and served best by computers. In this sense the book is about a new kind of architecture without architects.

It doesn't take much extrapolation to contemplate the computer-subversion of all the professions, a cheery institutional leveling that the Media Lab continues to this day, whether dealing with schools, broadcasters, or filmmakers. At Hennigan School the computers promote the students . . . and demote the teachers from the main event to appreciated assistants. More learning, less teaching. As for architecture, Ne-

groponte predicted computers would bring more designing, less archi-
tecting. With personal computers now, that is on the verge of occurring,
with people being given the architectural software tools to design their
own homes.

By the end of the book, Negroponte had turned the founding image
inside out:

> The last chapter is my view of the distant future of architecture
> machines: they won't help us design; instead, we will live in
> them. . . . While proposing that a room might giggle at a funny
> gesture or be reluctant to be transformed into something else seems
> so unserious today, it does expose some of the questions associated
> with possible cognitive environments of tomorrow. I strongly believe
> that it is very important to play with these ideas scientifically and
> explore applications of machine intelligence that totter between
> being unimaginably oppressive and unbelievably exciting.

By the time the book came out in 1975 (delayed by the too-early
use of computer-typesetting), Negroponte and Arch Mac had moved
beyond architecture. An interesting echo of what happened to the founding image was embodied in the "Put That There" room, which was a
personal computer with the person inside.

As the group took on the fragmenting world of communication
technologies, Negroponte kept the efforts centered by remaining focused
on the individual human and how humans converse with each other.
Richard Bolt recalls they were deliberately working with the root meaning
of "conversation"—"to keep company with." The machines had to tend
toward being convivial intellectual partners of humans, or forget it.

That impulse has a distinguished history. In 1950 Alan Turing
proposed what has come to be known as the Turing Test. Turing was
the British mathematician who introduced the idea of a universal computing machine in 1936 and who designed the first electronic computer
to break the German codes in World War II. In his 1950 paper, "Computer Machinery and Intelligence," Turing, noting that we judge people's
intelligence by their conversation, offered a pragmatic measure: "A ma-

chine may be deemed intelligent when it can pass for a human being in a blind test."

The Media Lab has projects that inadvertently have already passed the Turing Test. Chris Schmandt told me that some outsiders who encountered the "Conversational Desktop" and its predecessors on the phone had no idea they were conversing with a computer. It's a partial pass, because if the outsiders had probed, they would have quickly encountered the system's limitations, but in a way it's a more genuine test, being casual. Imagine defending yourself on a phone or by e-mail against someone determined to prove you're a computer. You'd probably lose.

Negroponte has his own test, much more demanding, where the computer and the human are the opposite of strangers suspicious of each other. He wrote in 1977:

> I coined the term "idiosyncratic system" to distinguish a personal computer from a personalized computer, one that knows its user intimately and can accordingly invoke all the necessary inferences to handle vagaries, inconsistencies, and ambiguities. I offered the following hypothetical scenario as an example:
>
> > "Okay, where did you hide it?"
> > "Hide what?"
> > "You know."
> > "Where do you think?"
> > "Oh."

At this level, conversation and intimacy are the same thing. That they're at the heart of all the Lab's activities finally seems so obvious that I feel my whole year of puzzling was no more, or less, than a conversation which began, "Okay, Nicholas, where did you hide it?"

Jerome Wiesner recalled a not-so-golden aspect of the RLE days in the '50s: "Most of what we thought of doing, we couldn't do, because we had to build our systems with vacuum tubes. Norbert Wiener and I, for example, started out to make a machine for communicating with deaf-blind children through pins, but we couldn't keep the damn machine running. Theory was inhibited by the hardware. I don't think that's the case today. I think we can build anything we can conceive of. So we're terribly knowledge-limited today.

"I see the Media Lab as a place for all these things which we dreamt about that couldn't become realities because the hardware didn't permit it, a place where we ought to exploit all the knowledge we now are acquiring about knowledge. When Nick talks about man-machine interaction, that's what it means to me."

9 FUNDING THE FUTURE, FINDING THE FUTURE

> One of the worst things that Xerox ever did was to describe
> something as the office of the future, because if something is
> the office of the future, you never finish it. There's never any-
> thing to ship, because once it works, it's the office of today.
> And who wants to work in the office of today?
>
> —David Thornburg

How exactly research organizations get money from
sponsors would be better documented if it were part of the underground
economy of crime. There are no books about it, no articles in business
or government magazines, no academic papers.

Jerome Wiesner and Nicholas Negroponte agreed that we might
have an opportunity to try something new and useful for this book. They
would do a joint interview with me about life on the fund-raising road
and shed a little light on the shadowy craft of high-ticket begging. Since
both of them are world-class fund-raisers considered particularly un-
beatable in combination, it promised to be a choice interview.

On the much-anticipated morning I set up the tape recorder on the
coffee table in front of Wiesner's corner couch and waited politely to
see if they would get each other going. Strained silence. I raised the
topic specifically but gently. Half-started sentences, vague generalities.
I barbed a few questions, like a mean journalist. They dodged with
practiced ease.

Finally a sort of discussion got going, but it was all in code and
whispers. Wiesner murmurs anyway, but this was beneath audibility.
And the lower he murmured, the more the customarily forthright Negroponte did. I moved the microphone from the table to between them
on the couch, hoping that its battery-boosted sensitivity would pick up
what I couldn't, four feet away. It didn't.

Partly I was seeing, though failing to hear, the product of long collaboration. Negroponte and Wiesner finished each other's sentences, echoed each other's words, referred to leading American corporations by the first names of their chief executive officers, and chortled companionably at whatever it was they were talking about. It was one of those "Hide what?" conversations opaque to outsiders.

For an hour I watched them leaning together and cooing like turtledoves. Their secrets are safe. In retrospect, an exposé was too much to expect. Money is still a taboo topic in polite company; "free" money is doubly taboo; New Englanders are secretive about money anyway, liberal New Englanders even more so, and liberal *academic* New Englanders . . .

What follows comes from a few things that seeped onto the tape that I've tried to decode into clear English, along with stronger statements from other conversations and other sources. Oh well.

☐ *Nothing Proprietary*
☐

■ The kind of deal the Media Lab makes with its sponsors is pretty clear. A 1985 article about the Lab in *Fortune* magazine explained, "The corporate sponsors have to figure out how to capitalize on its inventions. For their money they get a five-year key to the lab. None of the work is proprietary. Sponsors can wander around and ask questions about the different projects. Negroponte wants to avoid the fate of Xerox PARC, a lab that failed to find ways to communicate its inventions to its parent company."

There are some forty-five laboratories at MIT, ranging from $2 million to $10 million a year in operations. The $6-million-a-year Media Lab is the most recent and the only one permitted to have an academic component—meaning the Lab can hire faculty, accept students, and award degrees. And it is unlike many of the other labs in allowing no proprietary research, no secrets. I asked Negroponte one day, "There must be lots of people trying to fiddle that." He nodded, "Constantly. It's a hard one to sell sometimes. Some sponsors back off."

Negroponte's voice took on a certain relish: "You can call a company's bluff. You can say, 'You have two choices. You want to fund something for $300,000 a year, we'll give you an exclusive on that, and we won't show it to anybody else. But when you come to the Lab, we're going to put blinders on you and take you up to the little room and show you the work we're doing for you, and then we will march you right out of the building again. There happens to be $6 million of other stuff going on in the building, but you're not going to see any of it.'

"Or: 'Give us the same $300,000; we'll give you complete access to the full $6-million package, and all you have to do is let us show other people what we're doing for you. Which would you prefer?' Everybody so far has said they prefer access to the full package."

I wondered how a company would get its value then, if it was most interested in a particular line of research. Negroponte: "We do write reports for sponsors that only they see, but when we write papers for publication, everybody gets them. Real exclusivity comes with working closely with the Lab researchers, having conversations with them as the work goes on. I'm not saying sponsors slink into the building at midnight. They just have to keep in touch. The value of an idea to a company is often proportional to the energy they're willing to put into transferring it. If it really is that valuable, they've already taken it and run with it, so they've got a lead of anything from six months to God knows what."

General Motors' support of the hologram research at the Lab is an example of funding specific research. All the work done is public, but GM gets the license to use the technology developed under the grant. If others want to use that particular technology, they can license it from MIT. Such deals are written by MIT's cadre of deal-writers, who have a reputation. "MIT is the hardest to set up a contract with," Nat Rochester from IBM told me, "because they drive such a hard bargain. They want all the rights and all the money. Whatever it is, they want it. But it's worth it. You just have to hassle harder when you set up a contract with MIT." MIT holds the world record for royalties from a single technology—$19 million for licensing certain computer memory technology to IBM and other computer makers in 1955.

Negroponte said he never knew when a sponsor was starting to use something from the Lab: "That's their business." "But you must occasionally get offers," I said, "from a sponsor who thinks you're on an interesting track and 'here's a couple hundred thousand to take it a step further.' " Negroponte: "What we'll usually do is tell them no, we don't want to take it a step further, especially if it's close to being a product. The way something becomes a product successfully is if they run with it, don't tell anybody they're running with it, do a good job, and then drop it on the world all of a sudden. That has to be done in corporate secrecy, and we just can't participate in that."

That's part of the reason. The main reason is, product development is seen as too mundane. The skills involved in honing a product are not the same and not as educational as exploratory skills. A research direction is considered promising at the Lab only if it's far out (but not too far): far out enough to be original and amazing (preferably impossible-seeming) and without real competition ("If you can be scooped, you're working on the wrong problem"); far out enough to push the very edge of technology available or expected; but not so far out that it's deeply useless or infeasible. Whether something is practical versus theoretical is deemed irrelevant: inventing toward application and doing science toward increasing knowledge are seen as one activity.

One of Negroponte's most delicate tasks is matching up sponsor's interests with Lab interests. "We don't tell faculty what to do ever, period. That's not why they're here—they could go work for DEC or IBM or somebody." As a result, some research of interest to the Lab languishes for lack of a sponsor, and some potential sponsors don't connect because their main interest is not matched by Lab competence or curiosity.

"Do you encounter the not-invented-here syndrome?" I asked, meaning that some sponsors might resist ideas from outside their own shop. Negroponte: "Sure. But in so many cases we're providing an environment to seed sort of zany things happening that can't happen in their own corporation and they know it. And the rivalry is much less than it probably would be if we were developing products. If anything, the word isn't 'rivalry,' it's 'envy.' We get sponsors who say, 'Oh God, I wish I were young again and could be here instead of our drab place.' "

"How is this any different from corporate research centers like Xerox PARC?" I asked. Negroponte opined, "What's going to make something like the Media Lab work, for however long it manages to work, is in very large measure the bigger context, the bigger intellectual space of MIT and the excitement of young students. You're not just sitting in an isolated laboratory. The Psychology Department will have a lecturer in machine vision, we'll get word of it, and our people will go scurrying over there. Places like PARC get a few years where people spend guilt money and do a reasonable job, and you get some very interesting work, but it can't sustain itself. Finally people are hungry for something else. It's shown itself over and over again."

It's certainly true that being at MIT is like having a permanent ticket to an eight-screen first-run movie theater whose program changes every day. I'm not so sure that's good for concentration. On an ordinary Thursday afternoon and evening in the buildings around the Media Lab I attended a film-illustrated talk, "Evolution of an Imagemaker," a panel discussion, "Electronic Publishing: the CD ROM Option," a talk by Seymour Papert, "What's Next?" and a composer's lecture, "Some Technical and Aesthetic Considerations in Software for Live Interactive Performance." A fraction of what was available.

MIT and the Media Lab do succeed in singing a siren song to sponsors, especially alumni. Nat Rochester observed, "In an organization like IBM we get rather ingrown. There are more IBM people communicating with you, demanding things of you, than you can really cope with, so you tend not to have a very good picture of what's going on outside. In addition it's not legal in some ways to talk to people because of antitrust laws and because of IBM security—which turned out to be essential—so it's nice to be in close communication with a group that can really talk much more freely." (Compare this statement with one about Japanese corporations a few pages below.)

Jerome Rubin from Times Mirror said that his company was a sponsor "not only because we can see what they are doing, but because visits to the Lab and conversations with people there spark our own ideas. They're way ahead of their time, and that's great. That's what they should be doing." A liaison person from another sponsor commented, "It's probably not too hard to get your money's worth. For example, if you buy in for $100,000 and get to walk around and see all the blue sky thinkers, it is probably cheaper than funding a corporate position for a blue sky thinker."

A major instrument of MIT's bedfellowship with commerce is its

ILP—Industrial Liaison Program. For a yearly fee of $30,000 to $50,000 companies get to visit the campus and its sundry research activities. Each activity they visit receives a modest financial reward from the ILP office for the visit, so everybody is suitably motivated. The Media Lab is always one of the top two in ILP visits.

Negroponte finds potential sponsors primarily through his public speaking at conferences and trade organization gatherings. A typical courtship proceeds from conversation at the conference to phone calls and then letters, and then a visit to the Media Lab. With indication of serious interest, Negroponte schedules a visit to the prospective sponsor and a private performance for its senior people, sometimes with Wiesner or one of the Lab researchers along, depending on who has connections with the target people and their fields of interest.

At a typical lunch in the executive dining room after his talk Negroponte is challenged, "You said in your talk that we don't make intelligent use of color on computer screens. What's so wonderful about color?" Negroponte points out that typewriters used to have red ribbons to indicate negative numbers in financial reports, but with the advent of computers that convention was replaced by parentheses. "Even expensive four-color annual reports now use parentheses for the minus numbers, because they're less conspicuous. Wouldn't it be useful if in your financial reports and spreadsheets the numbers that were very volatile were, say, orange? And the numbers that were steady were blue? Then if the large numbers were blue and small numbers orange, you would feel pretty good. But if it was the reverse, you would have reason to worry."

The real question has been answered with blatant discreetness: Negroponte is bright and fast, and he understands about money. The endgame commences.

"Who suggests the amount?" I asked the shy fund-raisers in Wiesner's office. We do, they said. "How do you figure out how much to ask for?" I pressed. You feel that out, they said. A mutual friend prepares you. You figure how much they can use what you're offering, and how much they can afford.

"Is their word always good?" I asked. Wiesner squinted, "It's rare that somebody backs down. Only once did we have a management change

that cost us a grant. The fellow who ran M/A Com was a strange character. He insisted on running the company by satellite communication
from a house in Florida. Eventually they eased him out and the new
president was sufficiently mad that he had made the commitment without
consulting the board—that's the way he was running the company."
Negroponte mused, "It was small, it was a hundred K." (K is thousand;
he was saying "$100,000" in computerese.)

I asked, "How do you keep the funding going with a sponsor?"
Negroponte clearly had charge of that one: "It's variable. You tend to
build up a personal rapport with somebody in the company. When that
person moves on, you may have a built-in antagonism with the new
person who wants to do their own thing, and you have to rebuild relationships.

"What's the fastest funding you've gotten?" I wondered. Wiesner
smiled fondly. "The fastest was Kobayashi at NEC. In the afternoon he
said, 'Come back tomorrow morning, I have to talk to my board.' We
talked to the board. He said, 'Go out of the room.' He came out in ten
minutes and said, 'The board says okay.' " The NEC coup was a million-
dollar grant, half for the building, half for a "career development chair."
Endowing a faculty chair is always the most desired funding and the
hardest to nab—it takes a $1.5-million endowment to yield the yearly
$75,000 a full professor gets.

Things were simpler in the old days when all the money came from
Washington.

□
□
□ *From American Military to*
□
□ *Japanese Corporate*
■ If you wanted to push world-scale technology at a fever pace, what
would you need to set it in motion and maintain it indefinitely? Not a
hot war, because of the industrial destruction and the possibility of an
outcome. You'd prefer a cold war, ideally between two empires that had
won a hot war. You wouldn't mind if one were fabulously paranoid from
being traumatized by the most massive surprise attack in history (as the

U.S.S.R. was by Hitler's Barbarossa) or if the other was fabulously wealthy, accelerated by the war but undamaged by it (as the U.S. was by victory in Europe and the Pacific). Set them an ocean apart. Stand back and marvel.

American computer science owes so much to the Soviet space program. While America's German rocket scientists were curtailed in the '50s, Russia's German rocket scientists were unleashed, and in 1957 Sputnik, the world's first satellite twittering overhead in Russian, humiliated America. In direct response President Eisenhower established in 1958 a thing called ARPA—Advanced Research Projects Agency— at the very top of the Department of Defense with minimum bureaucracy, lots of money, and scientists in charge. When the American space effort spun off from ARPA and became the National Aeronautics and Space Agency (NASA), ARPA remained with a full head of momentum and funding, and an indefinite charter.

It became one of the all-time success stories of government-sponsored basic research, though never lauded in the popular press. The most prestigious work came out of the tiny Information Processing Technology Office (IPTO), a dozen people headed originally by J. C. R. Licklider, then Ivan Sutherland (twenty-six years old), then Bob Taylor (thirty-two years old), then Larry Roberts, then Licklider again, then Robert Kahn, and currently Saul Amarel. They funded basic computer science for nearly three decades, primarily at MIT, Carnegie-Mellon, Stanford, the University of Southern California, and the University of California, Berkeley. America's resulting world leadership in computer science has given the nation the edge in defense and in much of international commerce.

The price? By 1970 ARPA had an annual budget of $238 million, with $26 million going to information processing research.

Marvin Minsky, who ran the AI Lab on ARPA money, told me, "There were very few situations in funding history which were that stable. There was probably more freedom of research under ARPA than any other government agency, because they trusted the judgment of the people that they supported." "Why?" I asked. Minsky smiled. "Because they were us. For fifteen years the office down there was run by an ex-MIT person or equivalent. It was like having a patron."

In 1970 the political weather changed. In the course of Senate debates on ABM (antiballistic missile) research, three liberal Democrats—William Fulbright, Edward Kennedy, and Mike Mansfield—pushed through a rider on the Defense Appropriations Bill requiring that ARPA show direct military applicability in all the programs it funded. The Mansfield Amendment, as it came to be known, damped everything. Even the name changed; now it was DARPA—*Defense* Advanced Research Projects Agency.

Trust downshifted. Minsky recalled, "The tradition up to then had been that the proposal was the description of what we'd done the previous year. Now they wanted to know what we would do in advance, and that was absurd. For example, Terry Winograd's famous program, which was a great breakthrough in language and so forth, hadn't been in the proposals. Terry just did it. The successes of the Artificial Intelligence Laboratory were basically good ideas that students got, and you didn't get the students until the thing was established." Shortly Minksy and Papert quit running the AI Lab. Nevertheless the Architecture Machine Group got most of its money from DARPA right through the '70s. Negroponte: "It was our bread and butter for a decade, and I wish it would become again." Some of the holography and speech work at the Media Lab is currently funded by DARPA—10 percent of the Lab total.

One problem is, there's no serious alternative in government funding for large-scale sustained basic research. The NSF—National Science Foundation—supports basic research with many modest grants and gives considerable freedom for three years. Negroponte: "But when you come back to the NSF, you have no history. Your completed work doesn't count. Anybody over the age of thirty-five won't bother." Now that DARPA has spun off its "directed energy" research into the Strategic Defense Initiative (SDI, "Star Wars"), debate has been renewed about the agency's role. Should it develop knowledge primarily or weapons primarily? The fear is that fundamental computer research is adrift, spread too wide and shallow, not making the breakthroughs characteristic of the '60s and early '70s.

The debate continues at both ends of the funding. To an outsider like me, much of MIT appears politically liberal. I asked Negroponte, "When the hawks come to the doves for some nice technology, it must get odd at times." Negroponte nodded. "It certainly does, and Wiesner has spent his life agonizing over that. It's clearly the topic of a whole other book." In the 1960s MIT adopted a policy of no classified research on campus, which continues to this day.

I asked Wiesner and Negroponte why they shifted to so much corporate sponsorship. Wiesner began, "We want corporate sponsorship because we want flexibility—" Negroponte finished, "—which is ironic. It should be more flexible with the government." Wiesner continued, "We had a special constraint on us. We were not allowed to go to normal MIT sponsors. I think I invented that constraint, because there was a lineup of MIT building projects waiting and if we had stood in line and been competitive, this building might not yet exist." Rather than wait in line, they went to different theaters where there was no line: the film and publishing industries, and Japan, Inc.

"The Japan adventure started in 1978," Negroponte recalled, "as a major push to build the Media Laboratory. I had some contact with Matsushita, and Dr. Wiesner had some contact with Nippon Electric, which is now called NEC. We encountered a tremendous reception, which came to some degree from the vision of Koji Kobayashi, who is the chairman of NEC—the company slogan is 'C&C,' for Computers and Communications. What we were doing resonated with Kobayashi, and since he's such a leader in Japan as a whole, we were fuel for many of his arguments."

In 1980 two building grants from NEC and Matsushita were quickly followed by research contracts with NHK (Nippon Hoso Kyokai, the public television channel of Japan) and NTT (Nippon Telephone and Telegraph). Negroponte: "Once it started, everybody wanted in. There is a club phenomenon which is very strong in Japan. These giant companies—the Toshibas and Hitachis and so on—intercommunicate amongst themselves constantly. Often it's among classmates from the same university in different companies, because being from the same university has enormous meaning, much more than here.

"We would ask a company for $500,000 and they would say, 'You asked so-and-so company for $250,000. Why are you asking us for more?' Japanese companies are much more open. I've never signed a nondis-closure agreement there. And they show you more than here." Nondis-closure agreements prevent the signer from revealing company product development secrets. Negroponte has signed so many in America that sometimes he sounds like a man who has seen the future but can't talk about it.

I asked, "What value do the Japanese sponsors think they're getting for their money?" Negroponte: "What they believe they're getting is best described as the goose instead of the golden egg. The innovation that they see coming out of the United States comes from a style of think-ing that they don't have in their culture, or at least didn't have. What they thought that they would really be buying into wasn't the innovation itself—the golden eggs—but the method by which that was achieved, the style of thinking. And they thought that the best way to get that would be to send people on a regular basis to live in that environment and work in it." Accordingly the Media Lab now has fourteen Japanese research affiliates in residence, on paid sabbatical from their home com-panies.

"Are they learning how to be a goose?"

Negroponte: "Sure. There are some cultural problems that are built in because of the extreme homogeneity of their country. You could argue there is a blockage to the kind of creativity that comes from heterogeneous thinking and heterogeneous societies. But I'm not sure how much of the block is cultural and how much of it is what I consider a really lousy educational system.

"Japan has a problem which it's hard to imagine how they're going to overcome. In their entire education system there's so much serialist focus. There's no global or holistic or systemic thought. People aren't accustomed to trying to integrate lots of things. They're more accustomed to beating the hell out of a problem and fine-tuning things. Their goals as employees, what we would call their career path, is really measured by such variables as being on the company baseball team or having company housing close to the factory. There's not as much mobility in a corporation. So you go to the antenna department of a company like Sony for ten years, and it's the same guy there each year. He's been promoted, but in different ways, and he's still designing antennas. He's the best damn antenna designer in the world. They're superb at focusing on working bugs out of the pieces of a system, but not necessarily at putting them together in a larger system."

That may explain the appeal and importance of a global vision like Kobayashi's "C&C." In 1986, MIT Press published Kobayashi's book *Computers and Communications*, with a foreword by Jerome Wiesner. It's an interesting document. Not an autobiography or an as-told-to, it's a direct statement of program by the head of NEC since 1964, one of the world's leading action-intellectuals. Kobayashi declares:

> As the value of information rises progressively and the cost of information circulation falls, the economic equilibrium point will come down to a level where enormous quantities of information can flow. The so-called information society is nothing but a society that has reached this point. The advances of C&C technology ensure the coming of such a society, and we now stand in the transition period leading to the information society era.

Many have said such things, from Teilhard de Chardin (Catholic intimations of an information "noosphere") to the latest keynoter at corporate gatherings. The difference is, Kobayashi does it. In the mid-'60s he read a book by Princeton professor Fritz Machlup, *The Production and Distribution of Knowledge in the U.S.A.*, and shortly proclaimed that the " 'knowledge industry' represented the most appropriate corporate identity theme for NEC." Within a few years it was the theme of the entire Japanese industrial sector, leading, along with innumerable consumer electronic triumphs, to Japan's ten-year "Fifth Generation" computer intelligence project. America, partial source of the idea, scurried to keep up. The same thing happened with the idea of quality control, which was set loose in Japan by the American W. E. Deming. It's probably happening now with some ideas from the Media Lab.

Wiesner and Kobayashi were co-chairing a U.S.–Japan Computer Conference in San Francisco in 1978 when Kobayashi announced his C&C vision. "I stressed then," Kobayashi wrote later, "that computers would develop to distributed processing and that total communications systems, including switching and transmission, would follow digitalization." The technologies were forcing an overlap that soon would become a blending, much as in Negroponte's teething rings diagram.

Negroponte remembers where Kobayashi's C&C idea came from— a gap in America's systemic thinking: "He explained to me one day that he sat back and saw that IBM was precluded from going into the communications business by the antitrust suit that was in process, and that AT&T was regulated so it couldn't go into the computer business. He wasn't regulated. He saw his business as going into both of them. He was going to build a company that was the intersection of IBM and AT&T."

NEC prospered with C&C, building a conceptually linked line of tools from satellite communications to briefcase-portable computers. His is more of a world-scale vision than the Media Lab's, but Kobayashi shares the Lab's obsession with conversation. Of particular interest to him is "the problem of transborder data flow"—the damming, restricting, and confusing of information at national and language boundaries. His dream for two decades has been computerized simultaneous language translation of speech, and indeed NEC has become the world leader in speech recognition technology. "Throughout my fifty-six-year career at NEC, I have made it my mission to help create a situation that would make it possible for any person in the world to communicate with any other person at any place and any time. . . . Communication at the grass-roots level is the most powerful tool for deepening mutual understanding among nations." It may come.

Considering that fourteen companies, 18 percent of the Lab's sponsors, are Japanese, I asked Negroponte how far he was going to pursue that source of funding. He said, "We're slowing down a little bit because we don't want to be a complete arm of Japan. The Department of Defense worries about them spending too much on U.S. computer science." Three months after our conversation Negroponte was negotiating a multi-million-dollar deal with a Japanese university to clone the Media Lab in Japan through exchange of students and faculty, with U.S. government blessing.

The Media Lab *is* an arm of Japan, Inc., and vice versa. Negroponte's deputy at the Lab, Tim Browne, speaks fluent and forceful Japanese. When Negroponte or Wiesner go to Japan these days—every few months—

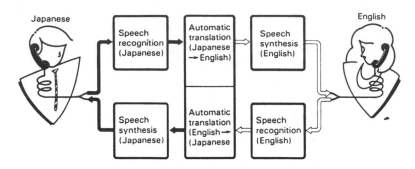

Koji Kobayashi's diagram of a simultaneous-interpretation telephone system, from *Computers and Communications*

they take along video demos with Japanese sound tracks and overhead transparencies with *kanji* captions. One of the delights of being on the Lab's e-mail system is the periodic reports on Japanese pop technology from a friend of Negroponte's in Japan named Sunakawa, one-paragraph descriptions of: a Cuff Button Microphone, Bar Code Books That Talk, an Electronic Pocket Date Book, Computer Games in Hotel Rooms, and such. The Terminal Garden cat is named "Necco" both for the New England Confection Company down the street and because *necco* is Japanese for "cat." Some Lab students sound like Korean War veterans with the odd bits of Japanese in their conversation.

Negroponte himself has written a book called *Human Interface* (1984), which appeared only in Japanese—the English original was destroyed. For the *Nekei Shimbun*, the Japanese equivalent of the *Wall Street Journal*, he wrote a series of eight columns which appeared as full-page features with a huge photo. During the series he flew into Narita Airport at Tokyo and the Japanese customs agent said as he approached, "I know you!"

□ *Right Exploiting*
□

■ The brash art of implementing other people's discoveries is at the heart of making good use of something like the Media Lab—by its sponsors, by readers of this book, by any innovators.

I grew up with the somewhat racist notion that the Japanese were "mere" imitators, exploiters of other people's ideas. The marketplace has already proven how unmere a talent that is, but if it hadn't, examination of Koji Kobayashi's *Computers and Communications* book would dispel the illusion. Jerome Wiesner wrote in the foreword:

> The success of NEC demonstrates that behind every great company there is an outstanding leader. Leadership is a mysterious talent, an amalgam of vision, energy, understanding of institutional goals and purposes, knowledge of the substance of the basic work involved, and a genuine concern for human beings. The nature of its role becomes evident in a comparison of mature Japanese and American firms. Their essential difference lies in the divergence between the philosophies expressed by the terms "good management" and "great leadership." American firms are built by visionary technical leaders, but as they grow and prosper they tend to fall under the spell of people whose major emphasis is good management. Even very large Japanese firms tend to retain leadership that places an emphasis on the technical aspects of the business. One component of Dr. Kobayashi's style, which emerges clearly in the narration, is his thorough understanding of the technical aspects of the fields in which his company operates.

"After they reach $500,000 a year," Wiesner grumbled to me one day, "American companies tend to be run by the bankers. After a billion a year, by the lawyers."

Kobayashi's book reads like a travelogue. "One day in July 1962 I was in Chicago. . . ." He switched on his hotel TV and saw a telecast from Paris via the new satellite Telstar which impressed him. "On my way back to Japan I stopped in Los Angeles. . . ." He stopped at Hughes Aircraft and learned about synchronous (geostationary) communication satellites. In due course NEC became a major satellite manufacturer. "Kobayashi travels constantly, and his antennae are always out," Wiesner observes.

Such travelers must have technical competence, or they won't know what they're seeing and hearing. I saw three kinds of sponsor visits at the Media Laboratory: by senior managers, by active researchers, and by a combination of both. The combination was the most effective. Senior managers alone often tended to wander around as I did, trying to disguise their bogglement. Active researchers alone had a wonderful time, and the Lab people enjoyed their visits most, swapping gossip and lore and trying new angles on the demos, but there may have been little company impact because the researchers were too junior.

Researchers and senior management traveling together would arrive at the Lab already high on the mix of young enthusiasm and whole-company consequence. The researchers would devour the Lab, explaining it along the way to the vice presidents in company terms, there would be no boggle, and a warm report full of ideas would go back to head-quarters. At the same time, because of the bilevel connection with a "customer," Media Lab research would be reinvigorated.

Many sponsors use the Media Lab as a way to stay abreast of what's going on—and what might be going on—in communications technol-ogy. It's a good strategy for many, apparently, but some organizations use that kind of peripheral scanning as a way to maintain their immunity to new information, preventing it from actually affecting their behavior by taking a little Media Lab now and then as a vaccine. That may not be all bad. A company doesn't want to come down with every case of Dense Media or High Definition Television or Smart Telephone that's going around.

Deciding which new diseases a company should come down with is what the Kobayashis of the world do.

The Media Lab has in its history a fine example of wrong exploit-ing—an excellent, simple idea, instantly applicable, available free to anyone, that has sat on the shelf in plain view of the world since 1971.

Called Fuzzy Fonts, it is a cheap, easy way to have much higher resolution print on computer and TV screens. Negroponte: "It's not subtle. When you see it, you gasp." He's right. Characters on the screen look just beautiful, like on paper, and you can read them even if they're tiny. On a TV set ordinary fonts are usually presented forty characters on a line, maximum sixty characters. Fuzzy Font characters are still easy to read at eighty characters per line, and you can go up to 100.

"Having to look at stairstep characters and jaggies should be against the law," declares Negroponte. "Aliased fonts should be an OSHA violation." Aliased fonts are what you see on almost all computers. Each square pixel (picture element) on the screen is either black or white: one information bit per pixel. The problems come when you're representing a sloping line and you see a jagged edge instead, or the serif at the tail of a character is smaller than a pixel and it disappears entirely.

"Anti-aliasing" smooths the jaggies by introducing a little gray in the right places. With two-bit pixels instead of one-bit you have the choice of black, white, or two shades of gray. That disappearing serif can be represented by a light gray pixel, and your eye reads it as a serif. It's cheap because doubling the resolution this way only doubles the cost, whereas doubling the resolution by increasing the number of pixels quadruples the cost—four jaggy one-bit pixels instead of one fuzzy two-bit pixel.

Negroponte: "I personally have exposed tens of thousands of people to Fuzzy Fonts since Paula Mosaides—I remember her name because she was Greek—got us started with this back in 1971. The only semi-convincing argument against it I've heard is from people who claimed that the eye seeks out crisp edges, and if it encounters nothing but fuzzy edges it gets much more tired. That turned out to be wrong. Acuity is

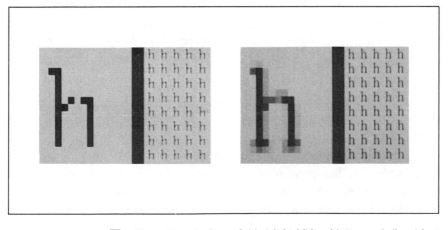

The serif at the base of this *h* is invisible with a normal aliased font (LEFT) but visible using the grays of a Fuzzy Font (RIGHT).

sharpness of the image; resolution is some measure of the finest level of detail that you can read. They are not the same at all. You can give up acuity and gain resolution.

"Now, IBM ran an experiment where they presented the reader a page with a number of typographical errors in it, and the person was supposed to read the page and find the typographical errors. They would do it on paper, then do it on a screen with different errors but the same number of them. With a normal IBM or Macintosh screen they were something like 60 percent less efficient than on paper. Then they anti-aliased the fonts and put in the same kinds of errors, and people came up with 98 percent of the efficiency of paper. So Fuzzy Fonts on a screen are the closest approximation to paper in terms of your ability to read them."

Another test had people bringing a line on a screen to just touching a circle on the screen. If the line and circle were anti-aliased with a little gray with two-bit pixels, the people were twice as precise. It is not just an aesthetic effect. Fuzzy Fonts may be the Media Lab's single most proven commercial idea. Why it had to wait till 1987 to become a product is a mystery. (Apple finally introduced Fuzzy Fonts on their second-generation Macintosh computers in spring, 1987, followed by IBM.)

The great contrasting case of *right* exploiting is what happened when Steve Jobs, then head of Apple Computer, visited Xerox PARC (Palo Alto Research Center) in 1979—what he grabbed, and how he ran with it. That one act changed the face of personal computing from techie-arcane to intuitively understandable. It created the Macintosh computer, whose success forced all other personal computers to emulate its interface tools and graphic richness. The grabbing could have happened any time from 1974 on, or it could have happened never. Hundreds of other people, including the management of Xerox, had the opportunity and didn't take it.

Though the episode is famous, no case-study analysis of it has ever been made. I called Steve Jobs, now head of NeXT, Inc., for his version of what happened that day in November 1979. He said, "When I went to PARC, I thought it would be an interesting afternoon, but I had no concept of what I'd see. Larry Tesler was my guide for an hour, to show me around. My mind was just totally blown. The minute I saw an Alto

(PARC's prototype personal computer) and the mouse and the multiple fonts, I *knew* that we had to have it. I came back to Apple a raving maniac about this stuff and I grabbed a bunch of people, in particular Bill Atkinson, and dragged them over there. Bill started to see it. Not too many other people got excited, but at least I got Bill excited."

Apple had a new computer in early development at the time called the Lisa. Jobs, by sheer energy and persistence ("It was like pushing a boulder uphill, but I was pretty tenacious and screamed loudly"), got the Lisa's direction changed in the next three months to copy and improve on everything he'd seen at PARC. He even hired his Xerox guide, Lawrence G. Tesler. The Lisa came out in 1983 and eventually failed because of its price ($10,000), but its successor, the Macintosh (at around $2,000), became Apple's leading product by 1986.

My researcher Deborah Wise talked to Larry Tesler, now head of Advanced Technology at Apple, to get his version of what happened when he guided Jobs around. Tesler was in Alan Kay's research group at Xerox in 1979, and was PARC's personal computer enthusiast "as defined by the market rather than by Alan Kay," meaning that Tesler had an early PET computer and attended Homebrew Computer Club meetings. "Alan Kay had been telling everybody that there would not be a mass market for personal computers until they were $1,000 or under and had more power than the Alto and were portable, which would be sometime in the '80s. And all the other experts at Xerox were saying that was all science fiction anyway, and the real thing to do was to concentrate on office networked workstations."

Since 1974 Xerox had been demoing the Alto computer with its graphic ("bit-mapped") screen and mouse and fonts and overlapping windows and icons and pop-up menus and paint program to visitors at PARC. According to Tesler, one group got the full demonstration and explanation, "and at the end one of the guys said, 'You get really good reception here.' He didn't even understand that the screen was not connected to an antenna." Most visitors saw that the Alto represented spectacular advances, "but very few understood either in depth or in scope the applications of what they were seeing."

Xerox executive visitors varied from well-prepared and highly astute to ill-prepared and baffled at how any of this would fit in with the copier business. Starting in 1976, Alto computers were produced in quantity (1,500 by 1979) and distributed nationwide around Xerox. That finally built support to get out a product. Tesler: "Xerox felt that their distribution channels were through their copier sales forces to businesses, and that their natural market was large installations at large companies and government. There was an overemphasis on networking, file server projects, and laser printing, and an underemphasis on user interface and personal applications. Office Automation was the goal of Xerox PARC, not personal computing."

Steve Jobs was able to have a close look at PARC because Xerox had put money in Apple, both as an investment and because Apple might be a potential manufacturer for a Xerox small computer. Tesler remembers how the group visiting from Apple was received: "The attitude of most of the scientists at Xerox was that these were a bunch of hobbyists and a waste of time—they really weren't very sharp and they were self-taught; their machine was a toy. I was excited to get to know these people and show them the ins and outs of the system. What was different about this group was that they really understood what they saw and the implications and got very excited and asked all the right questions and understood all the answers. These were obviously experienced and well-educated scientists, and very sharp. It was clear to me that they understood what we had better than Xerox understood it. Steve was leaping and jumping around the room yelling things. He kept saying over and over, 'Why aren't you doing anything with this?' The implication was— I don't remember if it was said explicitly—that if you don't, we will."

Apple did, adding its own embellishments along the way. The confusing three-button mouse was turned into a one-button mouse, the pop-up menus became pull-down menus from a "menu bar" at the top of the screen, and so on. The eventual result was a computer that admirals and kindergarteners could immediately understand, use, and love. Alan Kay called the Macintosh "the first personal computer good enough to criticize." Steve Jobs hired him too.

Xerox went after the wrong customer, the office instead of the individual. The eventual computer product from Xerox, the Star system introduced in 1981, was grotesquely overpriced and went nowhere. A few years later the company was surprised again when the Japanese, starting with Canon, seized a personal *copier* market Xerox didn't believe existed.

□ Users of the Future
□

■ The Media Lab has other value than just being the source of exploitable ideas. It's big enough and has a wide enough range of well-connected activities that it amounts to a kind of User's Group of the next generation of communication technologies. Future customers, in a sense. The value is not in market research, which the Lab assiduously avoids except for the television Audience Research Facility, but in what can be accomplished by users as designers.

Commercial designers go where the perceived market leads them. Amateur designers, user designers, go where curiosity leads them. It's the difference between convergence on the known and divergence from the known. Steve Wozniak, co-founder of Apple Computer, designed the original Apple computer in his spare time for his own pleasure and to excite his friends at the Homebrew Computer Club. Years later he remarked, "Somebody who's designing something for himself has at least got a market of one that he's very close to." That's the opposite of statistical market research.

Certain technologies attract quite powerful amateur interest. One is private aircraft, which has fostered a whole population inspired by the original "home-builders," Orville and Wilbur Wright. The Experimental Aircraft Association now has 100,000 members in fifty countries tinkering away in basement and garage and chilly hangar, being simultaneous designers, builders, and pilots of unique airplanes. Many now-commercial small aircraft designs began life as blueprints passed around among home-builders. The landing gear on all Cessna airplanes comes from a design by amateur Steven Wittman. The most original commercial designers, such as Phil Lear (of Lear-Jet) and Burt Rutan (of the world-circling "Voyager"), have risen to success on the enthusiasm of amateur supporters. The Experimental Aircraft Association has lobbied with great success to protect its members' rights to take serious bodily risk. User Group power.

My father was a ham, a radio amateur, one of the 1.5 million hams worldwide. The first thing they did, back in the early '20s, was establish, over government resistance, that shortwave radio was a viable means of communication. A measure of how worldwide they became is the fact that the first satellite not owned by a government was OSCAR (Orbiting Satellite Carrying Amateur Radio), launched in 1961. One of the most recent of a long series of technical innovations from the hams is "packet radio," a means of sending data communications error-free by radio, now put to commercial use by Federal Express.

Given the amateur origin of personal computers, it's no surprise that User's Groups have been a major force in that market. There are over 2,000 such groups in the U.S., led by the Boston Computer Society with 20,000 members. On teleconference systems like CompuServe and The Source, the fastest growth area of online services are the SIGs (Special Interest Groups) devoted to personal computers—CompuServe has nearly a hundred of them chewing away at the problems of sundry makes and models. Whether face to face ("F2F," as they say) or online, User's Groups are far the best source of current in-depth information on personal computers because books, magazines, even weekly tabloids can't keep up with the speed and variety of the field.

Smart computer manufacturers and software designers involve themselves deeply with the User's Groups, realizing that they're the major source of word-of-mouth publicity, good and bad, and that no one is more interested and skilled in improving their product than their customers. The groups have even been responsible for a whole new kind of product distribution, called "shareware" or "freeware"—you copy the software free (online or at a User's Group meeting), use it awhile (the manual is part of the program), and then pay for it if you like to the address given with the program. Some excellent word-processing, spreadsheet, and telecommunications programs are distributed this way. They are the fastest-evolving programs on the market because the designer/distributor (one person) is in constant direct touch with customers and has no burden of inventory.

As designers, users of all kinds diverge in pursuit of their own individual kinks and curiosities. But as users, as customers, they are where everything converges. In a fast-moving area like personal computers or communications technology, most new stuff arrives either ignorant of the other new stuff or seeking to obliterate it. It is the customer that determines the market leaders, the standards, the conventions, the acceptable prices. And customers smooth over innovation; connectedness in the market moderates big jumps, makes them fit in.

The Media Lab invents the future in part by being clever and free-spirited and in part by being a User's Group of the future, where holograms and flexoids and eye-contact computers and personal newspapers all hang out together, interfering creatively, adding up to an anticipatory whole even odder and more interesting than its parts.

The epigraph at the beginning of this chapter about Xerox's failing to commercialize effectively by forever pursuing the "Office of the Future" depicts exactly what the Media Lab has going for it with its "School of the Future," "Movies of the Future," "Vivarium," and so forth. One value of setting grand integrative goals like that is that they entrain worthy subgoals—they become "forcing functions," in Alan Kay's words. Xerox stayed bewitched by its grand goal—the Office of the Future—and let some of the magnificently accomplished subgoals like personal computing slip away. The tail should have wagged the dog and wasn't allowed to.

The Media Lab has a different function than a business. Chasing horizons is its job. It sells not what works, but what might work.

PART TWO

The Media Lab of the World

10 LIFE IN PARALLEL

The machines will get good enough at dealing with complexity
that they can start dealing with their own complexity, and you'll
get systems that evolve.

—Daniel Hillis

There is a revolution going on in computer science and
computer technology that almost amounts to a new beginning. "Parallel
processing" has been anticipated with theoretical faiths and doubts for
decades, but now it's arriving. It could mean major retooling in both
media labs, the MIT one and the world one. The pace of computer-
related change in society is likely to accelerate as a result.

Nearly all computers to date are "serial"—they do one thing at a
time, as quickly as possible, and move on to the next. This was the
"architecture" laid down by mathematician John Von Neumann in the
late '40s, the foundation on which the vast and otherwise various su-
perstructure of computer technology has been built. Changing that foundation changes everything. Parallel processors, as the term suggests, do
things concurrently and thus break out of the "Von Neumann bottleneck." One experimental parallel computer, at Columbia University,
was called "The Non-Von" in his honor.

The major reason to mess with all this is speed, always the primary
obsession with computer users. Stuff happening on five or a hundred
different paths at once can theoretically go five or a hundred times faster
than on one path. An even better reason to process in parallel is because
that's how animals compute—brains from sea slug to human have the
opposite of Von Neumann architecture. The web of neurons in brains
and other nervous tissue is so richly interconnected it's called "neuro-
pil"—like the pile of carpeting or a felt hat.

People at the Media Lab, like all who are involved in artificial intelligence, are impatient for workable parallel equipment because it can offer so much to image processing and other imitation brain activities. Marvin Minsky recounted how important having the best equipment is: "The AI Lab's high point was when it had the largest memory in any available computer. That was 1970. We had a half million words, and nobody else had a half million words. It was *the* place. We had people from all over the world who wanted to come there and try something. Then when we had the LISP machine it was unique for a while. If the Media Lab gets the Connection Machine, that would be a reason for really ambitious people to come and try new things."

The Connection Machine is the most massively parallel of all parallel computers—65,536 processors operating at once. It is a brand-new machine, introduced by Thinking Machines Corporation at $4 million. In July 1986 the Media Lab purchased the first one, initially at quarter-strength with 16,384 processors. The Connection Machine was invented at MIT, in the AI Lab, by a Minsky protégé named Danny Hillis. Minsky told me, "Danny made the idea so clean that it became almost a new mathematical object—very elegant, extremely simple in a way. He is a wonderful builder of things, very good at making things out of wire and balsa wood and beads." The Boston Computer Museum has a working computer that Hillis constructed entirely of Tinkertoys. His 1985 book, *The Connection Machine*, is a gem, technically profound but accessible to the lay reader.

I met Hillis one evening at dinner at the Media Lab and was invited to visit his shop for lunch the next day. It wasn't far to go, four blocks away in a renovated industrial building by the Charles River, one of dozens of MIT-related startup companies in the neighborhood. Danny Hillis looks even younger than his twenty-nine years. He has big cheeks, straight dark blond hair combed across his forehead, level brows over a bright gaze, and easy amiability. Running shoes below are matched by no tie above. The offices of Thinking Machines are upscale, informal, with the stirring feel of a place making a big, confident bet. We sat by large windows overlooking the Boston skyline across the Charles.

Some interviews take off. This one did, so I'll report the conversation straight, lightly condensed. If you like, you can watch for Media

Lab hallmarks of good conversation such as interruptibility, granularity, thread, graceful degradation, the lead passing back and forth, limited look-ahead, no-default, infinite database, shared environmental reference, mutual persuasion, and how the same question yielded different answers at different times. Hillis began with the artificial intelligence origins of his invention:

DANNY HILLIS: We have one example of intelligence, which fits in about a square meter of neurons. It's wadded up into a ball inside your head. And we know that it's able to do, by definition, the kinds of things that we call intelligence. On the other hand, in computers we've got these components which are a million times faster, and yet to give them something to do like looking at a picture and knowing that it's a picture of a chair or a desk takes them hours and hours, if they can do it at all. Not only that, but the more information you give the computer, the slower it gets. So it's a kind of paradoxical situation—if you try to make it smarter by giving it more information, you're making it stupider by making it slower. That's the Catch-22 that AI is in right now.

AI is at a funny place. You can look for areas where stupidity works, and that's what's called "expert systems," where just a little bit of knowledge is sufficient to get you through. The other area that people are going into is trying to figure out some tricky way of not having to look at all the knowledge—"backward search," "rule-based reasoning," "frames." It all probably has grains of truth in it, but it's basically a way of avoiding doing what's the right thing to do, just because you don't have enough computation power to look at everything or deduce every fact. If there weren't a third way out, that's probably what I'd do.

But there is a third way out. We have this existence proof in our brain of these slow components doing intelligence, and apparently they do it just by having a lot of them working together. If you look at the structure of that, it turns out you can actually build something out of electronic components which has that flavor. In fact it turns out to be a much better way of using electronic components.

The ordinary computer has this very funny design which doesn't make any sense anymore. Back when it was designed, the switching components were very expensive and very fast, and the memory components were very slow. One half of the room was these big expensive vacuum tubes, and you had to keep those busy. The other half of the room was big slow mercury delay lines or cathode ray tubes, and you only got a word out of them every once in a while. So the whole design was set up to balance that. You got out a word and did a lot with it with the vacuum tubes and you put it back in.

You can look at a silicon chip under a microscope and you still see those two halves of the room there. There's the vacuum tubes over on the right, which is the processor section, and there's the memory section on the left, doing almost nothing, spitting out something once in a while, while the processors are keeping very busy. It's just a leftover from what was at the time a very good balance in technology.

STEWART BRAND: If the world were optimal, which it never is, thank God, when would have been the time when the architecture might have caught on and converted?

DH: As soon as you started making the memory and the processing out of the same components, which is relatively recently—when magnetic core memory went away and got replaced by semiconductors in the mid-'70s. Everything got so much cheaper, you could print the things like pamphlets.

Usually what parallel processors do is, they take two stupid computers and work at breaking a problem in half and getting the two to work together and not step on each other's toes. If you use four of them, it gets more complicated. That process sort of bottoms out at about a dozen.

The Connection Machine is a little bit different. We assumed from the beginning that there wasn't a distinction between memory and processing and that you wanted tens of millions of things. A neuron is basically a memory/processing element, and the information, as near as we can tell, is in the connectivity. Nothing very interesting happens within one neuron. The interesting thing is the interactions between them. That led me to looking at systems where nothing very interesting happens in one memory/processor—it's so small, by itself it's just nothing. The computation takes place by the whole ensemble of things working together.

SB: "Connections" in terms of relationships or in terms of actual wire?

DH: It's not physical wiring, it's *as if* you had the little tiny processor/ memory units wired up in any pattern you wanted. So imagine you had a plug board that you could connect up, and if I have a processor here that's representing the concept of "apple" and one that's representing the concept of "red," and I want to know that apples are sometimes red, I just put a connection between those so that when I think of red I think of apple. Of course you don't physically do it that way, but conceptually that's what's going on. Physically there's a sort of telephone switching network between them. The hard technical problem that the Connection Machine solves is building that network.

(The way Hillis managed connecting the 65,536 processors is in a sixteen-dimensional hypercube array. That sounds exotic, but all it amounts to is that each processor is directly linked to sixteen others, and thus it can reach any other processor in the machine through a maximum of sixteen intermediary processors.

Because memory is distributed among all the processors, the whole machine is in a sense an active memory, capable of "data-level parallelism" rather than just "program-level parallelism." The way word gets around among all the processors is ingenious. Any processor can call any other by "slow" broadcasting. When the addressed processor answers back, a swifter "cancel" order goes out to stop the broadcast. The connection between those processors is then maintained for the duration of its usefulness, amounting to a "virtual network" customized for the problem, by the problem. Adaptable "hardwiring" like this around usefulness seems to be what neurons do.)

SB: How much attention are you really paying to neurons? Are they sort of a metaphor at this point?

DH: Completely a metaphor, and it's a bad metaphor because we don't really understand neurons.

SB: Why is the machine you're doing the size it is?

DH: Two kinds of people ask that question—some of them "Why is it so big?" and some of them "Why is it so small?"

SB: Which is the more interesting dimension?

DH: The reason it's so small is I can't build a bigger one with the current technology. This is a practical size to build. It brought us up above the threshold where you can really do a problem by assigning a processor to each piece of data. With 64,000 processors you can do real problems dramatically faster than you can do them on any other computer. It's up to a stage where you can solve problems that nobody can solve.

SB: That *nobody* can solve?

DH: Literally that's true sometimes, because unless you can solve them faster, you're not solving them. Predicting tomorrow's weather next week isn't much use.

SB: What's your competition, Crays?

DH: The neat thing about this machine is that it's at the beginning of the learning curve. It's easy to see how to build one ten times or a hundred times or a thousand times as fast, whereas the serial machines— the supercomputers like the Cray—are really getting hard pressed to get another factor of two, factor of three.

(What's limiting the Cray, and other computers of conventional architecture or limited parallelism, is the speed of the electrical signal. The supercomputers require heroic engineering—very close packing to reduce the distance signals must travel and ferocious cooling systems to enhance superconductivity and bleed the intense heat. Negroponte points out, "In one nanosecond (one billionth of a second) light only travels one foot." The current Cray 2 operates on a four-nanosecond cycle and does its central processing in a machine the size of a couch, clearly approaching its limit.)

SB: Are all of your advantages measured in speed?

DH: That's the easiest-to-sell advantage. I think that the most real advantage is that it's just a much more natural way to do computation. That's a hard sell at this point because people are so used to thinking of their problem in terms of what fits with what they're doing now. If you ask customers what they want, they say, "I want exactly what I have, only cheaper and faster."

SB: Is yours cheaper?

DH: Cost/performance-wise it is. But the real reason I believe in it and the company believes in it and is investing in it is it's more natural. Let me give you a specific example.

Take a physical simulation problem. You're calculating the flow of air over an airplane wing. Now, the way that that's done on a serial computer is, you first of all add a layer of abstraction on top of it—you say, "Let me try to write the differential equation for that." The differential equation of course is only an approximation of what's really going on. You say, "Now my problem is to solve that differential equation. Well, I can't really do that, so what I'll do is make an approximation of that differential equation by breaking the area up into spaces and have the differential equation for each one of those chunks, and then I'll solve that simplified discrete version of the differential equation." Then you say, "I can't really exactly solve it, I'll solve it using floating point approximation." By the time you've put all those layers of artificiality on top of it, you don't actually get a very good answer, though it's a useful answer.

If you want to sell a machine to somebody who's doing that, their definition of the problem is, "I want to do so many floating point operations per second." What they really wanted to do in the first place is figure out how the air flowed over the airplane wing.

The natural way to do that is, the air is a bunch of molecules bumping into each other, and you want to take hundreds of millions of molecules, bump them into each other, bump them into the airplane wing, and see how the air flows. It doesn't have anything to do with differential equations or floating point numbers or cutting up space. On the Connection Machine that's a very natural way to do it, because you use one processor to represent every air molecule.

SB: Does this mean you can handle modeling extremely turbulent and large systems, like planetary weather?

DH: Maybe. With turbulence specifically it looks like we can model some things that weren't possible to model before. We've already shown some successes in that area. It's so new, it's a different physics—you really have to decide whether you trust your model of the particles colliding and things like that.

SB: Do you think a different physics might come out of this?

DH: Oh yeah, absolutely. Just since we've had the first machine going we've had articles in *Physical Review Letters* on physics modeling, and articles in *Nature* on some vision stuff that was done on the machine, and this is before we've announced the product.

SB: How about synthetic holography like Steve Benton is doing at the Media Lab?

DH: Have you run into Carl Feynmann over there? He's figured out how to do synthetic holography on the machine.

SB: What other problem areas lend themselves?

DH: Well, design. It's being used right now to design its successor. You see that picture of a chip? (*He gestured at a mural-sized diagram of a computer chip on a far wall, looking like the street, water, and electrical system of a city.*) That's a design for a very simple chip. The neat thing about that chip is the method by which it was produced, which was: somebody wrote a very simple LISP program and compiled it into a chip. They said, "Make me a chip which does that," and the system completely automatically designed it—nobody drew any of those lines, nobody really even had to print out that picture. We could have just sent the software design off and had it fabricated into the physical chip.

SB: Is this sinister? Should we be worried? Is this the self-replicating robot that everybody has forebodingly foretold?

DH: You should always be worried about progress. Any new capability has a side of it you have to worry about.

SB: You worry about to what degree it feeds itself: do you have any runaways built in?

DH: Well, are you sure a runaway is bad?

SB: No.

DH: Yeah, I think eventually it will feed itself. I think you'll have these machines designing their successors, and after a while we won't understand how they work.

SB: Do you still understand now?

DH: Yeah, but it's getting on the edge of not understanding. With the next generation there will be a level of detail which has been designed automatically which we won't understand. We already get that in some of the AI programs—they surprise you by how smart they are sometimes, particularly if they're built by a bunch of different people and there are synergistic interactions between things people did.

SB: Actually synergistic rather than interfering?

DH: Of course you get interfering ones more often. Anyway, I don't see any reason why we're necessarily going to keep understanding it, which means we will have less control over it. Hopefully you can put in general principles that guide it, that make sure it's going to come out right. But you can never be any more sure of that than when you're designing a bridge—in a bridge we don't really understand what each one of those cables is doing, but we have enough general principles of design that we're pretty confident that it's not going to fall down.

SB: Do you over-design, the way builders do?

DH: Absolutely. In fact that's a lot of what structured programming and things like that are. It's a kind of over-design, to make sure that you keep control of what's happening, or catch it immediately when something happens that's not what you expected.

SB: I'm wondering how good this will be at modeling lifelike processes. I'm working with Alan Kay on the Vivarium, where the idea is to have creatures with lives of their own in virtual worlds.

DH: One thing that I'm really interested in is the connection between the kind of learning an individual does and the kind of learning an ecology does as it evolves.

SB: Yes, please. That's my main interest. Say more about that.

DH: That's getting very close to exactly what the machine was designed for. Each of these processor units—which you can think of as either creatures or ideas—they're in some sense competing with each other, growing according to how successful they are, breeding with each other according to how successful they've been, and sort of exchanging either genetic material or subparts of the ideas. I think that approach is one of the most promising to actually lead toward an intelligent adaptive system. Computationally it's just completely infeasible on the old kind of computer.

SB: Why is it more feasible on this kind?

DH: Because you can essentially be doing millions of operations at once. Even on this first machine that we built, we're doing thousands of millions of instructions a second (MIPS) instead of millions of instructions a second—billions instead of millions. If you take the speed ratio of the very fastest supercomputers versus this machine, it's kind of like the difference between a bicycle and a supersonic jet. It's qualitatively different. That means you can try a whole new category of experiments. The speed and the naturalness become the same thing. It's really a very artificial thing to say, "Now we're going to change its strength according to how successful it was; now we're going to . . ."

In a Vivarium sort of environment what you're talking about is a bunch of individual entities which can be a little bit themselves, but mostly the interesting thing happens through their interactions. That's how I just described the hardware. The problem and the hardware are almost the same thing.

(One day I logged onto the Media Lab's e-mail system and found a message from student Steve Strassmann to the Vivariumites: "As I got on the plane in Dallas after Siggraph [an annual computer graphics gathering], I was suddenly possessed by a furious desire to draw hair. It is probably feasible to render fur, hair, steel wool, etc., realistically on the Connection Machine, using a particle-

system-based idea. This is a neat project because: 1) nobody's done it; 2) it takes advantage of the Connection Machine's big win, non-local communication; 3) it's vital to the Vivarium." He proceeded to outline a hair-rendering algorithm, taking account of length, color, curling, interaction, clumping, etc. "The user specifies the growth of hair in a 3D scene by a cursor dipped in 'hair tonic,' and painting 'growth hormone' paint onto objects." He figured that a hamster, with about 13,000 hairs, would be the biggest thing he could draw with a hair per processor on the 16,000-processor Media Lab Connection Machine, but he can grow the hair faster than hamsters can, in microseconds.)

DH: Computation should be like electricity. You plug into the wall and use as much of it as you need whenever you need it. I think that is the direction we're heading in. Which might make you unhappy.

SB: Why?

DH: Maybe I'm extrapolating too much. You have to understand, I give you credit for making the counterculture decide that computers were okay and on their side. As I see it, it could have gone either way, and you pushed it over to the right side. What I'm talking about now goes against decentralist ideas. Let me make the analogy to electric power. Microcomputers are like batteries, they're nice but they're limited. Imagine if your refrigerator or your house lights had to run off a battery. The interesting thing about this parallel technology is you can build an arbitrarily large source of computing power, and I think people will use it in a utility sense. I think personal computers will be not such an important mode of computation anymore. They'll still have their place, but the sort of computation you'll have in your home appliances will draw on that central source of computation when they need it.

SB: You'd see a national grid or an international grid similar to the present electrical one?

DH: Yeah, to some level of detail.

SB: So there'd be fiberoptic umbilicals coming into the house.

DH: Probably a single fiberoptic is as much bandwidth as your house and all the people in it could absorb. It just makes a lot more sense. You want everything to have a certain amount of intelligence sometimes. You want your alarm clock, when you shout at it to shut up in the morning, to decide whether or not to shut up based on what you said, and the rest of the time you want it to sit there, stupidly ticking away. That's sort of analogous to your refrigerator—when the motor starts up, it draws a big surge of current.

I think people will see for a while this trend continuing of decentralization of computers, because of the diseconomies of scale of large computers. But then I think when this technology goes in you'll get much more of a practice of shared communal computing resources.

(I asked Negroponte one time how much longer the phenomenon of computers constantly getting faster, cheaper, and smarter would continue. He replied, "There's an interminable period ahead to saturate parallel processing. If you really master it, there is no saturation. You just keep on throwing more processors in.")

SB: An office building would have a computer and that's part of what you rent?

DH: Or maybe even the city would, or would have several, like the electric power plants, and you switch between them. If the communications problem gets solved—and I don't see any reason why fiberoptics isn't going to just be the solution to that—and the architectural problem of how to use those resources gets solved—and I think the Connection Machine is the solution to that—then I think things will go in that direction. The whole idea that software should be something like a book that you keep around your desk (and you might not have the right one) has got to go away. It's just too awful. Really, you want the computer to be able to do anything it knows how to do. Everything that anybody's ever told the computer how to do is a tremendous amount of knowledge, and you want to be able to draw on that knowledge. That's got to be shared, and the step from that to sharing the hardware is a small one.

SB: Is the military jumping at this stuff? They usually jump at things first.

DH: The military is paying for the development of all the interesting parallel computers. They're interested in it just for sheer speed. They're the same people that funded all the AI research—DARPA.

SB: What are the major parallel architectures that are being worked on now?

DH: There's an awful lot of machines that are putting together a dozen microprocessors or a dozen minicomputers. I couldn't even list them. I don't really regard that as a true parallel machine. But they're going to be economically important over the next few years, and there'll be a lot of startup companies that sell those. There are a smaller number of projects that have massive parallelism. The extreme version is the Connection Machine. There's a project at Cal Tech called The Cosmic Cube, which is 256 microprocessors talking to each other. There are a bunch of projects where you wire up around a specific problem. For instance there's a project at Goodyear Aerospace that's a two-dimensional thing for doing image processing.

(According to a 1986 article in Technology Review *by Michael Dertouzos, head of MIT's Laboratory of Computer Science, there are some fifty known groups working on multiprocessor projects, about equally divided between universities and private companies. Many of the projects worldwide were stimulated by Japan's highly publicized Fifth Generation project, started in 1980. The European Economic Community responded with an equally well-funded project called ESPRIT, and America set up the business-sponsored Microelectronics and Computer Technology Corporation (MCC) in Texas. The National Science Foundation declared in 1986, "The top priority, right now the very single priority in the research community . . . is parallelism." DARPA, with its millions, launched a nationwide Strategic Computing Program, with emphasis on parallel processing research. Thinking Machines has a $3 million contract from DARPA for the Connection Machine.*

The stakes are reflected in a remark at the end of Dertouzos' article: "Technological leadership in the information revolution is, in my opinion, ultimately linked to geopolitical strength."

He adds, "The government has become increasingly preoccupied with possible leaks of research to military adversaries and commercial competi-

tors. . . . However, because of the freedom that such research requires, this trend toward increased management could do far more to damage innovation than to accomplish the intended goals. As a result, the United States could cede leadership in information technology to Japan."

The physical Connection Machine has a geopolitical look, possibly slightly satirical, almost certainly influenced by the movies. Darth Vader black, it stands nearly six feet high, wide, and deep, a ominous cube of cubes. Rows of red lights flicker and glow behind black smoked-glass panels. In contrast to characterless conventional mainframe computers, it is a charismatic machine.

The one at the Media Lab was initially used for animation, holography, and compressing movies onto compact disks. Vivarium creatures, including flexoids, were expected to inhabit it soon.)

SB: What's the connection between what you're at here and Marvin Minsky's "society of mind"?

DH: That's the kind of theory that fits well on this machine. I was working closely with Marvin this whole time. The fact that Marvin was thinking in that direction and the fact that this machine fits with it is no coincidence.

SB: Is there any programming going on that would carry it further than that?

DH: For the "society of mind" specifically, no. With genetic evolving-algorithms we are doing some things. We're looking for a good domain to try some of them out. Do you know how to play Go?

SB: Unfortunately, no.

DH: It's a very interesting game. People used games for a while in artificial intelligence, but it turns out that most games were solvable without intelligence. They're in this expert-systems category—great applications of stupidity. But Go has not yielded to that technique at all. The very very best Go-playing programs are not even better than somebody who's been playing Go for a week.

SB: Do human Go players and chess players have much in common?

DH: There are a lot of people that know both. Go players tend to be pretty disparaging of chess. I know how to play chess better than I know how to play Go, but I can see why Go is fundamentally a much more interesting game. Chess is a very tactical game. Every move is very important. The whole game can fall apart on the basis of one move.

Whereas with Go, much more of the knowledge is general principles of trading off offense and defense and being conservative versus being aggressive. There's ideas like "boundaries" and "friendliness," "influence" and things like that. The rules are much much simpler than chess, but the implications are much more complicated. You can sort of draw a moral from each game. It's not a tactical game. If you play too hard, if you play just to win a situation, then you lose the game, unless you keep a sort of perspective about the whole thing. It's a game of balance and attitudes. You can tell what mood somebody's in by how they play a Go game. If you can get somebody angry at you, then they lose the game. Go genuinely requires intelligence, unlike these other games like chess which can be played with intelligence but can also be played in a different way.

SB: I want a computer that gets jokes. I'm interested in context and content, all these things that make jokes go, and emotions like delight.

DH: That's a good benchmark for AI. It's hard to imagine something that could genuinely tell what was funny and what wasn't without being intelligent.

SB: If octopuses can have moods, why can't computers? You can see I've been auditing Jerry Lettvin's Animal Physiology class.

DH: Jerry Lettvin is the one that talked me out of being a neurophysiologist. When I first arrived at MIT I had read the paper Jerry did with McCulloch and Pitts on "What the Frog's Eye Tells the Frog's Brain." But I don't remember names. My first night at MIT I went down to a party at the housemaster's. I walked in, and there was this guy—I remember thinking of him at the time as a 300-pound Jewish Benjamin Franklin—sitting on the floor and pointing at the freshman students that had just walked in the door and saying, "What are you interested in?"

Whatever it was they were interested in, he would tear it apart. He got to me. "What are you interested in?" "Neurophysiology." He said, "Echh, that crock of shit. I defy you to tell me one decent piece of work that has ever been done in that field." So I started telling Jerry Lettvin about what the frog's eye tells the frog's brain.

He said, "Yes, and how did they do that?" I was very proud of myself because I was the first one who'd gotten a word in edgewise, and I had the facts at my fingertips and was engaging this guy in real conversation. Then after I was dangling out there, he says, "Don't you see what's wrong with that?" "What do you mean?" So he begins to tear the paper apart, how there's no way this data could have led to that conclusion, this conclusion contradicted that conclusion, this data couldn't have been measured anyway—"Do you realize how hard it is to get a probe on an individual neuron, and do you really think they did it on the same one twice?" Eventually he gets me to say, "Well, I guess I jumped to conclusions there."

He said, "Now I ask you, should that paper ever have been published?" I said, "It sounds like it shouldn't have." He said, "Doesn't it sound like the people who wrote it must have been either dishonest or idiotic?" I said, "I guess so." He says, "Thank you, that's all I wanted to hear you say," and he starts talking to the next person. And of course everybody slaps me on the back and explains to me who I was talking to.

But he eventually did convince me, when I had more serious conversations with him later, that the kind of questions I was interested in asking weren't going to be answered in neurophysiology, and he suggested that I go over and talk to Marvin Minsky. And when I actually did, Jerry shook his head and said, "Out of the frying pan and into the fire."

SB: What can't the parallel machine do?

DH: This kind of parallel machine is good at problems that are large because the amount of knowledge is large, because you can assign processing to each piece of knowledge. There are problems that are difficult problems that just have a tiny amount of data, and this would not speed those kinds of problems up. I'm pretty sure that problems of intelligence can be solved by these slow components working in parallel. It might very well be that there's a kind of intelligence that goes way beyond what people can do, that you would want to do if you could imagine it, and there's no guarantee that *that* would be a parallel problem. But we can't even do the things that we can imagine yet.

SB: Is this a case where the hardware is ahead of the software?

DH: The hardware was designed from an approach to the software. We started out with an idea of how we would like to write programs and then invented hardware that would do that. There's a direct embodiment of that software in hardware, and that's why it's a more natural fit.

SB: Are you getting a co-evolution between hardware and software?

DH: Absolutely. After having done that embodiment, we looked back at the software we wanted to do and said, "Gee, we were still locked into the old way of looking at things." I make fun of the physicists who model the model of the model of the model, and I think of that as their problem, but of course I do the same thing all the time. It's hard to get rid of your idea of how to do it versus what it is you wanted to do.

Another example is, some people were working on document retrieval. They said, "What we want to do is a very quick relational database query." But after a while you step back and realize that really what you wanted is to find articles that interest you on a certain subject. That's different than doing a database retrieval with keywords and that sort of thing. For instance, typically you've got some article and it's about right, and you want to find the other articles that are like it. You essentially put one article in each processor. The one you've got says, "Here's what I'm like," and everybody looks at that and says, "How much am I like that?" and then they order themselves in the order of how much they are like the other article. That whole operation takes fractions of a second for tens of thousands of articles. If you can do that very fast, then you can easily adjust it. "Oh, yes: that's what I meant; that's what I meant; that's not what I meant. Now do it again on the basis of that knowledge." It's fantastic how fast you can get at information that way.

SB: Do you have to start over with new computer languages and basics like that?

DH: I'm not sure how long we'll stick to this, but all we've done so far is extend conventional languages. I think as we get thinking in the terms of the machine we'll completely change how we express problems.

SB: It'll be interesting to see what convergence you get with things like brains.

DH: It will be. We're doing some neat neural-network simulations. There's been a surge in progress. There was a period when there was something called "perceptrons" a long time ago, and that sort of died out. The nice thing about them was they learned to do whatever they could do, the sad thing about them was they couldn't do much. There's now a much more general class of neural networks that in principle—maybe not in practice—can do anything you would want to do, and people have gotten them to learn learning algorithms that let them eventually learn to do those things. Now the question with "in principle" and "eventual" is whether in practical time they'll work. People have never really been able to do non-trivial experiments on ordinary machines. We're doing some much bigger, more interesting experiments now, so we'll see.

SB: Vision-type stuff or what?

DH: No, for instance there's this guy Terry Sejnowski who takes strings of written text from a storybook and puts in the phonemes of somebody reading that story. When you do that for the first couple of pages, the machine learns the connection between the words and the sounds, which is very complicated. Then you let it read aloud the next few pages on its own. Things like that are starting to show some pretty impressive success. You eventually get sort of understandable English, including all the weird spellings. It's not an easy job.

SB: Minsky said out loud the other day that it'll take four or five years of steady effort to come up with the computer languages that really take advantage of parallel machines. How does that relate to the stepwise co-evolution you're doing now?

DH: As soon as you get beyond one barrier, what you find out is where the next barrier is. I think we've opened up a barrier that is going to let us make a big spurt of progress—in the same sense there was a spurt of progress in AI when the first kind of computer came along. It changed our perception of ourselves, but it didn't solve the problems. I think probably this is going to just get us another step, but it's going to be a very exciting next five or ten years.

SB: What happens after five or ten years?

DH: Then everybody understands what the issues are. It becomes more an established paradigm of how to do things, it becomes more a question of filling in the chinks. But it's not like now, when you feel a floodgate opened up, or like you suddenly landed on the promised land and you're free to explore.

SB: Dr. Wiesner said the other day that back in the RLE days theory was years in advance of the equipment. He said now that's flipped, and the equipment is way out in front of the theory. What if the equipment is accelerating faster than theory is?

DH: I think there's something about the equipment, though, that's going to lead you to a different kind of theory. If you look at computer science, it's rotten and ugly compared to physics. In physics, you start with big systems and study them by taking them apart and getting to a finer level of detail. In computer science we're starting with the pieces and putting them together and looking at the implications of that. It's synthetic versus analytic.

What makes physics look beautiful, so you can write down "$f = ma$" (*force equals mass times acceleration*)—those lovely linear laws? It's not because anything that simple is going on at the bottom level. It's because when you have the cumulative behavior of billions of things together, then what you can describe is the gross trends of the system, the average behaviors, the simple linear properties, the net effect of all of that mass. It's the net effect that's beautiful and simple and elegant.

If you started with quarks or something like that and had to get from there to $f = ma$ by going through particle physics and chemistry and structures of solids and so on, and had to discover that there were "objects" and "forces," then things would look pretty messy for a while.

SB: Would they look messy forever?

DH: Well, after a while you get things big enough so all the messy effects cancel each other out, because that's what messiness is, in a sense. Galactic scale is much neater than the scale we operate on—you don't worry about electromagnetism, you don't worry about the nuclear forces; chemistry is irrelevant. It's just gravity and mass, and it's all beautiful.

SB: Do you have a sense of what's beyond parallel?

DH: I think there's two directions. On the hardware I think you're probably going to get change from electronic technology to some other kinds, which is going to open up bigger, better, cheaper kinds of possibilities— maybe more chemical or biological kinds of production techniques. That will happen and it will have a big impact, but it's a kind of engineering.

I think that the more interesting thing that will happen is when you begin to get the process feeding back on itself. The machines will get good enough at dealing with complexity that they can start dealing with their own complexity, and you'll get systems that evolve. I think in the long run that's going to be a much more important kind of a change than the other one.

SB: How long is that long run?

DH: I don't know. It's easy to predict things in the couple-of-years time-scale. It's easy to predict things in the hundreds-of-years timescale, because there's certain things that just sort of have to happen. To say in between is harder. I think the process of machine evolution will lead to things we can't imagine right now. I think I'm not going to get to be immortal, but maybe my children will. They may be made out of different stuff than I am.

SB: On that note, let's get some lunch.

11 THE POLITICS OF BROADCATCH

Your Honor, we cannot accept this photograph in evidence. While it purports to show my client in a hotel bedroom with a woman not his wife, there is no way to prove the photograph is real. As we know, the craft of digital retouching has advanced to the point where a "photograph" can represent anything whatever. It could show my client in bed with Your Honor.

To be sure, digital retouching is still a somewhat expensive process. A black-and-white photo like this, and the negative it's made from, might cost a few thousand dollars to concoct as fiction, but considering my client's social position and the financial stakes of this case, the cost of the technique is irrelevant here. If Your Honor prefers, the defense will state that this photograph is a fake, but that is not necessary. The photograph *could* be a fake; no one can prove it isn't; therefore it cannot be admitted in evidence.

Photography has no place in this or any other courtroom. For that matter, neither does film, videotape, or audiotape, in case the plaintiff plans to introduce in evidence other media susceptible to digital retouching.

—Some lawyer, any day now

Social, political, economic speculation is something the Media Lab ostensibly avoids, figuring it takes one set of skills to create news, another set to interpret news, and they can interfere with each other if you try to blend them. True enough.

Fortunately the reader and the writer of this book need suffer no such limitation. We can speculate, pontificate, editorialize, fantasize, and fret. We'd be derelict if we didn't, considering the multifarious import of what the Media Lab is up to. In a book of mostly fact, what follows is mostly opinion.

☐ *Information Wants to Be Free*
☐
■ Information also wants to be expensive.

Information wants to be free because it has become so cheap to
distribute, copy, and recombine—too cheap to meter. It wants to be
expensive because it can be immeasurably valuable to the recipient. That
tension will not go away. It leads to endless wrenching debate about
price, copyright, "intellectual property," and the moral rightness of casual
distribution, because each round of new devices makes the tension worse,
not better.

Consider the dilemma of a personal computer user who paid $600
for an excellent spreadsheet program called "Lotus 1-2-3," which, if used
adroitly, can help run a million-dollar business on greased rails. The
program can be copied *perfectly*, with a little fiddling of the copy protection, in a few minutes for the cost of a couple of blank floppy disks,
$10 or so. Bad behavior, right? Wrong. That copyability is considered
so much a part of the value of the product by the market that Lotus and
nearly all other software producers were forced to drop copy-protection
schemes in 1986 and 1987 because non-copy-protected competitors were
grabbing the market. (Note: piracy—reselling without permission—is
bad and illegal; copying for local handiness, like xerox copying, is quasi-
legal and good, in my view.)

One software maker, Borland International, offered a copy-protected version of a "desktop utility" program called "Sidekick" at $55
and a non-copy-protected version of the identical program at $85. Guess
which version outsold the other five-to-one. The copy-protected version
was not only more of a hassle to work with, because of the inflexbilities
and incompatibilities that go with any such scheme, but also it offended
users by broadcasting mistrust and defeating the very malleability of the
medium. They paid $30 extra for freedom. As personal computers become
more powerful, it becomes ever easier and cheaper to copy ever more
valuable programs. Each time a problem like this gets partially sorted
out, new technology ups the ante.

Consider the astonishing phenomenon of "digital sampling" in the
music business. Thanks to new technology you can now take any sound—
a falling tree, somebody's complex guitar strum on a CD—and make a

virtual instrument out of it, reproducing that sound at any pitch, in any combination, any tempo, on a standard electronic keyboard. "We got Dorothy Darrow's curves!" said one famous musician, David Bristow, of another famous musician, the opera soprano, one day in a talk at the Media Lab. He meant that the spectrum of Miss Darrow's remarkable voice was captured electronically and is now playable on a Yamaha DX-7 keyboard.

How digital sampling has become a problem was explained in the August 2, 1986, *Billboard*. Attorney Bill Krasilovsky observed, "Copyright laws only cover the sequence of notes in a composition, not the actual notes within that sequence. It takes a redefinition of all the terms." Krasilovsky was hired by the American Federation of Musicians Local 802 to look into the use of a sampled conga drum sound for the "Miami Vice" sound track by Jan Hammer. The original conga drummer, David Earl Johnson, said, "I'd like to get paid for that. . . . He's got me and my best sounds for life, and there's no compensation." Similar borrowings include Led Zeppelin using the late John Bonham's kick drum sound, and The Art Of Noise re-employing Buddy Rich drums.

"Listen to the radio, and you'll hear Phil Collins' gated snare-drum sound on dozens of records he's had nothing to do with," commented a sales director for one of the sampling gear manufacturers. In fact they're not Phil Collins' gated snare-drum sounds. ("Gated" means the acoustic space changes.) Collins nabbed the sound from former fellow band member Peter Gabriel, who developed the gated drum sound with engineer Hugh Padgham. Both Collins and Gabriel, who remain friends, have been accused in the press of stealing the gated drum from each other.

Anybody can do it. The cheapest sampling equipment, from Casio, is now under $100. Information wants to be free.

Information wants to be expensive. In the mass market hundreds of millions of dollars that are collectable or not collectable are involved in each of these copying areas. A major reason the Media Lab is being sponsored to pursue "Paperback Movies" is the magnitude of VCR piracy. The June 16, 1986, *Billboard* reported:

A recent check of 350 videocassette rental outlets in Tokyo, carried out by the Motion Pictures Assn. of America (MPAA), revealed that 250, or 71 percent, were handling pirated tapes. . . . The MPAA check showed that pirate tapes of "Rocky IV," not yet released in Japan and with no authorized videotape versions available in the U.S. or Japan, have been available in Japanese rental outlets since mid-March.

If the MPAA wants statistics, it should check such places as Kenya, Sri Lanka, Indonesia, the Caribbean. In early 1986 *Variety* reported that among the 100 million videocassette users worldwide, some 46 percent of video transactions involved illegal copies. Still, maybe a few years of "free" movies is a dandy way to develop a market. The producers can find a way to charge for it later, once the appetite and audience is in big enough concentrations to be worth the trouble.

Each new kind of information provider has to get used to the idea of leakage, just as book and magazine publishers had to go through denial, outrage, panic, lobbying, and eventual accommodation when xeroxing came in. (That very use of the trademarked name "Xerox" as a verb with a lowercase *x* is a leakage that vexes lawyers.) Information wants to be free. When that's totally denied, customers go elsewhere, or they blandly break laws they consider unjust. The more new media proliferate, the more choices customers have, and the more leverage they have on producers by the ability to shop elsewhere.

But producers are not without resources. Item: in some countries (Germany, Austria, Scandinavia) blank tape of any kind has a surcharge which is divided as "royalties" among the appropriate producers. Item: the U.S. is considering requiring "decoder" devices in all consumer taping equipment that would defeat efforts to duplicate copy-protected products. Item: while all judicial decisions are in the public domain, multimillion-dollar Lexis succeeds in charging handsomely for them by owning copyright on *the page-breaks* (the real value, of course, is in the indexing and searching). Information wants to be expensive.

For some while to come, copyright law will be in an uproar. With parts of electronic publishing such as e-mail, teleconferencing, and personal guidance through databases, copyright sometimes feels like an old statute against swearing on Sundays. Ithiel de Sola Pool traced the problem in his *Technologies of Freedom*: "The recognition of copyright and the paying of royalties emerged with the printing press. With the arrival of electronic reproduction, these practices became unworkable. Electronic publishing is analogous not so much to the print shop of the eighteenth century as to word-of-mouth communication, to which copyright was never applied."

What *do* you charge for information? How do you collect payment?

People will not pay for quality of information. A trivial phone call costs exactly the same as an important one. Good books cost no more than bad books. A carefully read newspaper costs exactly the same as one consigned directly to the bottom of the birdcage. The finest new TV drama from the BBC costs the same as a re-re-rerun soap opera (nothing). In none of these can you get your money back if you're unhappy: producers won't pay for quality of information either.

The legal and billing practices on this go back to telegraph days. Telegraph was treated in law as a common carrier, like transportation. It had to provide service without discrimination, it had to be licensed and regulated. But, wrote Pool:

> a basic principle [was] established in telegraph law that the carrier, if not grossly negligent, was liable only for the value of the undelivered physical message, not for the value of the information contained in it. In contrast to transportation common carriers, who could be held liable for the value of the lost or damaged cargo, the message carrier moved something that had no obvious or intrinsic value that the carrier could recognize.

If a Kodak developing lab inadvertently destroys or loses the roll of film with the priceless pictures you took of a tidal wave hitting Alaska, Kodak will apologize and replace the roll of film. (If I were wrong about that statement, I'd find my ass in court. Information as message rather than as cargo can have a very high valuation.)

People won't pay for quality of information, because the valuing is retroactive, but they will pay for quality of *source*, because the constancy (reliability) of source makes value somewhat predictable. As a magazine publisher I was always amazed that people would pay good money *in advance* for the unknown issues of next year. Subscriptions work well as a way of paying for information. Cable television, as mentioned earlier, failed and failed in its early experiments on a "pay-per-view" basis. It wasn't until the customer paid a monthly fee for the total service, irrespective of use, that cable took off.

Pool predicted that subscription-type billing would work best for electronic publishing, and he's been right. Most online services charge a flat monthly fee, along with a hourly fee for use to keep the amount of traffic manageable. As star performers develop on teleconference, e-mail, and database online systems we can expect their remuneration to match their past, not present, value—their reliability as source. My friend Art Kleiner told me one time of a poet's economic analysis: "In his *ABC of Reading* Ezra Pound compared reading a passage to cashing a check. Its value depends on something you are drawing against behind it. In the case of information, you are drawing against the reputation and expertise of the person who is writing or speaking. This contradicts something I wanted very much to believe when I was a teenager—that wisdom equaled wisdom no matter who was saying it."

Likewise, computer software publishers are finding that a program is not a commodity that they can sell and forget about, it's an entering into a long relationship with the customer, extending through panic phone calls for help by the user and new updated versions of the program by the publisher, often based on customer complaints and suggestions. Soon I won't be buying Microsoft "Word" for word-processing, but subscribing to it.

Thanks to credit cards, billing can be managed even with complex information relationships such as the multi-source "Personal Television" and "Personal Newspaper" services the Media Lab is inventing. In an information-centralizing culture like France you might get one monthly information bill from French Telco. In information-decentralizing cultures like I hope America is, you'll get a tangle of bills such as the American phone companies currently send, and a program in your home entertainment center will sort them out and arrange for payment.

Harvard's Benjamin Compaine has a nice analysis of the economics of broadcast in his 1982 book, *Who Owns the Media?* It begins with the idea of information as a "public good" ("good" not as the opposite of "bad" but as in "goods and services"):

A public good to an economist is one which has essentially no marginal cost associated with adding distribution. The best example is a television broadcast. Once the fixed costs of production have been incurred and the show is sent over the air, there is no difference in expense to the broadcaster if one household or 21 million tune in to the show. Thus, television (and radio) advertising is not sold at its marginal cost, since that is zero. Price always exceeds marginal cost.

The "product" of the media differs from most commodities, which are private goods. Every orange, for instance, has a cost, and each one adds weight in shipment. . . .

In print media, the information content is really the public good, while the physical product—paper and ink—is a private good. . . . The incentive, therefore, for broadcasters and publishers is to increase circulation or audience for a product, since that adds little or nothing to marginal costs while justifying higher marginal revenue from advertisers in the form of higher advertising rates.

So everything aims at total popularity. The Media Lab would like to mess with those economics, because the result at present is that "bestseller" books are too easy to find, all other books are too hard to find, and the most perfectly targeted books aren't sold at all. The same with television, radio, magazines, and daily news. Mass media, driven by mass advertising, is a form of cultural monocropping. Such cornfields give short-term high yield, but as ecosystems they're boring and fragile, and they deplete the cultural soil.

The Invited Persuader

■ If the technology of mass information distribution shifts from broadcast toward broadcatch, toward more control by the user, advertising has to shift with it. Negroponte divides ads into "advertising as noise" and "advertising as news." Advertising-as-noise—"Marlboro-type ads whose information content is zero"—he figures will not do well in the new environment of highly customized media. It's too easy for the user/viewer to edit around them. "Commercial-zipping," it's called with VCRs.

But advertising-as-news, such as an announcement of a sale at a store the customer is interested in, or any ads that pay attention to the user's interests, Negroponte expects to flourish in highly personalized media. "Suppose the system knew—or I let the system know—that I'm an avid windsurfer, I do a lot of skiing, I drink Scotch, I buy a lot of white wine, I travel a great deal, and I own a BMW. The person who's selling the advertising space now goes to Johnny Walker and says, 'You were paying us $100,000 a minute. We're now going to charge you $200,000 a minute, but everybody who's going to see your ad is a Scotch drinker.' "

In other words, the advertising you want can reach you in greater depth than ever, while the advertising you don't want will be screened out more easily and actively than ever.

Meanwhile a third kind, what might be called "reverse advertising," advertising by the customer, can open up enormously in truly interactive media.

That's why American newspapers have lobbied so fiercely and successfully against electronic telephone directories on videotex-like services. Ithiel de Sola Pool wrote:

A bogey haunts the boardrooms of newspaper publishers: the possible electrocution of classified ads. If the 31 percent of advertising revenue that these ads bring in is lost to competitors offering want ads on videotex, newspapers will be in crisis. . . . Readers can call up precisely those listings that meet their needs, such as three-room apartments below $400 within twenty minutes of downtown. The listings can be instantly updated or purged. If a job is listed in the electronic want ads, it is still open. . . . Electronic yellow pages make sense, too. Instead of just looking up a listing of restaurants, subscribers could get a listing of the kind of restaurant they want, with information on the day's special or the current waiting line, and could even have an interactive way of making a reservation.

Only 20 to 30 percent of newspaper revenue comes from circulation. All the rest is from advertising, which is why newspapers are so vulnerable. They've been losing advertising share to electronic media for a long time. Print media had 53 percent of American advertising dollars in 1935 but only 34 percent by 1981. Newspapers are major sponsors of the Media Lab in part because they have to look at becoming an electronic medium themselves.

An intriguing place to research how want ads can be electrified is on the so-called "sex boards"—home-based computer bulletin board systems like "Dial Your Match" that exist by the dozen in every major American city. Some are explicit and raunchy, some romantic, some gay, some straight; some are free, some you pay a modest fee to join. Like the "personal" ads in newspapers, they are an ultimate form of self-advertising, but the computerized interactivity offers advantages that newspapers lack.

When you join a sex board, via your personal computer of course, you answer an online questionnaire about your age, weight, sexual preferences, jokes you find funny, and such oddments as whether you're the kind who stays to watch the credits at the end of movies. The system then shuffles through its members to see who best matches what you're looking for and lists them in order of likelihood, along with how often they log onto the system and whether their mailbox has room for a message from you. There are public conferences where chat and flirtation go on, and private e-mail where the nitty-gritty of phone numbers and evenings available this week can be worked out. They are brave, friendly-feeling, amateur services full of enthusiasm. No wonder the French national e-mail system took off on this wavelength. The sex boards are truly advertising as conversation. There's no reason similar services couldn't exist for buying, selling, renting, or swapping cars, homes, jobs, sailboats, pets, lawyers, or flower seeds.

I asked Negroponte how come he had no sponsorship from advertising firms. Answer: "They don't have capital. They're cash flow oriented." For forty years the fraction of the American economy spent on advertising has remained constant at about 2 percent of the Gross National Product. That means that when advertising fattens one medium, it starves others, and the changes can come with considerable suddenness.

In these days of diminishing network clout, the search at advertising firms is for "nontraditional" advertising and "segmented" markets.

The economics of new media will be determined even more by advertisers than by subscribers, if the past is any indication. It also turns out that advertisers play a crucial role in the politics of information. Anthony Smith wrote in *The Geopolitics of Information* something you might not expect in a book subtitled "How Western Culture Dominates the World":

> Advertising, so overwhelmingly dominated by the U.S., is an important historical factor in the West's version of a free press. Until well into the nineteenth century most of the European and American press was subject to various forms of political and governmental patronage; not until the present century was it possible, in many parts of Europe, for newspapers to operate under a banner of political neutrality. It was advertising that enabled the doctrine of impartiality or objectivity to take root in newspapers.

My father was an advertising man. I never gave him the credit he deserved for being a defender of freedom of the press, a bastion of liberty. On the other hand, I have had columns in major newspapers censored because the advertisers in those newspapers complained about what I said. (Nothing political; I was explaining how the reader could get some products much more cheaply by mail order.) Also advertisers inevitably narrow whatever medium they subsidize, because the editor *has* to serve the already identified and paid-for audience. Exploration outside the predictable is punished, and so is any form of criticism of the audience other than teasing.

All media routinely declare they are independent of their advertisers. One reason they have to keep saying it is everybody knows they're lying. The other reason is to shame the advertisers as much as possible and back them off. Editors are well aware that the actual value of the publication/program to its readers/viewers/listeners is in inverse proportion to the amount of pressure that advertisers get away with. *The New Yorker* is a valuable read; most camera magazines aren't.

Advertisers are more freeing as sponsors than governments because of the difference between many small pressures, some of which offset others, and one big pressure. The many small pressures permit variation, which is the engine of adaptability and growth. One big pressure, however principled and well-intentioned, is stultifying always.

☐
☐ *Information Wants to Be (Politically) Free*

■ "Although there are other nations that have a relatively free press, the United States is unique in allowing all forms of transmission of information to be privately owned," wrote Benjamin Compaine in *Who Owns the Media?* The telephone and telegraph companies, book publishers, newspapers, magazines, radio and television broadcasters and networks, many communication satellites—all are privately owned. Even the post office has private competition in UPS and Federal Express.

The wellspring of all that entrepreneurial zest is one clause in a political document. The First Amendment to the U.S. Constitution, as ratified in 1791, reads in part, *"Congress shall make no law . . . abridging the freedom of speech or of the press."* That strong statement has been diluted since, as we'll see, but it declared the principle radically, early, and with the force of law. Political decisions shape communication forms.

Until 1950, radio in Japan was a government monopoly with no commercial users, and only the medium-wave frequencies were employed. When radio was privatized in 1950, a market suddenly opened up for radio and then television receivers, which primed the whole Japanese electronics industry. Koji Kobayashi wrote in *Computers and Communications,* "Clearly the release of radio waves was a pivotal event that set off a burst of activity that revitalized postwar Japan. In this sense it is quite significant that every year on the first day of June a grand 'Radio Waves Day' celebration takes place to commemorate the promulgation of the Radio Waves Laws."

All the roads of the Roman Empire were one gauge; so are all the railroads of the U.S. (same gauge, incidentally). One cart, one train, fits all. Empires like standards and are good at enforcing them; it's one of the genuine advantages of empires. The hidden cost, of course, is the loss of variability that drives adaptability, but that can be borne by the larger grain of other nations, other empires. Where standards and decrees about communications run into trouble is when they are handed down from on high without public experimentation and debate, as New Math was handed to the schools, as a particular High Definition Television production standard was almost handed to the world in 1986 at Dubrovnik.

Many communication decisions, such as which format will be standard for VCRs (VHS, Beta, or 8mm), are played out in the market, usually to pretty good effect. But many, like allocation of broadcast frequencies and rights of privacy and copyright protection, are legislated or simply decreed (as metric conversion was, for example) out of public sight until too late. The freedom of the press, of public communication, is ill guarded when that happens.

"Homeostasis" is the biological term for maintaining balance in a system and preventing harmful excursions. MIT's Norbert Wiener declared in his seminal 1948 book *Cybernetics*, "Of all [the] anti-homeostatic factors in society, the control of the means of communication is the most effective and the most important."

Political forms shape communication forms. The Soviet planned economy, Pool reported, made it easy to wire streets and apartment houses for loudspeakers. "So for forty years the wired speaker was the dominant device for radio entertainment in the Soviet Union. Not till 1964 did the number of regular radios in the country come to exceed the number of wired loudspeakers. Decades later, development in China followed the same course." To this day, according to *Newsweek* in 1986, copy machines in the U.S.S.R. are kept locked up, and direct-dial long-distance phone service is prohibited, "apparently because it threatened to overwhelm KGB surveillance."

In the U.S. there are 25 million personal computers. In the U.S.S.R. there are a few thousand, most of them without printers. Computer technology in the Soviet Union is estimated to be seven to ten years behind the free-press West.

Enter the videocassette recorder, apparently a mere entertainment medium. There are said to be 2 million imported VCRs in Russia and some 300,000 in Poland, with plenty of rental movies available. Predictably, a VCR proletariat is emerging, and dissidents such as Poland's underground publisher Nowa are beginning to produce their own video-cassettes. The *Washington Post* reported, " 'Videos provide a way for people to gather together, have discussion about what they see, and make decisions about their activity,' the Nowa activist said. Unlike under-ground books and printing presses, moreover, VCRs are legal in Poland; those who watch them are unlikely to be raided or arrested by police."

Influence goes both ways between politics and communications. Communication forms also shape political and organizational forms. This is especially true of new media. If the government gets them first, as Nazi Germany did with radio, you get a top-down bias in the political process. If citizens get them first, as happened with VCRs in Poland, you get a bottom-up bias. Technology moves faster than laws. All new technologies are outlaw areas. All new communications technologies are political dynamite.

It would be interesting to do a communications analysis of revo-lutions. The American Revolution was in the hands of printers (hence freedom of the "press"), with Tom Paine's pamphlet "Common Sense" selling 120,000 copies in three months. Ayatollah Khomeini's revolution in Iran was spread by audiocassette tapes, copy machines, and telephone; no one bothered to take over a broadcast facility until the Shah left. By contrast, in the Philippines the crucial battle in the overthrow of Fer-dinand Marcos in February 1986 was for the government-owned Channel 4 television station. The live broadcast of Marcos' inaugural ceremony was cut off in mid-gesture by the rebels and replaced by a John Wayne movie.

Political change in nations with highly centralized communications is almost forced to be convulsive, because local and short-term adapta-tions don't have a chance. A country whose communication system is paid for by advertisers and users (directly, rather than through taxes) is less revolution-prone. It has micro-revolutions going on the whole time, most of them inconsequential. Even the consequential ones, by building piecemeal, can change the system in large ways without chaos.

The question raised by the work at the Media Lab is whether that technological populism may be growing even finer-grained and more adaptive than ever. Interactive media such as Personal Television, Per-sonal Newspaper, Papert's computer-rich School of the Future, and the

Vivarium are highly governed by the individual. Are these developments natural extensions of what goes on in a market economy and a democracy, where individual choice ultimately governs?

I hope so.

But for a "politics of broadcatch" to take hold will require more than just the enabling technology. It doesn't need encouraging (though a little basic science can go a long way). It does need defending. It may require shedding some habits America has accreted about regulating communication technologies. The First Amendment guaranteeing freedom of the press needs to be inspected, debated, and enforced anew in light of new meanings of the word "press."

Most of the groundwork for that has been done expertly by Ithiel de Sola Pool in his 1983 book, *Technologies of Freedom: On Free Speech in an Electronic Age*. Pool, who died in 1984, helped found the Political Science Department at MIT, wrote on the social impact of the telephone, and did research on U.S. elections, cable TV, Soviet propaganda, and Third World economic development. His book was the single most helpful text in preparing the book you're reading and the one I would most recommend for following up issues raised here. His interpretations of what's really going on with new communications technologies are the best in print.

The main argument of his book, to do it summary injustice, begins as follows:

> The new communication technologies have not inherited all the legal immunities that were won for the old. When wires, radio waves, satellites, and computers became major vehicles of discourse, regulation seemed to be a technical necessity. And so, as speech increasingly flows over those electronic media, the five-century growth of an unabridged right of citizens to speak without controls may be endangered. . . .
>
> In fact this country has a trifurcated communications system. In three domains of communication—print, common carriage, and broadcasting—the law has evolved separately, and in each domain with but modest relation to the others.
>
> In the domain of print and other means of communication that

existed in the formative days of the nation, such as pulpits, peri-
odicals, and public meetings, the First Amendment truly governs. . . .

In the domain of the common carrier, which includes the
telephone, the telegraph, the postal system, and now some computer
networks, a different set of policies has been applied, designed above
all to ensure universal service and fair access by the public to the
facilities of the carrier . . . : it is obligated to serve all on equal
terms without discrimination.

Finally, in the domain of broadcasting, Congress and the courts
have established a highly regulated regime, very different from that
of print. On the grounds of a supposed scarcity of usable frequencies
in the radio spectrum, broadcasters are selected by the government
for merit in its eyes, assigned a slice each of the spectrum of frequencies, and required to use that assignment fairly and for community welfare as defined by state authorities. . . . For broadcasting,
a politically managed system has been invented.

"Fuck that." I can say that here in a book but not on a television
talk show. In the Radio Act passed in 1927, Section 29 decreed, "No
person within the jurisdiction of the United States shall utter any obscene, indecent, or profane language by means of radio communication.'"
It's still the law. Hams (radio amateurs) and CB radio users can't swear
either. It's okay to curse on cellular telephone, however.

Since radio stations had to go through elaborate charades with the
Radio Commission (now the FCC—Federal Communications Commission) to get and keep their licenses, they bent over backwards (or for-
wards, depending on your metaphor) to please the government. Pool:

In the early 1920s, censorship of speakers by radio stations themselves, sometimes called "private censorship," was common. As
early as 1921 an emergency switch in the studio of a Newark station
was used by the engineer to cut off speakers in mid-sentence if their
material was deemed unfit for public ears. Subjects treated in this
way included birth control, prostitution, and cigarettes.

You could also be cut off or barred from the air for opposition to chain stores or Prohibition, criticism of the government, or being Norman Thomas, the Socialist. Norman Thomas wrote many influential books unhindered; his publishers did not need a license from the government.

Just a problem of the naive early days of radio? Frank Stanton's reminiscences at the Media Lab about running CBS gave more recent perspective. A student asked him about government interference in the media by the Reagan administration, and Stanton began, "There's much more freedom today than there was a decade ago. The direction, at least in this administration, has been to keep hands off controlling the news. It could change very quickly I think.

"Newt Minow told me a story about when he was chairman of the FCC. The old Huntley-Brinkley news team took a very hard line on the administration one night. Minow had just gone to a dinner party, and the White House called. He came on the phone, and President Kennedy said, 'I want those men off the air!' Minow swallowed his tongue and said, 'May I come see you in the morning?' Kennedy: 'I want them off the air!' Next morning Minow went in to see the President and said, 'Have you had a chance to think about it?' The President said, 'Yes, and I recognize I can't do that.' But it's the kind of thing that scares you.

"My wife used to say at seven-thirty at night when the phone rang, 'Please don't take the call, because you won't get back to the table until nine o'clock.' Frequently it was President Johnson in those days, calling to say, 'Why do you do this to me? You're killing me!' and take me apart. I never told the news department about that because I saw my role as being a sort of a buffer zone between Washington and the people in the newsroom.

"If you step on the toes of enough Congressmen night after night, they can make life pretty miserable for you." Stanton told of a busload of nuns who drove from Rhode Island to see Senator John Pastore to complain about a movie they saw one night at 11:30 p.m. on television. Pastore and an assistant saw the movie and were shocked. The Senator called the heads of the three television networks to his office. "He said, 'I want to institute a process of clearance of everything you put on the air through the Trade Association.' He asked each of us to think about

how it was going to be set up and come back within two days. Two of
the three networks went along with it. It never got into the press. That
could happen again. Can you imagine what would happen to entertainment if you had to go through that kind of a process with our whole
schedule?"

The irony is that the premise which underlies government control
of broadcast media has evaporated. Broadcast spectrum of radio frequencies is not scarce, hasn't been for years, and is growing ever less so. Radio
and television channels can be closer packed and more localized; both
radio and television receivers continue to improve dramatically; frequencies can be reallocated (the transfer of two unused UHF television
frequencies could provide a city with a thousand radio stations); multiplexing permits multiple signals over the same piece of line; compression
techniques such as the Media Lab is working on reduce bandwidth requirements markedly; cable television has taken broadcast out of the
"air" entirely; satellites are offering whole new broadcast frequencies (Ku
and Ka); satellites can be more closely spaced in orbit; and the coming
of fiberoptic cable inspires talk of "infinite bandwidth."

Pool suggested that the major source of spectrum "scarcity" is the
government itself and reproposed a scheme from the '50s that government
auction off spectrum the way it does water rights and public lands. It
would be more equitable, it would reward and therefore enoucrage efficient use of spectrum, and it would get government out of licensing and
censoring electronic communications in violation of the Constitution.
Reagan's FCC Chairman Mark Fowler supported exactly this policy before he left office in mid-1987.

In Washington, D.C., there are twenty-three radio stations (licensed and regulated), eleven television stations (licensed and regulated) . . . and two daily newspapers, both of them fully protected by
the First Amendment. Which is the scarce medium?

Continuing Pool's argument, the current "convergence of modes"
of communications technologies—the Media Lab's founding symbol of
overlapping circles—has put the different bodies of communications law
into conflict. The system is no longer trifurcated into print, common
carrier, and broadcast. Pool gives an example of the kind of squirming
this can lead to. In 1969, when the FCC was busily regulating everything

about cable television, it required that any coverage of a political candidate offer equal time to rival candidates. The American Newspaper Publishers Association then inquired pointedly whether that requirement would apply to them when they started sending newspaper copy over cable. The FCC emitted so tortured a ruling of yes-but-no that it was ignored by everybody.

Pool points out that "the first defensive tactic by the owners of an old medium against competition by a new one is to have the new one prohibited. If this does not work, the next defensive tactic is to buy into the attacker." Thus the growing phenomenon of "cross-ownership," where publishing and broadcasting are carried on by the same corporation, often on a huge scale. Worried about communication monopolies, the FCC forbade any one company from owning a broadcast and print medium in the same city. It sounds reasonable, but it prevents the very kind of service the Media Lab is exploring. Pool:

If a newspaper wishes to improve its service by coupling its print offering with an online database, or with a newsreel, one could only cheer this result. Certainly the preservation of the press, a goal that everyone proclaims, is better served by encouraging the print media to make imaginative use of multimedia opportunities than by enjoining them from doing anything but putting ink on paper in an obsolete conventional way.

To conclude Pool's argument, he was most concerned with what might happen to electronic publishing:

If computers become the printing presses of the twenty-first century, will judges and legislators recognize them for what they are? At issue is the future of publishing. . . . Videodisks, integrated memories, and databases will serve functions that books and libraries now serve, while information retrieval systems will serve for what magazines and newspapers do now. Networks of satellites, optical fibers, and radio waves will serve the functions of the present-day postal system. Speech will not be free if these are not also free.

A hint of the kind of chilling that can occur came late in 1986 when President Reagan's National Security Council declared that certain scientific and technical information publicly available on electronic databases should be classified "sensitive" and restricted. Book burning is book burning, whether it's done electronically or with a match. The principle is that simple. The issues, of course, are not. Debate and redebate of the political requirements on communcations will go on as long as the technologies advance, which shows signs of being forever.

One abiding need is for a balance of centralized and decentralized in any system. Pool: "Freedom is fostered when the means of communication are dispersed, decentralized, and easily available, as are printing presses or microcomputers. Central control is more likely when the means of communication are concentrated, monopolistic, and scarce, as are great networks." You want both. Each is a relief from and a corrective to the other. And with the coming technologies of broadcatch, each is more intimately connected to the other. " 'Prime time' becomes 'my time,' " Negroponte predicted.

One can foresee a new communication principle as fundamental as freedom of speech and press. It's related to the right of privacy, which must indeed be redefended in a communication-rich world, or individuality and variation will diminish. This would be *the right of access*. You may not choose to reach everyone, or be reachable by everyone, but the connection should be possible. As Pool points out, this would require "universal connectivity, directory information, agreed standards, and a legal right to interconnect." Ensuring all of those are suitable activities for government and intergovernment agreements.

Much of what we are defending the right to communicate, of course, is lies, including some new kinds.

□
□ *Digital* Faux

■ "You tell me the *National Geographic* moved a pyramid? Oh boy, what a mistake. They're the wrong magazine to do that. And a pyramid!" Media analyst Russ Neuman was enjoying my report of *National Geographic* using digital retouching techniques to slide the Giza pyramid sideways a bit in a photograph so it fit better on the cover of their February 1982 issue.

There has been almost no press about the coming of digital retouching, perhaps because the press itself is implicated. In 1985 Kevin Kelly and I did a cover story on the subject for *Whole Earth Review* which turned up the following, randomly collected. *Popular Science* used the technique to put an airplane from one photograph on the background from another photograph for a cover. *World Tennis* had Bjorn Borg and John McEnroe back to back in dueling costumes on their cover, apparently in one photo together but actually joined by digitial retouching from two photos taken on separate occasions. In a book of photographs called *Idylls of France*, by Proctor Jones, prominent telephone poles and lines were surgically removed from one picture of a Basque shepherd, and litter in a stream was disappeared from another picture. The 1984 annual report of Huntington Bancshares had a sumptuous photo of downtown Columbus, Ohio, featuring their headquarters tower. The picture also showed the tower of their major competitor, Bank One, but the thirteen-foot-tall sign on Bank One's building was evaporated, and Huntington Center's own parking lot and its cars were turned into a bright green lawn. The cover for the *Whole Earth Review* issue, naturally, was a snapshot I took of three flying saucers buzzing downtown San Francisco.

The technology for doing all this was pioneered at MIT by William Schreiber and Donald Troxel—Schreiber now heads the Advanced Television Research Project at the Media Lab. It began with a 1969–79 contract from Associated Press to solve AP's problems with the differing wirephoto standards between the U.S. and the rest of the world. Schreiber and Troxel invented a laser photo facsimile system and then an "Electronic Darkroom" for AP. Photographs and slides were read by a laser scanner in minute detail, translated into digital form, and stored in a computer, where the images could be reshaped and edited at convenience. Nearly every AP picture you see in newspapers is digital. So are all the photos in *Time* and *USA Today*, for the same reason: so they can be sent by satellite to distant printers for far quicker distribution than used to be possible. How much do those publications fiddle with their pictures? There's no way to tell.

Schreiber told me, "It became obvious that digital retouching could be made absolutely undetectable—as opposed to analog retouching (dodging, airbrushing, etc.), which you can almost always see if you look very carefully. If you have a picture represented by a discrete set of numbers, and you change some of the numbers, you may not be able to tell that that was not a natural image." I asked whether you couldn't use another computer to detect suspicious redundancies in a retouched image. He doubted it: "You could get around that by introducing some random perturbations." Since the computer-manipulable pixels can be smaller than the grain in the film, there is no limit to how persuasive the detail can be in a retouched photo.

The technology was refined subsequently for gravure printers. It is now common in "electronic color pre-press systems" used in most high-quality printing. The leading manufacturers of the equipment, at $250,000 to $1 million a system, are Hell in West Germany and SciTex in Israel. It's so widespread that the kind of expensive retouching that used to be the sole province of advertisers and catalog makers is now a standard editorial tool.

Voices from the SciTex room: "Kick up that blue a little more." "Let's see the whole thing with more contrast. More still. Can you mute the sky a bit?" "Uh oh. Brown eyes, blue blouse. Try the blouse in green. No, darker." "It's great except for that guy with the weird look behind them. Could he go away, please?" "You don't like that guy, how about this guy instead?"

Photography, in effect, has become a form of *faux*. That's the exquisite art of faking marble or wood with paint, enjoying a vogue these days. The word, pronounced "foe," is French for "false." It's a wonderful art; you can fake kinds of marble and wood that don't even exist, except that they do exist. As *faux*.

Kevin Kelly wrote photography's epitaph:

We've been spoiled by a hundred years of reliable photography as a place to put faith, but that century was an anomaly. Before then, and after now, we have to trust in other ways. What the magazines who routinely use these creative retouching machines say is, "Trust us." You can't trust the medium, you can only trust the source, the people. It's the same with text, after all. The only way my words are evidence is if I don't lie, even though it's so, so easy to do.

Photographs of missiles in Cuba, of Oswald smiling with a gun, of burning monks in Vietnam, of a burning nuclear reactor in Russia, of a nuclear weapons factory in Israel—photographic reproduction is a political instrument. Its new flexibility has not been examined in public forums.

Quite soon it will also be a personal instrument. Electronic still photography is coming to the world. Sony halfway introduced an electronic camera called the Mavica (magnetic video camera) in 1981 and then withdrew it because the resolution was still too low. The Media Lab, in a project for Polaroid, is developing ways to boost resolution through continuous sampling of the image by not having a shutter.

Negroponte: "Basically, it's going to make cameras into computer peripherals. You'll play with the images in the computer, sequence them and store them, make albums, do all of your retouch stuff." The Media Lab proposal to Polaroid suggested, "One could envision photographing 'the family' before the Arc de Triomphe, wherein the results include no cars circling Place de l'Étoile, and no other tourists in the scene." And then, I presume, you'd be able to print out the result in living, lying color. I'm perturbed; Negroponte isn't.

Television, as you may have guessed, is already far gone. The local weatherperson on Channel 7 gesturing at the weather map or satellite photo is gesturing at a blank wall. The image is inserted by a technique called Chromakey. The gesturer is watching a monitor and adjusting his hand in the picture accordingly. The intrepid on-the-scene reporter speaking so forcefully may be holding a microphone which is erased along with hand and arm, live, at the station. CBS shows the wider screen of the Japanese HDTV it's supporting in some of its studio-to-studio interviewing. The wide screen has a wide live image, but the extra part is not real; additional curtain or other innocuous background is "cloned" in electronically.

Studios that are trying the Japanese HDTV production system for real are finding that it is far easier and more believable for faking things than standard TV. Referring to the composite images he was making with HDTV Ultimatte, one producer told *Broadcasting*, "They give it a rich look beyond reach for me in 16mm, and not even found on 35mm. It is absolutely seamless." He had just saved thousands of dollars in "location" shooting, not hiring extras, not dressing streets in period costume.

Tom Wolzien, vice president at NBC for editorial and production, is one of the few who has publicly raised questions about the ability to change video news footage with the new digital retouching equipment. He told a University of California, Berkeley, seminar on the changing technologies of newsgathering, "Once this new technology gets out there, we're going to have a helluva time telling what's real and what's unreal."

Some people are upset about the computer "colorizing" of classic black-and-white movies. That one doesn't bother me, because it's overt, and the viewer can always turn down the color control if feeling purist. The kind of thing worth being bothered about, I think, was addressed by David Zeltzer at the end of his talk to the Vivarium students about where computer animation is heading.

"You could do the fantasy movie 'Dark Crystal' on your own machine at home," Zeltzer mused. "We would take the whole Hollywood movie-making industry and make it into a cottage industry. One craftsman could make a movie instead of armies of technicians and gaffers and best boys. People won't know what to do with that yet. I don't know what to do with it. I'm a little afraid of it.

"What happens if CBS has one of these machines that can generate real-time animation of photographic quality? You look at two TVs— one's got a picture of Ronald Reagan shaking hands with Gorbachev, and the other set has a picture of Ronald Reagan punching Gorbachev in the nose, and you can't tell them apart. One's on videotape and one was synthesized on a computer. We already don't believe in film anymore. What's going to happen to electronic newsgathering when the validating function of videotape no longer exists? Television will no longer be a verification medium. Who's going to control that?

"How do we put governors on these fantasy systems so that people don't fantasize the wrong things?"

□
□
The Important Philosophers
□
of the Twentieth Century
□

■ Marvin Minsky knows exactly whom to ask about technology and fantasy problems. He keeps up with their literature, seeks their friendship, visits their homes. On the snowy Sunday afternoon at Minsky's home I asked him why he was so interested in science fiction writers.

"Well, I think of them as thinkers. They try to figure out the consequences and implications of things in as thoughtful a way as possible. A couple of hundred years from now, maybe Isaac Asimov and Fred Pohl will be considered the important philosophers of the twentieth century, and the professional philosophers will almost all be forgotten, because they're just shallow and wrong, and their ideas aren't very powerful.

"Whenever Pohl or Asimov writes something, I regard it as extremely urgent to read it right away. They might have a new idea. Asimov has been working for forty years on this problem: if you can make an intelligent machine, what kind of relations will it have with people? How do you negotiate when their thinking is so different? The science fiction writers think about what it means to think." Other writers he pays close attention to are Arthur C. Clarke, Robert Heinlein, Gregory Benford, James Hogan, John Campbell, and H. G. Wells. If Minsky had his way, there would always be a visiting science fiction writer in residence at the Media Lab.

Science fiction is *the* literature at MIT. The campus bookstore has a collection as large as some science fiction specialty stores. Every computer science student knows and refers to John Brunner's *Shockwave Rider*, Vernor Vinge's *True Names* (Afterword by Marvin Minsky), William Gibson's *Neuromancer*. The world's first popular computer game, "Spacewar," was created at MIT's Project MAC in 1961 by student Steve Russell and his fellow hackers based on the *Lensmen* series of space operas by "Doc" Smith. Tod Machover at the Media Lab composed an opera called "Valis," from a science fiction story by Philip K. Dick, which debuts at the Pompidou Center in Paris and then will travel to MIT.

Somewhere in my education I was misled to believe that science fiction and science fact must be kept rigorously separate. In practice they are so blurred together they are practically one intellectual activity, although the results are published differently, one kind of journal for careful scientific reporting, another kind for wicked speculation.

Every now and then you'll see a work that really combines both, examining scientific news and imagining social consequence in one breath. The most exceptional of these recently is a 1986 work called *Engines of Creation*, by Eric Drexler. I first came across its subject at a meeting of the Nanotechnology Study Group at MIT, at which author Drexler and Marvin Minksy were speaking. I came out giddy, blind-sided by a future even more revolutionary than what's coming in computers and communications.

The premise of the study group, and of Drexler's book, is that we are rapidly acquiring the technical ability to craft individual molecules out of atoms, and when that is accomplished, it will change everything we know. "Nano" means "one-billionth" to indicate the unimaginable tinyness of engineering involved. It is a realm of true alchemy, where substances can be reconfigured and shaped at will. Minsky states in his foreword to Drexler's book, "Nanotechnology could have more effect on our material existence than those last two great inventions in that domain—the replacement of sticks and stones by metals and cements and the harnessing of electricity. . . . *Engines of Creation* is the best attempt so far to prepare us to think of what we might become, should we persist in making new technologies."

The first part of the book is a closely argued survey of work in physics, materials science, medical science, and computer science that is converging at the scale of the molecule. Technology will proceed quickly, rewarded at each step of further miniaturization, until it reaches a level of nanomachine that Drexler calls "the assembler breakthrough." "Because assemblers will let us place atoms in almost any reasonable arrangement," he writes, "they will let us build almost anything that the laws of nature allow to exist. . . . With assemblers, we will be able to remake our world or destroy it."

Once this level is approached, the technology can move with awful speed. The assemblers will self-replicate, making millions of themselves, all operating at the blinding speed of the infinitesimal. They will rapidly mature the kinds of artificial intelligence being glimpsed in massively parallel computers like the Connection Machine. One handout from the Nanotechnology Study Group foresaw "sub-micron computers with giga-hertz clock rates, nanowatt power dissipation, and RAM storage densities in the hundreds of millions of terabytes per cubic centimeter." In other words: whole computers smaller than a millionth of a meter, going at millions of cycles per second, on billionth-of-a-watt energy, with memory in the trillions of bytes.

Utter plastic, utterly brilliant.

The "assembler breakthrough," the enthusiasts proclaim, could come "in twenty years, plus or minus ten years." Engines self-assembled of diamond, human immortality, zero pollution, space suits as alive as the wearer but immeasurably tougher and more sensitive—the speculation in the book is good heady technological forecasting, done with a sci-entist's training and a science fiction writer's imagination and flair.

Impressively, Drexler doesn't leave it there. The book is warning as well as promise. The whole last half of the book, starting with a chapter titled "Engines of Destruction," is about the political process of controlling nanotechnology. It's like trying to design a solid container for a quart of universal solvent. Some new political and intellectual forms may have to arise.

"All panaceas become poison" is the theme of most science fiction. Too much of anything wonderful becomes terrible. Part of the real re-search on any new good thing is discovering how much is too much, how fast is too fast.

☐
☐ *Metacomputer*
■ Artificial intelligence and nanotechnology are not the only potential runaways in progress. The rich human connectivity that the Media Lab is inventing toward also has harmful excesses waiting to be explored. New technologies create new freedoms and new dependencies. The free-doms are more evident at first. The dependencies may never become evident, which makes them all the worse, because then it takes a crisis

to discover them. Crises of large complex systems can be nasty, if the system hasn't had time to mature a lot of checks and balances.

If there is a single science fiction story most pointedly expressive of the future the Media Lab is inventing—of the hazards of totally addictive total connectivity—it is "The Machine Stops," by E. M. Forster. Yes, the one who wrote A *Passage to India* and A *Room with a View.* It was 1909, he was thirty, he was incensed by the optimistic materialism of H. G. Wells' *The Time Machine,* and he wrote a brilliant fictional riposte that hasn't dated a line in eighty years.

The story concerns a woman in a hexagonal cell, an ultimate Media Room, in electronic contact with thousands of people. She's impatient when a tiresome son she hasn't seen since he was born interrupts her, as he seems to have no interesting ideas to offer, just unseemly criticisms of the Machine that connects them and a demand that she come see him personally. She is extremely busy, she explains, she has a lecture to give in five minutes. "The clumsy system of public gatherings had been long since abandoned; neither Vashti nor her audience stirred from their rooms. Seated in her arm-chair she spoke, while they in their arm-chairs heard her, fairly well, and saw her, fairly well." Her lecture, ten minutes long, is well received.

In their uniform perfect rooms, everyone lives underground. Finally she visits her son, an arduous journey managed entirely by the Machine, and he tells her of a visit to the surface and his realization that only the Machine lives, that the people are dying. " 'The Machine develops— but not on our lines. The Machine proceeds—but not to our goal.' " Disgusted by his heresy, she warns him he is doomed and returns in relief to her room. "But there came a day when, without the slightest warning, without any previous hint of feebleness, the entire communication system broke down, all over the world, and the world as they understood it, ended." As the world-sized Machine destroys itself with all its humans, the son and mother meet a last time, the son gasping in triumph, " 'I am dying—but we touch, we talk, not through the Machine.' "

Everyone at the Media Lab would protest that Forster's Machine is exactly what they're seeking to prevent. Yet it is a Connection Machine right out of Danny Hillis's fantasies; an Architecture Machine as Negroponte finally pictured it, in which one lives; an Electronic Publishing

Machine that engages everyone's intellect; a kind of Vivarium in which virtual reality takes over. Like all computers, it crashes, but the computer, and the crash, have grown too big for repair by a lulled humanity.

Of course that's what attracts us to a Media Lab. The Lab flirts with dangers like living with addictive connectivity, total entertainment, and out-of-the-body experience. It inflates hubris and then mocks it. And through reinventing the media it seeks to ensure that communication systems are human-based in their very texture.

The world Machine is coming anyway, with or without the Media Lab. Earth is already wholly integrated. The coins in your pocket know about the price of oil, about apartheid in South Africa, about the Pope's opinions on birth control, about the Soviet space program, about dollar/yen exchange rates. All that will advance now is the rate of knowing, the structure of new immediacies.

We can anticipate calamities of the emerging, accelerating world information systems—sabotage, financial crashes, cultural pillagings, *faux* news stories, entertaining dictators. We must hope that such information disasters occur early and often, so that caution is built into us and into the systems.

While computers probe and imitate the "society of mind," they are also shaping the mind of society. Computers and communications have already blended so far that they are one activity, still without a verb to express what it does. We don't even have a word for the nervous activity in the body—it's not "thinking," "sensing," or "talking." All the chemical and energy activities in a body (or a society) have a word for their sum action—"metabolism"—but there's no equivalent word for the sum of communications in a system. The lack of a word signals a deeper ignorance. We don't know what constitutes healthy communications.

If humans are most distinguished from other organisms by the elaborateness of their communications, then the coming of new levels of world communications implies the arrival of something more than human. Cyborg civilization, maybe, or a cognitive planet. Politics, even more than usual, is lagging well behind the process.

12 THE WORLD INFORMATION ECONOMY

A Nobel Prize is waiting for the person who figures out the economics of information.

—Jay Ogilvy

Curious situation: there is a world economy, but not really a world body politic. That anomaly grows steadily more acute as the metamorphosis of communications technologies accelerates economies worldwide and confuses politics worldwide. Many of the changes are so large we can't see them, but we'll be feeling their effects for fifty years. For the most voluminous form of electronic communication doesn't just earn money, it *is* money.

That picture emerged from a conversation I had with professional world watcher Peter Schwartz while I was at MIT. During a visit to the Media Lab, Schwartz commented that the entire world economic game was changing drastically because of changes in communications technology. You could see it in what was happening with four major areas that were starting to affect everything else. What areas? He held up four fingers: "Finance, electronic entertainment, computers, and telecommunications."

From 1981 to the end of 1986 Schwartz was in London, heading the "Business Environment" section of the strategic planning division of Royal Dutch/Shell, an oil company, one of the world's three largest corporations. (The other two are General Motors and Exxon; each of the three turns about $100 billion annually.) Since Shell has some 160,000 employees in several hundred operating companies in 120 countries, its interests are definitively global. Shell's "business environment" is the contemporary history of the world. In recent years Shell has gotten the reputation of being uniquely right about predicting and preparing for such world-wrenching surprises as the oil price collapse in 1985, and Schwartz is in the middle of that reputation.

The interview was in his hotel room on Harvard Square, Schwartz and I hunched over a table by the window. Resting on Schwartz' bed and occasionally lobbing in comments was Jay Ogilvy, formerly director of research of the Values and Lifestyles Program at SRI International. In 1987 Schwartz and Ogilvy were hired as strategic advisors by the London Stock Exchange to develop scenarios for the future of world finance markets. Both of them clearly take abiding pleasure in thinking about the world's aggregate squirreliness. Schwartz, forty, has a red beard, liquid brown eyes, the politics of a former Peace Corps worker (Ghana), and the articulate rap of someone who has made a lot of "presentations."

□
□ *World Money*
□

■ "This century was shaped by the structure of industrialism," Schwartz began. "A set of rules was enshrined toward the end of the nineteenth century about how life and the world was to be organized. It led to the cities, it led to the kinds of technology we have, it led to the economic structures that we have. They were very deep structural rules that later became organized and never really questioned.

"Now our technology has progressed so that increasingly the wealth-creation process has to do with information instead of with the material manipulations of manufacturing. That is, the value added in the transformation of stuff has to do with our capacity to understand and use information in various ways. If that's the case, then you have to ask yourself, how're the rules of that system going to be written? The way they're going to be written is just in the practical steps that people take.

"The principal information technologies—the means—we're talking about are telecommunications and computing. So what will drive this change? Well, as the manufacture of things like textiles and steel and automobiles were the really driving, organizing structures out of which industrialism emerged, the two great systems that will dominate the new information-rich system are finance and electronic entertainment on a worldwide scale. How finance and electronic entertainment evolve will affect everything else. Technology is like water and follows the path of least resistance; they're the path of least resistance.

"In the case of finance there are three things going on. The markets are becoming global, they interact, which drives globalization further, and they're *huge*. The newest numbers I've seen show that in 1986 international foreign exchange transactions reached $87 trillion. $87 trillion. Twenty-three times the U.S. Gross National Product."

"What's the history of that number?" I asked. A trillion is a million millions.

Schwartz: "Before the '70s it was one, two, three trillion a year, max. It reached $65 trillion in 1985—double the figure for 1984. What happened was a combination of the international volatility of the dollar and the huge outflows of capital from industrialized countries after the first OPEC crisis. Back when the dollar moved a tenth of a penny over three weeks, currency arbitrage was no game to play. But when the dollar moves three or four cents a day, and you've got a billion bucks here, five billion bucks there, there's good reason to move money from Tokyo in the morning to Paris in the afternoon. You're talking really serious money—tens of millions profit absolutely risk-free. Then that process fed on itself and started accelerating."

The *Washington Post* reported in August 1986 about the daily volume of international money exchange transactions: in Tokyo $48 billion a day, New York $50 billion, London $90 billion. Those three markets are so placed that the sun never sets on the wheeling and dealing. A New Yorker can stay up all night and lose his company's shirt in Tokyo before breakfast. Until the early '70s, national governments were able to assure fixed rates of exchange by being the major players in the game. Now the exchange rates float, changing from minute to minute. The *Post* concluded, "With the continuing integration of the world's national economies, exchange rates have joined the list of things that nobody controls."

It is a peculiar kind of economic activity. Schwartz: "That $87 trillion is several times the Gross World Product. It's not trade volumes, it's not physical activity that is driving the value of currencies any longer;

it's this electronic money sloshing around the world in *vast* quantities. Trade is only about ten percent of that $87 trillion; it's trivial. Movement of money itself is the game. The shift is fundamental."

"How consequential is that?"

"Quite consequential." Schwartz' intensity increased another notch. "One, just for the stability of the economy, it's an extremely difficult system to manage. The fluidity and scale of the process are so large that the U.S., which is the biggest economy in the world, represents only five percent of it—not much leverage. Secondly, because of the reversal of the relationship of exchange flows versus trade, the scope for domestic economic management is much less. A country can't just adjust its domestic inflation rates to affect its exchange rate anymore. And third, we don't understand it. At Shell we've just done an analysis on the new kinds of financial instruments—ruffs and swaps and various ways of doing international finance—and what is absolutely clear to me is that it is a system out of control, that nobody really understands.

"People innovate new mechanisms, and these mechanisms are tried, and they're commercially viable—coaggegrating money and reselling it in a different way, and so on—but nobody knows what the consequences of that are. Nobody knows how to regulate that, nobody knows what the meaning of that money is. And every time in history, the thing which precipitated a depression was the collapse of the meaning of money. When these mechanisms evolve that way, completely out of control, there is enormous danger."

"The danger is what?" I wondered. "A worldwide credit collapse?" Phone the bank and nobody answers for a couple of weeks. When they finally do, everything you own has a different value.

Schwartz: "Yeah, that would be a perfect example, and that's quite plausible. The problem is that it could begin in relatively trivial ways and then ripple through the system in ways that people didn't understand. The whole Latin American debt crisis—one of the reasons it occurred was that there was significant 'interbank lending' that was in effect involuntary. There were just mechanisms that had been set up for moving money from here to there, and nobody really questioned it. What was actually happening was a lot of short-term money over the course of two or three months suddenly flowed into Brazil. I mean a few tens of billions of dollars; their debt went from about $60 to $90 billion in six months, and they didn't even know it. Nobody knew it. It just went whoosh. No individual bank could observe it. This bank was lending to that bank to cover this trade credit, to cover that trade credit, and it just began to flow without anybody raising a question.

"Now, I should tell you that I have been worrying about this issue since the late '70s, but a major financial crisis keeps not happening, even though the system has been getting massively more electronic and interconnected that whole time. We're starting to refer to this as 'resilient fragility.' The system appears more fragile than it is. It's often the case that complex systems produce resilience in unpredictable forms—even in unrecognizable forms: you can't find what's producing the resilience even though you're looking for it."

"Presumably," I presumed, "when the system either crashes or conspicuously threatens to crash, then out of that comes the new game and new rules."

"That's exactly what's always happened." Schwartz nodded. "Now this issue is being taken seriously enough by enough policy makers, including the banks and so on, that they're really beginning to think about how you manage this kind of system. It's being addressed by things like the Group of Thirty. The Group of Thirty is the thirty old wise men of the financial system—the former heads of the World Bank and the big private banks and a few economists and so on. They meet from time to time to make pronouncements on the structure of the financial system. The Institute for International Economics, a few of the private banks, are beginning to think about these management questions. But coming back to information technology: finance is not one of the biggest customers of communication services, it is *by FAR* the biggest customer."

I couldn't picture it. "What's the medium of all that transfer of electronic money?"

Schwartz: "Essentially one computer in one location talking to another computer in another location, very very rapidly, in vast volumes of data, over land lines, satellite lines, because it's a twenty-four-hour-a-day game."

It sounded to me like some casino of the gods located high in hyperspace: "Does any of this have anything to do with anything, or is it just speculation on speculation? Where does it connect to the world short of when it crashes?"

Schwartz: "Two ways. One is, it's an activity just like oil or anything else. Wealth is created and activity is generated, and real money is made and lost. But, more importantly, it really determines the conditions of access to capital, it helps set interest rates, it says who's got the money and who doesn't. The basic patterns of trade in terms of access to capital, liquidity, and so on, are profoundly affected by that."

The $87-trillion question: "What's the future?"

Schwartz: "In the United States we have one mechanism, the Federal Reserve Bank, which acts as the overseer of all money in the United States. The federal government says, 'We control the currency, therefore we've got the lever on the system.' That's basically right, and something similar is true for virtually every individual sovereign country in the world. No such mechanism, I think, could exist internationally. Not for a long time to come. Can you imagine a genuine international currency with a body to supervise it, to which sovereign nations willingly give up part of their sovereignty?

"More likely is a far more complex structure, in which you have multiple currencies in some form of complex basket, with the interplay of several large institutions. It might involve an evolution of the current International Monetary Fund, the Bank of International Settlements, and the World Bank, along with the central banks of the three major countries—Germany, Japan, and the United States—all of them forming some kind of relatively tight (not loose, like now) confederation of management. The individual countries would have a lot of influence and so would the individual institutions. That group would establish: (a) exchange-rate regimes, and (b) those criteria that will determine the validity of a country's money—essentially what amounts to credit-worthiness. And that will be quite significant because that will in turn set the global inflation rate."

"This would happen over twenty years, or what?"

Schwartz: "Twenty years at the outside; even as soon as five to ten years. We're beginning to see movement in that direction. The U.S. has just shifted its position drastically. From: absolute opposition to any increased role for the international institutions, and any structure of exchange rates and financial regimes, *at all*—'Free markets rule entirely, and these international institutions are a bunch of commies run by the European socialists and we're not interested in participating.' To: 'Our domestic economy is profoundly affected by the consequences of not playing in that game, so we think it's important that the game is structured appropriately, and we will now play to help structure the game.' That was the shift from Don Regan to Jim Baker at Treasury."

"It sounds like a shift from, 'We don't want to play because it's a fucked game,' to 'We want to play and we want to dominate.' "

Schwartz: "It has not gone that far, but that's the reality. If we don't play, there's no game. If we do play, we're still the biggest gorilla on the block by a *long* way—80 percent of world financial transactions are dollar based. The U.S. is the key player."

There is a global computer. So far it's functioning primarily as a global cash register.

It's fair to say the world financial future is inventing itself without Media Lab participation. On the other hand, Andy Lippman has some ideas about signing checks remotely and establishing identity and preventing forgery electronically. That would have impact: worldwide losses to forgery are said to be $4 billion a year.

On to show biz.

□ *World Entertainment*
□

■ "Electronic entertainment" for Schwartz includes all forms of recorded music and drama—videocassettes, audiocassettes, record albums, CDs, DATs—and all forms of electronic broadcast—television and radio. The field is one he's been close to. He's a friend of musicians such as The Grateful Dead and Peter Gabriel, and he helped shape the script of the 1984 movie "War Games," about a young hacker unwittingly playing an all-too-real Thermonuclear War. ("Interesting game," the computer concluded, "the only way to win is not to play.")

"If you look at the market for electronic entertainment," Schwartz began, "it's overwhelmingly young people. And the demographics of young people in the world are just exploding, particularly in the developing world—China, India, Latin America, Southeast Asia. In Mexico 50 percent of the population is under fifteen.

"Then, you have the changes in the technology of both recording and distribution—VCRs, satellites, CDs, all that stuff the Media Lab is involved in—so the world market is now accessible in a way that it wasn't ten years ago. Thirdly, you now have not only a worldwide market but a worldwide series of sources. The largest film industry in the world is India, by far. The second largest is Hong Kong. The United States is third."

News to me. "That's measuring by what?"

Schwartz: "By any measure—volume of cash, total films made. In India it's mostly by Indians for Indians, but a lot of it is export. Most of it goes to the Third World. You go into a video shop in Lagos, Nigeria, and you will see walls of films, 90 percent of which you've never seen before. They would never be in any video store in the United States. First of all, many are not in English; secondly, they're rotten films; third, most of them are adventure, comedy, love stories, dumb sorts of things— a lot of them are horror or Indian westerns. Indians *love* westerns—there are hundreds and hundreds of Indian cowboy movies. Indian Indians playing American Indians, and Indian Indians playing American cowboys, speaking, of course, Hindi."

"How much of the stuff coming out of India and Hong Kong is in English?" I asked.

Schwartz: "An overwhelming amount. If they want to get an international market they have to do it in English. Then they are able to sell almost anywhere, and people can dub or put in subtitles. As I've heard the numbers—this is from the British Film Board, so take it with a grain of salt—something like 60 percent of all films worldwide are in English."

"The language of science is the language of entertainment," I mused. Two successive English-speaking world empires, British and American, the first truly planetary empires, had a life span covering the building of rapid (later instant) world communications. Their legacy is a world language. Most people's second language is English. One by-product is that people whose first language is English increasingly have no second language at all, which narrows their minds. California recently declared

English to be its "official language," enforceably so—rather cheeky in a state whose constitution was originally written in Spanish and English.

Schwartz: "You go to Eastern Europe and hear rock bands, and they sing perfect English, even though they don't understand a word. There's a rock band I know of in Hungary called Locomotiv GT—the biggest rock band in Hungary. They're flawless English speakers because they know if they want to get *any* kind of market outside of Hungary, or even inside, they have to do it in English.

"One of the interesting things that the British have not yet picked up on is that this could be their salvation. They've got this English-language advantage, and they have an *incredible* talent pool in entertainment. But all the big British movies that you've seen recently were made with American money. 'Gandhi' was American money, 'Chariots of Fire' was American money. Almost none of the money on either of those two Academy Award winners was made in Britain. The British see this as trivial. They're interested in saving their automobile industry; they're not interested in feeding their entertainment industry. Here the world is *hungry* for English-language entertainment. . . . God, if Britain decided to get on a roll with this and really put some money behind it. . . . You know where the best special effects facilities in the world are? Britain. You know where studio work for 'Star Wars' was done? A studio outside of London. It wasn't done in Hollywood."

I asked, "With American electronic entertainment, how much of the market is overseas?"

Schwartz: "Something like 35 percent of the video revenue from American films now is outside the U.S. It's quite substantial. You figure that the U.S. film industry is about $9 billion a year, half from the box office, half from VCRs."

Time magazine reported in June 1986 that five of the top ten music singles in England at the time were by black American musicians, two-fifths of France's box-office receipts went to American movies, most of the forty-seven radio stations in Lima, Peru, played American music, and ten of sixteen movie theaters in Nairobi, Kenya, had American films.

Ogilvy commented from the bed, "So far as I can see, the U.S. can't win for losing. On the one hand we are number one players in the game and everybody wants our stuff, and on the other hand the more we put it out there, the more we're accused of cultural imperialism. There's no winning that."

Schwartz picked up the original argument: "The point is, there's this vast entertainment business going on that we don't even see. It's extremely profitable and also very fluid. A lot of the communications infrastructure that will be linking things is going to be a function of what finance wants on the one hand, and what the electronic entertainment media want on the other. Everything else will in a sense be piggybacked on that. The rules for satellite allocation, for bandwidth allocation, for regulatory structures, how one makes money, how you put together finance, and so on, will be focussed around those two industries.

"It's just like how oil became the dominant medium of the international transfer of energy, and that set the international energy price. Then the gas business, the coal business, the nuclear business all had to conform to what the oil industry did, intentionally or unintentionally, by way of structuring the game.

"An economist in Paris, Albert Bressand, says there was the world oil shock in the '70s, the world banking shock in the '80s, and we can expect a world information shock in the '90s. It will come when the information providers decide to revalue what they produce, and that attempt, however it turns out, will change the game."

While a hardware manufacturer like Kobayashi at NEC applauds the coming of the information age, urging on higher information flows and cheaper costs for ever more valuable information, "software" manufacturers like Hollywood and the music industry feel control and money slipping away. They are bound to try to grab them back. But how? Schwartz figured they would do the same as the oil companies and try for vertical integration—own the whole process from oil discovery to gas tank, from writer to theater seat or TV set or headphone. There is indeed a lot of that going on already as Hollywood studios buy up VCR rental shops, theaters, television stations, even a "fourth" television network (FBC—Fox Broadcasting Company). Schwartz: "There will be some cottage industry companies that produce films like 'A Room with a View,' but the main films will be produced by great production machines that turn out endless variations on themes—'Cobra 17,' 'Rocky 42.' "

But integration by itself probably couldn't produce a world-jarring "Information Shock." Schwartz wondered if some kind of technological gatekeeping might do it—if everything were funneled through tightly controlled supersatellites, say. I thought that fiberoptic cable would be a likelier gatekeeper medium, especially if the Media Lab was successful in hooking people on sensorily rich, highly interactive entertainment forms that wanted a lot of bandwidth. Schwartz thought that computer-intelligent "ticket-takers" might emerge that could extract income from information flows with great subtlety and reliability. We both predicted that the emergence of widely agreed communications standards would make gatekeeping more possible. Neither of us could imagine a really complete lock on commercial information ever being achieved.

Nations haven't succeeded in controlling information in the new media environments. Why should companies?

☐☐ *Fading Nations*

■ In Anthony Smith's *The Geopolitics of Information* is a remarkable statement:

> The whole history of the nation as a political unit of mankind has been predicated upon territoriality; the technology of printing came into being in the same era as the nation-state and both seem to be reaching the end of their usefulness in the era of the computer; it is physically impossible to impose upon data the same kinds of controls that are imposed upon goods and paper-borne information, though the world will inevitably continue to try to do so for some years. . . .
>
> The problem is simply that there is no room in the long run for conflicting information doctrines within a world which is becoming increasingly interconnected.

That observation from 1980 is corroborated by Peter Schwartz' recent studies.

One commercial phenomenon that fascinated the strategic planners at Shell was the world success of the Italian clothing chain Benetton. Schwartz: "They're *staggeringly* successful. Benetton really operates as if there's a kind of world uniform. There's a sort of 'color of the week,' and because of the media, that color sweeps the world very quickly. There must be five or six thousand Benetton shops worldwide. You walk into one and you'll see the same colors and designs you would find in any Benetton shop anywhere in the world on that day. The colors will change by next week. Benetton's computer analysis shows what is selling in terms of type, price, and color of every Benetton item all over the world, every day. They dye 15 percent of their colors every day on the basis of the information they get that day."

I opined, "It sounds like fashion is an electronic entertainment medium that operates on a very tight feedback loop. So does world news. How well does news get around?"

Schwartz: "Now we get into one of the most interesting public policy debate issues—the control of the flow of information, including news. The question is, will there be technical mechanisms by which governments can prevent information from flowing across their borders? Clearly governments outside of the United States, with almost no exceptions, reserve unto themselves the right to determine what their citizens will see. This is true for Britain, I might add."

I wondered, "Is that one shifting at all? Do other countries see the U.S. as just being crazy continually, or do people see a free press as having some corrections built into it?"

Schwartz: "No, I think most of the world still believes it is appropriate for the government to control what people will know. It's really quite amazing—to me at least, having grown up in the United States. Regimes nearly everywhere are—a term which is not well known in the United States—*dirigiste*. French word. Literally, it means state direction. It isn't socialism, it isn't fascism, it's essentially the idea that part of the central role of the state is to direct society—as opposed to take care of a few things and let everybody else take care of themselves, which is the U.S. philosophy. Most every other country in the world is in some sense *dirigiste*.

"The debate is always in these terms: 'If we permit private media, even if people like it, and it competes successfully with our state media, we may be degrading the quality of our public. They will be getting poorer information, less culture, less of the things which they ought to have.' The debate in Britain right now, for example, is: is independent television pulling down the BBC, which is supposed to be the flagship of high quality news and so on? Everybody is saying, 'Oh, BBC news has deteriorated to compete with ITV news, and, gee, maybe we should cut ITV news and not permit them to do certain things so we can preserve the BBC.' That sort of debate goes on in France, in Italy, in Holland. Commercial success does not guarantee further growth."

Ogilvy piped up from the bed, "Say something about transborder data flows."

Schwartz: "That's a huge issue. For example, Shell is not permitted as a company to ship computer data to Brazil. And we're not allowed to take computer data out of Brazil. We cannot establish a communication link between our computer in Britain and a computer in Brazil, because they want to be able to control what we send down that line. The result in various places in the world, as you would expect, is that there's a huge subculture of illegal phone lines and intermediaries running trucks across national borders carrying cans of data tapes."

"What does all this do to politics?" I asked. "Will the governments get more control or less?"

Schwartz: "I think inescapably less. They can push against the river a bit, but it's an incredibly powerful river that's coming at them. They can channel it a bit, but not completely. The kids are going to listen to rock 'n' roll. People are going to watch 'Dallas' no matter what."

Hmm. Maybe we're already seeing the first effects of the restructuring that Schwartz is predicting from world electronic entertainment. You could make a case that there is a worldwide loosening of communication controls going on. In China students have demonstrated for a freer press. In the U.S.S.R. a top dissident like Sakharov was permitted a public hearing (via Voice of America, deliberately unjammed that night). In Italy, France, Spain, West Germany, and Britain, television is being opened up to more private ownership, and advertising is beginning to take off, along with its customary freeing and, in some eyes, degrading of program content. Even strait-laced Indian television has discovered advertising and the allure of popular soap opera programming. There is talk in Europe of broadcasting shows Europe-wide simultaneously in a number of languages, and interest there has revived in direct satellite TV broadcasting, which ignores national boundaries. In late 1986 the America-based firm of BBDO negotiated the first major deal in global advertising—Gillette paid millions to media baron Rupert Murdoch for TV time in seventeen countries on three continents.

If that trend continues, what effect would it have on generations growing up in a denationalized entertainment environment? Schwartz: "We've spent a lot of time talking about the role of information and computing in education, but by far the dominant curriculum in education today does not take place 8 a.m. to 3 p.m., it's 4 p.m. to midnight, when the kids watch television at home. Actually the teaching time at school is probably only about four hours. They've got seven hours later on of much higher quality (in the sense of access to communications), much more potent information, which completely overwhelms anything they get in the classroom. The second-order consequence is in some sense like what we were talking about with the inversion of trade and finance. Electronic entertainment will be the dominant educational medium that will shape global consciousness."

Global consciousness is not everybody's idea of a good thing. Apart from the draining of national sovereignty inherent in the global cash register, there is the threat of the global jukebox and the global movie projector weakening cultural identities worldwide. Nothing, apart from physical home turf, is as ferociously defended as a group's unique sense of who it is and what constitutes right behavior. But the means of physical defense of territory are well known; the means of electronic communication defense have to be invented while the damage is being done, and all the skilled inventors work for the invaders.

A Spanish ecologist, Ramón Margalef, wrote in 1968 after a lifetime of observing the transactions between ecological subsystems, "It is a basic property of nature, from the point of view of cybernetics, that any exchange between two systems of different information content does not result in a partition or equalizing of the information, but increases the difference. The system with more accumulated information becomes still richer from the exchange." In terms not just economic, the rich get richer and the poor get poorer. That imbalance is exactly what Seymour Papert and Negroponte were trying to redress when they worked at the World Center for Personal Computation and Human Development in Paris. Their personalizing technology showed promise; the institution failed (it finally closed its doors in 1986).

Different cultures will defend themselves in different ways. Some will join the game, exporting their own music (Jamaica), or finer films (Australia), or cheaper, high volume films (Hong Kong), or snazzier equipment (Japan, Taiwan, South Korea). Some will build high, fierce walls against electronic invasion with tight political controls, and pay the price of isolation. Some will lie low and let it all pass over them. Some will be flattened. The world will continue to be a patchwork of different communication regimes, but the sheer traffic will erode everyone.

In 1985 a vice president at Hewlett-Packard, Charles House, put the following message online to a group of corporate executives with whom he was teleconferencing on the subject of global scarcity and abundance:

> We were in Guaymas, Mexico, several weeks ago, riding through a small poverty-stricken area with a guy from Chicago. He was busy denigrating the area, "Who could stand to live here, you wouldn't know anything about the world, it is so squalid, etc." I was busy taking pictures of houses perhaps 25 feet square with a 1954 Chevy pickup in the driveway and a satellite dish on the roof. An area of perhaps 1,000 people, with about 50 satellite dishes!
>
> He said, "What do those dishes do, anyway?" I said, well, these people can get 130 TV channels from at least seven nations in five languages, and in addition they can get sub-carrier FM stereo. In other words, they have Quebec, Venezuela, Mexico City, all of America, BBC, and even Japan occasionally; and they get the Chicago Symphony as clearly as you do.
>
> He was stunned. Then he said, "What do they think when they see all that, and they look at this, where they live?" And I was silent, and my wife was silent, and he was silent.

The way things are shaping up, Third World nations are likely to get communications primarily by satellite while the affluent nations are being wired with fiberoptic cable. Audiences of satellites will be more passive recipients of more attenuated signals, because satellites are almost entirely one-way traffic: down. Fiberoptic audiences could be more interactive, in Media Lab terms, with much richer signals. The passive might be made more passive, the active more active, in full view of each other. That could be a recipe for violence. New communications technologies are political dynamite.

As the significance of territoriality fades, and nations fade, what will be the new grain of variety?

☐☐ *The Global City*

■ Marshall McLuhan declared that the world is in the process of becoming a "global village." His theory was that visual literacy fragmented humanity into specialties which collected in cities, but all that would be reversed by the "tribal drum" of electronic communications, and village-style connectivity would return on a planetary scale.

The image reflects his theory accurately, but it bears no resemblance to the actual experience of global connectivity, which is utterly urban. The world's villages remain wonderfully various and distinct; the world's cities are more alike every year. They are so intensely linked with each other that they increasingly act, and look, like boroughs of one large city which is situated everywhere and nowhere.

One creation of the supercity is the multinational corporation, which was only made possible, Peter Schwartz claims, by international telephone service and the jet airplane. While nations fade, the world corporations are increasing robustly, many of them now larger in financial terms than many nations. The world supercity is not the capital of anything, except itself.

Global transactions are not conducted at a leisurely rural or even suburban pace but on the schedule depicted by the Texan phrase for haste: "in a hot New York minute." The pace of cities and the pace of computers were made for each other. "What I want, I want now." Computers deliver in milliseconds.

It's interesting that we have no *sense* of this new configuration, beyond perhaps the kaleidoscope of images on the evening news. Harlan Cleveland, the head of the Hubert Humphrey Institute of Public Affairs in Minnesota, encountered the dearth in a graphic way, which he reported by e-mail to a group I was working with:

> I have wanted for some time to find a map of information flows around the world. The other day I had an hour to kill between appointments in New York City, so I dropped into the Rand-McNally map store and asked for such a map. My request created quite a stir, and virtually every employee was called into consultation. They brought out all sorts of maps showing flows of food and feedgrains, oil and coal, weapons and manufactures—but finally admitted that they had no map of information flows and didn't think their competitors had one either.

One would want such a map to be animated, depicting the flows in time series, showing where are the ebbs over time and where the floods and where the ancient streambeds, and how rapidly the torrent is growing. Other maps could show what is borne on the currents: what *kinds* of information are increasing, decreasing, blending? Are there emergent phenomena in massive information flows, perhaps the communication equivalents of tides or turbulence or vaporization?

The science fiction writer William Gibson (*Neuromancer* and *Count Zero*) imagines that all who live by computers will one day commingle in a jointly created virtual reality—"mankind's unthinkably complex consensual hallucination, the matrix, cyberspace, where the great corporate hotcores burned like neon novas, data so dense you suffered sensory overload if you tried to apprehend more than the merest outline."

Whether or not it ever becomes that hallucinatory, the supercity can be a handy place to live as well as do business. You can park anywhere. Science fiction writer Arthur C. Clarke told *Video Review*, "I've lived in Sri Lanka for thirty years, but I don't know if I could have remained here and kept up with current technological developments these past ten years without my computers, satellite-dish TV and home-video gear. They keep me in touch with the world." (He *should* have a dish. He invented communication satellites. Some are calling the geosynchronous orbit where those satellites reside the Clarke Belt.) Urbanity no longer has anything to do with proximity to tall buildings.

In America AT&T is being successfully pressured to provide "English-equivalent" phone service for Spanish speakers and two Asian languages still being determined. Dial a certain number, and you can do absolutely anything in your own language that you could do in English. The supercity, if it's a good city, will attract and preserve ethnic groups, including ones far removed from their home territory. As nations fade, cultural mythologies may increase in intensity to maintain humanity's requisite variety.

Work in the computerized global city will not be like work in the cities that industrialism created. Schwartz and Ogilvy waded into that one. Like McLuhan, they expect that the idea and practice of "jobs" will diminish.

Ogilvy sat up on the bed: "I'll give you an example of the kind of thing you might be getting at, under the rubric of 'form follows function'—Drucker's argument about the form of the modern corporation following the function of the reproduction of standardized, replaceable parts in manufacturing. So you get the bureaucratic corporations where all the lathe operators have to be doing the same thing, and therefore men have to be telling the same thing to their vice presidents.

"But what if the function is no longer chung-chung-chung standardization producing the same-same-same? If the function is the production of information—and the definition of information is 'a difference that makes a difference'—you're not doing the same-same-same anymore. Now you're turning out a different different difference, because if it's not different, it's not information."

Schwartz: "I'll give you a concrete example. Financial services. How do you compete among banks? The difference is in offering differential service, and the way they get that differential service in theory is how they manipulate and manage information. The perfect example was how

Merrill Lynch stole a market by creating the cash management account (SRI invented it for them). That became an intrinsic, though invented, value within the system. 'Jobs' go fluid in that kind of environment. I think it's a bit more like game players in an elaborately shifting set of games.

"You can see it in the oil industry in the shift of power from the people who find and produce and refine oil to the traders. Producing oil is basically industrial, and all its values are industrial values—things like economies of scale, for example. Trading—everything is information flows, speed of reaction, differences that make a difference, 'I know something you don't know.' Increasingly the game in the oil business is trading. We're going to see that as the driving force in a number of industries. So where before the engineer was the hero that drove the company, now he's a functionary necessary to produce oil that the trader can really make some money with."

"Like the farmer," I said.

"Exactly. Farmers don't make much money, but the commodity brokers sure do."

I pursued it: "Farmers pretty much stay in one place. Commodity brokers slither around?"

Schwartz: "Yeah, a lot, because of course what traders look for is information, and they travel to find it. Another reason is, the money is so big. A successful trader can get such a huge premium that people are constantly offering them vast amounts of money to move, and it happens all the time. Whereas a petroleum engineer's pretty much a petroleum engineer."

Not all that encouraging a picture. It suggests that farming, oil producing, manufacturing will be turned over to robots, after considerable pain among people who live by those lines of work, and the pillars of civilization—even more than now—will be people who live by their deals. That really could build a vast consensual hallucination from which the waking up would be no picnic.

Schwartz expects ten years or so of turbulence followed by a new stability. World birthrates, except for Africa, are plummeting, so demographic patterns should stabilize about the turn of the century. He expects a new communications infrastructure, shaped by finance and electronic entertainment, to eventually settle down as new increments of change don't offer that much new advantage and there's more to be gained from refining the existing structure. Also, no doubt, stability will look attractive after a decade of turbulence.

I asked, "So the decisions that are made now we're going to live with for forty years?"

Schwartz: "Or a half-century. That's why I think this game is so interesting right now. These rules are just being written, and not in a conscious way."

Ogilvy added, "What gets me is how utterly inappropriate our basic economic categories are. We need to recast the concept of property, for one thing, because in Marx's terms property is by definition *alienable:* that is, unlike your elbow, which is you and not yours, property must be transferable to another (*alia* equals other). I sell you the cow. You got the cow. I don't have the cow anymore. I sell you information. You got the information. I still have the information. That's one anomaly. Another anomaly: intrinsic in information is the 'difference that makes a difference'—*to a receiver.* So the condition of the receiver is an important part of whether a given signal is or is not information. Is it news or isn't it news? Well, that depends on the receiver and the receiver's ability to understand it. That's not true of a ton of steel. It's not true of a ton of wheat. A third anomaly is the notion of depreciation, the very notion of inventory—information doesn't depreciate the way physical things do."

I said, "Depreciation of news is instant."

Schwartz said, "But something like 'Gone with the Wind' doesn't depreciate, it *appreciates.* 'Gone with the Wind' is worth much more today than it was when it was made."

Schwartz is right: we don't understand the game we're playing. I'm not so sure he's right that the game will settle down. With a world economy and no world body politic, it could be that upheaval in world communications will continue to accelerate at exactly the rate of technology growth. The world economy of the past ninety years did not suffer prolonged accelerations, but it was not primarily an information economy. Engines without governors rev up and explode; economies without theories may do the same. The structure of the world information economy is being determined by traffic rather than policy in part because there's no world body politic, in part because there's no workable theory of what's happening.

The wired world is a teenager with a new car, taking dumb risks, finding new freedoms. It's a privilege to be around self-discovery like that, but grueling, and sometimes tragic.

13 QUALITY OF LIFE

What needs to be articulated, regardless of the format of the
man-machine relationship, is the goal of humanism through
machines.

—Nicholas Negroponte

Communications technologies converge at the world
and at the individual. The Media Lab assumes that if it helps take care
of the individual, computer-augmented individuals will take better care
of the world. The Lab would cure the pathologies of communications
technology not with economics or politics but with technology. That's
the underlying goal of every Lab project this book explored, as well as
ones it did not explore.

When Nicholas Negroponte and I originally discussed what this
book might be about, he suggested, "It's about quality of life in an
electronic age." A few months later he added, "It's a primer for a new
life-style." Later still he mentioned, "I was still in my pajamas at ten-
thirty this morning after I had been doing Lab work, through e-mail on
my computer, for several hours. Maybe what we're talking about is 'The
right to stay in your pajamas.' "

Run that image as a film clip—the director of the Media Lab rising
from the dark-finished thirteenth-century canopy bed that he and his
wife, Elaine, found in the south of France for a few hundred dollars,
mumbling good morning to their touchy bulldog, Piccadilly, flipping on
a Macintosh computer on the way to the shower, rotating in the hot
water blasted from the five shower heads while listening to a shower
speaker rinse him with the morning news, strolling back by the Macintosh
to see if any e-mail is particularly urgent, then heading for tea in the
kitchen that Elaine's *faux* work has made a place of rich marble and

trompe l'oeil non-doors, then back to the computer for a few hours of pajama-clad work.

This is not the picture from E. M. Forster's "The Machine Stops" of the compulsive communicator in her tiny standard cell. Negroponte cherishes and encourages individual eccentricity, and so does most of the work at the Media Laboratory. He told one corporate audience, "Some of us enjoy a privileged existence where our work life and our leisure life are almost synonymous. More and more people I think can move into that position with the coming of truly intimate technology, a fully integrated electronic presence for everybody."

A classic piece of handwaving.

□ *Personal Renaissance*
□

■ Is there any reason to believe that Personal Television, Personal Newspaper, Conversational Desktop, access to an infinite library of Electronic Publishing, a Vivarium of one's own, and a fiberoptic connection to a Connection Machine would encourage Personal Renaissance?

There is. We have already seen the arrival of personal computers make multitudes broader in their skills and interests, less passive, less traditionally role-bound. That's renaissance. We've seen people use VCRs to stop being jerked around by the vagaries of network scheduling, build libraries of well-loved films, and make their own videos. We've seen satellite dishes by the quasi-legal million employed to break the urban monopoly on full-range entertainment. None of those effects were predicted except by a fanatic few. The success of each of the technologies— personal computers, VCRs, and backyard dishes—came as an unwelcome surprise to industry market researchers.

Each violated what was known about audiences. No wonder. Each made audiences into something else—less "a group of spectators, listeners, or readers" and more a society of selectors, changers, makers. The same revolution Seymour Papert is fostering in the schools, to free the kids from deadening passivity by giving them computer power, has been going on at home with similar tools.

Another place to look for evidence is in the fifteen years of e-mail and computer teleconference usage that began with the ARPAnet which linked all the major computer research centers in the early '70s (inspired and paid for, of course, by DARPA). My experience with the medium is that e-mail creates writers. I've seen dozens of professional writing careers begun with total inadvertence by people chatting away online, being encouraged by their friends, then being quoted in print somewhere, then getting paid for it, and then they're hooked. Because their writing began as conversation, it's good writing. The magic ingredient is instant reinforcement by peers. Every time you say something useful cleverly online, somebody says "Bravo."

Marshall McLuhan used to remark, "Gutenberg made everybody a reader. Xerox made everybody a publisher." Personal computers are making everybody an author. E-mail, word-processing programs that make revising as easy as thinking, and laser printers collapse the whole writing-publishing-distributing process into one event controlled entirely by the individual. If, as alleged, the only real freedom of the press is to own one, the fullest realization of the First Amendment is being accomplished by technology, not politics.

Ithiel de Sola Pool reveled in what electronic publishing is doing to books:

> One change that computers seem likely to cause is a decline of canonical texts produced in uniform copies. In some ways this change will signal a return in print to the style of the manuscript, or even to ways of oral conversation. . . . A small subculture of computer scientists who write and edit on data networks like the ARPAnet foreshadow what is to come. One person types out comments at a terminal and gives colleagues on the network access to the comments. As each person copies, modifies, edits, and expands the text, it changes from day to day. With each change, the text is stored somewhere in a different version. . . .
>
> Computer-based textbooks may exist in as many variants as there are teachers. . . . Each teacher will create a preferred version, which will be changed repeatedly over the years. Or in a literature or drama course one exercise might be to take a text and try to improve it. Reading thus becomes active and interactive.

Pool worried that this will make computer access to the world's literature extremely problematic, because the literature won't hold still. Perhaps CD ROMs storing vast quantities of text unchangeably will solve that problem.

Asian cultures that rely on ideographic writing have been hampered by the sheer richness of their character alphabets—Chinese has more than 50,000 characters, for example. Over half of the fax machines in the world are in Japan, used to send ideograph messages graphically rather than through the hard labor of keyboards. But Koji Kobayashi notes in *Computers and Communications* that an intelligent new generation of word processors has "the possibility of breathing new life into Japanese culture. . . . The recent development of the word processor can be said to have profound cultural and historical significance similar to the invention of Japanese *kana* about 1,000 years ago, which in fact triggered the spread of the Japanese language from the nobles to the entire nation."

Newsweek reported in August 1986:

At a linguistic symposium in Tokyo in May, delegates from several Asian countries . . . proposed the development of a "new character culture" in which ideograms would serve, in effect, as a lingua franca for most of East Asia. The Chinese-character renaissance has begun, and it promises to change the very fabric of Asian cultural and economic life. This linguistic revival has been sparked by recent innovations in word-processing technology, which have produced computers that write, reproduce and transmit Chinese-character texts much as their Romanized-language counterparts do.

That's not just computer-enhanced individuality, it's computer-enhanced uniqueness of culture. Negroponte is waving his hands in the right direction.

We have only another decade or so of carrying on about computers as the big new bad/good thing. They're about to disappear from view the way motors did. Engines were cause for wonder and speculation when they ran ships and railroads. Nobody called the automobile or truck a personal railroad, but that's what it was, and people still were impressed.

Then motors got smaller and disappeared into lawn mowers, refrigerators, toothbrushes, wristwatches, and nobody (except nanotechnologists) speculates now about what motors will become or worries much about what they are doing to human dignity or economic inequality. Special-purpose microprocessors are burrowing into nearly everything from skyscrapers to humans (in pacemakers, organ implants, prostheses, so far).

Technology marches on, over you or through you, take your pick. The Media Lab is committed to making the individual the driver of new information technology rather than the driven. It does so by focusing on "idiosyncratic systems" that adapt to the user, by encouraging computation in real time and communication out of real time. Computation in real time means the human can interact live, "converse" with the machine, oblige it to function in human terms. Thus the push at the Lab for real-time computer animation, holography, and speech interpretation.

Communication out of real time, as with Personal Television and the Conversational Desktop and Electronic Publishing, means the individual human schedule prevails over the institutional. "Prime time becomes my time." VCR time-shifters have already discovered that one. E-mail and a smart telephone can handle your message traffic at your convenience, unchained from a 9-to-5 office.

A surprising amount of readiness for such apparatus is in place. The third-largest purchase that Americans make is for home entertainment equipment (first is the home, second is the cars). Banks are beginning to make Home Entertainment Loans. People have learned to run complex electronic entertainment equipment, and they're getting used to replacing it periodically with new generations of gear. If they do office work, they're becoming skilled computer jockeys, and the personal computer has already blurred the distinction between home and office (also between home and school).

Russell Neuman at the Media Lab predicts that only 10 percent of people will use home entertainment equipment interactively, and those only 10 percent of the time. The Lab is well served by a house conservative on these matters, but I'll bet he's wrong on this one. My researcher, Deborah Wise, discovered that "In 1900 Mercedes-Benz did a study that estimated that worldwide demand for cars would not exceed one million, primarily because of the limitation of available chauffeurs." Passenger passivity was an assumed constant. Wise added, "In 1908 the Model T democratized the motor car. By 1920 there were 8 million Model T's in America."

The imagined necessity of a chauffeur was based on two assumptions: one, that only people who could afford chauffeurs could afford automobiles; two, that driving a horseless carriage would take as much expertise as driving a horsed carriage. Both of those were correct, but only for a brief time. Likewise now with interactive high tech for the home. Very powerful electronic devices are becoming steadily cheaper, easier to use, and more rewarding. Computerized chauffeurs are being built in.

However: new freedoms, new dependencies.

We can exteriorize much of our information and habits into these machines, but then what happens? Negroponte is bullied by his digital wristwatch. He complained to me, "There's too much data in it. It's got phone numbers in it, telex numbers, credit card numbers. I can't buy a new watch, and I hate this one. It's not pretty, it certainly doesn't go with a dinner jacket, but I wear it anyway. If I forget it, it's a major disaster. I am the prisoner of this watch. That seems to be symptomatic of a larger phenomenon as things become increasingly intelligent. One has to worry about their intercommunication, which nobody's worried about so far. I should be able to change watches, and this watch would tell the other watch everything it knows, but there is no International Watch Protocol Standard yet." Sure enough, a few days later his watch battery ran down and the data evaporated; he was information-crippled for weeks.

Programming these machines to match one's habits and preferences can be tiresome, but it's also usefully revealing. It forces you to be conscious about everything you would like the machine to do, which can be an opportunity to change habits while your mind is on them. Once the machines are programmed, you can be unconscious again and do what they're knowing, probably more, better, and easier than before, but in time you will upgrade to a new machine, and that is an ordeal exactly the equivalent of moving house. When I mentioned to Jerome Wiesner that I was shifting my work environment from one kind of personal computer to another, he commiserated, "I think that nobody should have to learn a new machine after the age of twenty-seven." It's not just what you have to learn, it's what you have to teach the machine. More powerful machines require more teaching. That's something the Media Lab would like to reverse: more powerful machines should be able to learn from you on their own.

There's another threat in the coming of beautiful high-definition television and Personal Television that selects only stuff it knows you will love. "Imagine what it would be like if TV actually were good," Marvin Minsky warned. "It would be the end of everything we know." We viewers could easily advance from the condition of couch potato to couch fungus. Some religious group that works hard and forbids watching television, like the Amish, would take over.

Personal renaissance is not guaranteed by Media Lab technology, but computerized personal hell isn't either. People will try each, as usual, explore all the addictive possibilities, and the survivors will post warning signs at some of the gateways. I share Minsky's belief in sloppy corrective programming: don't fix the bug, just put in some code that notices when it's about to happen and head it off.

Negroponte posted one sign of a wrong direction for intimate technology in *The Architecture Machine*. He quoted a parody of conversation with a computer that was printed in the August 1967 issue of *Datamation*, by B. W. Boehm:

PROFESSOR: What time is it?

COMPUTER: I did not catch the last word. Or was it two words?

PROFESSOR: What is the time?

COMPUTER The dime is a copper coin worth one-tenth of a dollar. The word derives from the Latin decem, meaning . . .

PROFESSOR: No, no. What is the time? The time?

COMPUTER: It is 8:30 p.m., Thursday, December 5, 1985. We have been having some trouble with your linguals recently. Sometimes I can't tell your d's from your t's. Let's practice them. Watch the display screen for the intonation pattern, and repeat after me: "Teddy's daddy toted two dead toads to Detroit."

PROFESSOR: Teddy's daddy toted. . . .

That category of offense Negroponte called "unethical robots." Designing *ethical* robots is a long and interesting problem. We have enough trouble designing ethical human beings. Maybe practicing on robots will help.

And never discount the technical fix. A lip-reading computer would do better. So would a semantically astute one that could infer what the professor wanted.

But how do you fix problems that are too big to see?

☐
☐ *Communication Ecologists*

■ The human communication environment has acquired biological complexity and planetary scale, but there are no scientists or activists monitoring it, theorizing about its health, or mounting campaigns to protect its resilience. Perhaps it's too new, too large to view as a whole, or too containing—we swim in a sea of information, in poet Gary Snyder's phrase. All the more reason to worry. New things have nastier surprises, big things are hard to change, and containing things are inescapable.

We don't know yet how ignorant we are. The metaphor "ecologists of communications" may itself be misleading. If preservation is an issue, for example, it's a different kind of preservation than the ecological mandate of preserving existing habitat. It may be more a question, in the fast-moving communications world, of preserving *options*—room for individuals, cultures, technologies, and communication regimes to adapt.

Does the idea of "toxic information" mean anything? One can immediately imagine condemning pornography or enemy propaganda as toxic, pollution, contamination! We already do. Yet pornography keeps turning up wholesomely in the robust growth of new technologies like VCRs, e-mail, and instant photography. And what shall one do about enemy ecologists who regard our propaganda as toxic? Two centuries of lively experience with the practice of free speech and press in America suggests that most information that might be considered toxic can be handled by the public kidneys. Yelling "Fire!" in a crowded theater (unless there's a fire) has proven toxicity, however. There's insufficient time to sort out the truth of the matter before serious harm is done; could that happen in the crowded theater of world communications? Inevitably. The advanced technologies of information are equally the technologies of disinformation.

I'd like to see some enterprising Media Lab student fabricate an utterly persuasive video of the President of the United States—his worried face, his forceful voice—giving a broadcast beginning, "This nation is at war. . . ." There's a thesis in it, as they say. Produce the terrible lie; show it around; then think about it. Preventive maintenance begins with the question, "What's the worst that could happen?" We haven't begun to ask.

I'd also like to see Minsky's idea realized of a visiting professorship at the Media Lab for science fiction writers, funded perhaps by a George Lucas or a Steven Spielberg or a Hollywood studio. Communications technologies want rigorous, dramatic speculation about where they might be going and where they might go wrong.

We don't know how badly our metaphors fail us. When I started this book project I was planning to compare the sudden wiring of the world to the folding of the cerebral neocortex that made the human brain. The notion is an old and common one. In 1817 Senator John C. Calhoun declared, "The mail and the press are the nerves of the body politic." Marshall McLuhan wrote of the "global network that has much of the character of our central nervous system. Our central nervous system is not merely an electric network, but it constitutes a single unified field of experience." He was wrong about that. The "society of mind" takes great pains to divide experience into workable fragments opaque to each other.

I still thought that the importance of structure in the brain was a usable metaphor when I interviewed MIT neurophysiologist Jerome Lettvin for supporting data. He was as supportive to me as he was to the freshman connectionist Danny Hillis. "Let me tell you how bad it gets," he said quietly. "There was a case at one of the hospitals here just a few months ago that has scared the hell out of everyone. It was the leader of a motorcycle gang, a good talker. You don't become head of a gang without having some talents. Wild guy. He died in an accident. His brain came to autopsy. The cortex was completely unorganized. It was roughly the kind of uncorrugated cortex you find in a whale or a dolphin. It was not a human cortex in any sense. All of the lamination that we have so carefully documented—none of it was there." Lettvin went on with other anomalies: cut into a spinal cord and reduce pain, cut a little further, pain returns; a tadpole had its brain surgically rotated left to right, the frog functioned fine; a torn-off cricket leg can sense and position itself above an acid bath—how does it have position sense? "It is not that these are exceptions that demonstrate that there's a rule," he concluded. "These are exceptions that destroy anything that you care to say."

Okay, the world communication system is not a nervous system. The major similarity they have is that nobody knows how either one really works. "Global consciousness" not only doesn't work politically, it doesn't work as a metaphor. We can stop creating the Earth in our own image. It is something far more alien and interesting than that. Even more of a frontier than Hillis's Connection Machine is the connection machine of the world. Come to think of it, that metaphor may be more workable. Alan Kay, Marvin Minsky, and Danny Hillis are interested in modeling ecologies on the Connection Machine; maybe they could generate some connectionist ecologists along the way who can help look at world communication problems.

They could examine, for instance, the problem of narrow-minded robots in the global cash register. World stock markets, especially the highly electronic American markets, are showing new levels of extreme volatility because institutional investors' computers are investing mindlessly when triggered by certain formulaic combinations of events. In the minute-to-minute environment of financial markets a trend, even a random perturbation, can turn into a meaningless avalanche. As Peter Schwartz describes it, "The behavior of the market is driven by the behavior of the market," which is all that the robot investors are watching. But if you're in financial markets in a big way, you *have* to have robot investors to keep up with the hectic pace set by everybody else's robot investors. Question: do we just debug the robots until they work better, or do we set up some bigger computer as traffic cop, or do we enforce a slower pace so humans are still in the loop? (Global weaponry has been facing similar problems.)

This is part of a general problem of robots. They usually only know about things that they have been told about. In 1986 a huge and worrisome absence of ozone was discovered over the South Pole. The *International Herald Tribune* reported, "NASA scientists found that the depletion of ozone was so severe that the computer analyzing the data had been suppressing it, having been programmed to assume that deviations so extreme must be errors. The scientists had to go back and reprocess the data going back to 1979."

Another kind of problem may have to do with uniformity versus variety. Overly rational systems, including social structures such as armies, prisons, schools, and hospitals, easily become obsessed with uniform simplicity and tidiness. Besides being brutal and boring, they are inefficient and unstable as ecosystems. Complex information systems will generate variety out of sheer self-defense, if allowed to. This is where the "idiosyncratic" systems the Media Lab favors can be a salvation. The fairly trivial arrival of VCRs has already enriched the variety of movies being made. Personal Television doing computer-intelligent broadcatch could have a similar effect on TV programming. Electronic Publishing seems to be offering a far wider variety of authorship than New York publishing. And so on through the Lab. Ecologists of communications, like biological ecologists, may well wind up promoting diversity as a sign and protector of information-system health.

Like biological ecologists, communication ecologists are likely to inveigh against harsh rapid changes. Debugging takes time. Every change in a system requires associated changes nearby, and they take time to sort out, or violent disruptions occur. The forgotten thing about new communications technology is that there is no special hurry. These are luxuries, by and large. The world is not threatened by their absence. The technologies seem to be self-accelerating, and so is the market for them, but the *need* is not. If they are so wonderful, then they are worth bringing in lovingly, adaptively, gradually. Communications growth needs to keep moving or it could go static, but if it goes too fast it could generate massive resistance or crash by misadventure. The Media Lab inventing ten, twenty years into the future is proper conservative behavior. It's a way of probing into the future instead of lurching there.

Ecologists of communications, I imagine, would warn against having all one's eggs in one basket. We can be grateful for the vast dispersed populations of peasant and tribal cultures in the world who have never used a telephone or a TV, who walk where they're going, who live by local subsistence skills honed over millennia. You need to go on foot in Africa, Asia, South America to realize how many of these people there are and how sound they are. If the world city goes smash, they'll pick up the pieces, as they've done before. Whatever happens, they are a reminder that electronic communication may be essential to one kind of living, but it is superfluous to another.

I trust and hope that some urban curmudgeons also will tune out— read books, write with a pen, talk only face-to-face, and use the wealth of time and money they save to carve their own sweet path through nonvirtual reality.

☐☐ *Humanism Through Machines*

■ Computerists in general and Media Lab researchers in particular have a conspicuously unscientific relationship with their machines and programs. They anthropomorphize freely. A program is said to "know" about this and that; the machine needs a minute to "think" about certain kinds of problems; if malfunctioning, it may be described as "sick." Everybody knows better, but there's something comforting in the practice, and it bends research in the right direction.

Allison Druin, the Vivarium student with an art rather than programming background, would implore her workstation computer when something wasn't coming up right, "Come on, be *nice* to me!" Programmers nearby would roll their eyes, but in effect the Media Lab as a whole is insisting, "Come on, be *nice* to her!" and it applauded her building a huge furry computer interface with a lap, a face, and a personality.

Negroponte's goal is "ultra-personalized intimate technology—

everything made to order." In Jay Ogilvy's terms, Media Lab devices are the opposite of industrial machines. Their function is not the production of same-same-same, but the endless creation of a "different different difference, because if it's not different, it's not information." The idea is not to arrive at variety as rich as the variety of human beings, but to start from there and expand even further.

The Media Lab is inventing the technology of diversity. Some institutions that enjoyed industrial-style uniformity will no doubt regard it as the technology of perversity. That happened with personal computers—corporations fought them, unions fought them, the Soviet Union still is fighting them. But personal computers were a technology of separation originally; almost a survivalist mentality surrounded them. Current Media Lab technology enhances connectedness, yet it also manages to enhance autonomy. Kids at Hennigan School help each other more now, but the variety of student behavior there is also demonstrably greater since Seymour Papert's computers showed up. A player-listener of a Tod Machover piece of living music will be joined to the composer closer than with any other music form, but each listening-performance will be unique.

Connecting, diversifying, increasing human complexity rather than reducing it—these are instruments of culture.

As a university enterprise and an expression of an ethical vision, the Media Lab seems already to be a clear success. It's too early to tell whether it will be one of the great laboratories like Wiesner's RLE, Edwin Land's Polaroid, Xerox PARC, Los Alamos during the war, or Britain's National Institute for Medical Research, but in the terms of the bet made by the Lab's sponsors, they got a win. The Lab is doing a spectacular job of whetting appetites for juicy new technologies, as they hoped.

I was charged, in doing this book, to help the Lab think about what its emergent academic discipline might be, and in that I've failed completely. What would you call it, "The Department of C&C"? Maybe someone will coin a word for the new activity that joins communicating and computing, and that's what it will be the department of. Pragmatically, I suppose, the proof that it's a department of something will be when other universities and colleges have one too, whatever they name it. Such departments are likely to vary a good bit, to be fuzzier, less turf-bound, more collaborative than the staider, steadier disciplines. They're apt to be effectively the Department of New Stuff, part of the parent institution's dazzle factor, like sports. Having failed in my charge, it suits me fine if the uncertainty continues indefinitely. This is the grand intellectual discipline of Mumble Media Mumble.

"I began to think of communications as one big set of things," said Jerome Wiesner.

As for the media lab of the world, some serious choices are in the process of being made. A major one is whether human individuals will be the experimenters in the world lab or the experimentees, users of the future or mere consumers of the future. It will take a long political, economic, and technological process to work that out, but we can decide now which way we want it to go.

It seems the question "How will we directly connect our nervous systems to the global computer?" may have an answer. If Nicholas Negroponte's Media Lab has any say, we'll connect to the global computer exactly the way we connect to each other, through full-bodied, full-minded conversation. The world as we communicate with it does not have to be overwhelming. It can be an old friend.

I would add one further requirement for properly humanistic machines. The most ethical of all tools are tools of adaptiveness, tools that make tools, tools that remake themselves. Our machines have to welcome us inside them and help us hack around in there. A world of experimenters equipped with such tools can always do the right thing about the roster of technological futures being offered at any time: invent better ones.

Workers of the world, fan out.

BIBLIOGRAPHY

Brand, Stewart
  Two Cybernetic Frontiers
    New York: Random House, 1974.

Compaine, Benjamin M.
  *Who Owns the Media: Concentration of Ownership in the Mass
  Communications Industry*
    White Plains: Knowledge Industry, 1979, 1982.

Drexler, Eric
  Engines of Creation
    New York: Doubleday, 1986.

Drucker, Peter
  Innovation and Entrepreneurship
    New York: Harper & Row, 1985.

Forster, E. M.
  The Eternal Moment and Other Stories
    New York: Harcourt Brace, 1929, 1956.

Gibson, William
  Count Zero
    New York: Ace, 1987.

Head, Sydney W.
  World Broadcasting Systems: A Comparative Analysis
    Belmont, California: Wadsworth, 1985.

Hillis, Daniel
  The Connection Machine
    Cambridge: MIT, 1985.

Kobayashi, Koji
  Computers and Communications
    Cambridge: MIT, 1985, 1986.

Lambert, Steve, and Suzanne Ropiequet, eds.
  CD ROM: The New Papyrus
    Redmond, Washington: Microsoft, 1986.

Lammers, Susan
  Programmers at Work
    Redmond, Washington: Microsoft, 1986.

Langer, Suzanne K.
  Philosophy in a New Key: A Study in the Symbolism of Reason, Rite, and Art
    Cambridge: Harvard, 1957.

Levy, Steven
  Hackers: Heroes of the Computer Revolution
    New York: Dell, 1984.

McLuhan, Marshall
  Understanding Media: The Extensions of Man
    New York: McGraw-Hill, 1965.

Margalef, Ramón
  Perspectives in Ecological Theory
    Chicago: University of Chicago, 1968.

Minsky, Marvin
  The Society of Mind
    New York: Simon & Schuster, 1987.

Negroponte, Nicholas
   The Architecture Machine
      Cambridge: MIT, 1970.

Negroponte, Nicholas
   Soft Architecture Machines
      Cambridge: MIT, 1975.

Papert, Seymour
   Mindstorms: Children, Computers and Powerful Ideas
      New York: Basic Books, 1980.

Pool, Ithiel de Sola
   Technologies of Freedom: On Free Speech in an Electronic Age
      Cambridge: Harvard, 1983.

Smith, Anthony
   Goodbye Gutenberg: The Newspaper Revolution of the 1980s
      New York: Oxford, 1980.

Smith, Anthony
   The Geopolitics of Information: How Western Culture Dominates the World
      New York: Oxford, 1980.

Wiener, Norbert
   Cybernetics: Control and Communication in the Animal and the Machine
      Cambridge: MIT, 1948, 1961.

Wildes, Karl L., and Nilo A. Lindgren
   *A Century of Electrical Engineering and Computer Science at MIT,
   1882–1982*
      Cambridge: MIT, 1985.

Wolfe, Tom
   The Pump House Gang
      New York: Farrar, Straus, 1968.

INDEX

FOR THE BEST IN PAPERBACKS, LOOK FOR THE

In every corner of the world, on every subject under the sun, Penguin represents quality and variety—the very best in publishing today.

For complete information about books available from Penguin—including Pelicans, Puffins, Peregrines, and Penguin Classics—and how to order them, write to us at the appropriate address below. Please note that for copyright reasons the selection of books varies from country to country.

In the United Kingdom: For a complete list of books available from Penguin in the U.K., please write to *Dept E.P., Penguin Books Ltd, Harmondsworth, Middlesex, UB7 0DA.*

In the United States: For a complete list of books available from Penguin in the U.S., please write to *Dept BA, Penguin*, Box 120, Bergenfield, New Jersey 07621-0120.

In Canada: For a complete list of books available from Penguin in Canada, please write to *Penguin Books Canada Ltd, 10 Alcorn Avenue, Suite 300, Toronto, Ontario, Canada M4V 3B2.*

In Australia: For a complete list of books available from Penguin in Australia, please write to the *Marketing Department, Penguin Books Ltd, P.O. Box 257, Ringwood, Victoria 3134.*

In New Zealand: For a complete list of books available from Penguin in New Zealand, please write to the *Marketing Department, Penguin Books (NZ) Ltd, Private Bag, Takapuna, Auckland 9.*

In India: For a complete list of books available from Penguin, please write to *Penguin Overseas Ltd, 706 Eros Apartments, 56 Nehru Place, New Delhi, 110019.*

In Holland: For a complete list of books available from Penguin in Holland, please write to *Penguin Books Nederland B.V., Postbus 195, NL-1380AD Weesp, Netherlands.*

In Germany: For a complete list of books available from Penguin, please write to *Penguin Books Ltd, Friedrichstrasse 10-12, D-6000 Frankfurt Main I, Federal Republic of Germany.*

In Spain: For a complete list of books available from Penguin in Spain, please write to *Longman, Penguin España, Calle San Nicolas 15, E-28013 Madrid, Spain.*

In Japan: For a complete list of books available from Penguin in Japan, please write to *Longman Penguin Japan Co Ltd, Yamaguchi Building, 2-12-9 Kanda Jimbocho, Chiyoda-Ku, Tokyo 101, Japan.*